PEACE AND VALUE EDUCATION
FOR
VIKSIT BHARAT @2047

About the Editors

Prof. (Dr.) Lokanath Mishra, M.Sc. (Math), M.A. (Eco.) M.Ed., Ph.D. (Education), D.Litt. (Education) presently working as Professor and Head Department of Education, Mizoram University (A Central University), Aizawl, Mizoram. Previously he was working as Director, Faculty Development Center, Mizoram University, Principal in the rank of professor in Vivek College of Education, Bijnor (UP). He had been trained on Leadership for Academicians Programme (LEAP) through University of Pennsylvania, USA under Pandit Madan Mohan Malvya National Mission on Teacher and Teaching (PMMMNMTT), Ministry of Education, Government of India. Prof. Mishra was the Senior fellow of ICSSR, New Delhi. Prof. Mishra published 143 papers in reputed Scopus indexed National and International Journals. Prof. Mishra has published 20 (twenty) books and 32 chapters in an edited book related to Education, Teacher Education, Adult Education, Research, Peace Education, Tribal Education and Teaching of Mathematics.

Dr. Rashmirekha Das, M.Sc. (Geology), M.Ed, M.Phil, Ph.D. in Education from Sambalpur University and continuing Post Doc. in Education from University of North Carolina, Greensboro, USA. She has published 13 papers in Scopus indexed journal and one book Her areas of interest in peace education, Tribal education, Text book preparation. Dr. Das can be reached at rashmidas.edu@gmail.com

Dr. Mikael L. Chuaungo, M.A (Education), B.Ed. and Ph.D. in Education from Mizoram University. He is presently working as Assistant Professor in the Department of Education at Government J. Buana College, Lunglei, Mizoram, India. His research interests encompass constructivist pedagogy, integration of technology in education, and the challenges of Massive Open Online Courses (MOOCs) in India. He has contributed to several peer-reviewed journals and has actively participated as a resource person in national workshops focused on school-based action research and constructivist lesson planning. For correspondence, Dr. Chuaungo can be reached at mikael.chuaungo@gmail.com

PEACE AND VALUE EDUCATION
FOR
VIKSIT BHARAT @2047

Edited by

Lokanath Mishra
Rashmirekha Das
Mikael L. Chuaungo

CONCEPT PUBLISHING COMPANY PVT. LTD.
NEW DELHI - 110 059

ISBN: 978-93-6344-282-5

First Published 2025

Published and Printed by

Concept
Since 1974

Concept Publishing Company Pvt. Ltd.
A/15-16, Commercial Block, Mohan Garden
New Delhi-110059 (India)
T: +91-11-41101460
E: publishing@conceptpub.com, *W*: www.conceptpub.com

Cataloging in Publication--Courtesy: D.K. Agencies (P) Ltd. <docinfo@dkagencies.com>

Peace and value education for Viksit Bharat @2047 / edited by Lokanath Mishra, Rashmirekha Das, Mikael L. Chuaungo.
pages cm
Contributed articles.
Includes bibliographical references and index.
ISBN 9789363442825

1. Peace--Study and teaching--India. 2. Values--Study and teaching--India. 3. Conflict management--India. I. Mishra, Lokanath (College teacher), editor. II. Das, Rashmirekha, editor. III. Chuaungo, Mikael L., editor. IV. Title: Peace and value education for Viksit Bharat at 2047.

LCC JZ5534.P43 2025 | DDC 303.6071054 23

Preface

This humble piece of work has seen the light of day thanks to the blessing of the goddess MAA MANGALA. We bow our head to her for her mercy.

Today's peace education is not in any way peace education in the sense of creating learners—the human is both teacher and student, even though very few have access to it. The current peace education means human rights education, tolerance education, pacifist education, and education for non-violence. It means that the present peace education, as value education, is done through indoctrination and regimentation. Knowledge about these values is dictated to the learners by peace educators, positive attitudes towards these values are inculcated in their minds and they are trained in how to practice the skills of these values. They use dialogue and discussion to teach these values of peace, considering pedagogy as the methodology, even though it is a totally negative education of peace.

Hence, the whole world today needs a better type of peace education which would be beneficial to all. Indeed, true education is peace education, and peace is the product of true education. Hence, the ultimate aim of real education is to attain or to bring peace to individuals, which would be reflected in their surroundings or in the local to global society through these peaceful individuals. Therefore, the product of true education, i.e. peace, is used with education to give more emphasis for naming it as peace education. Thus, true peace education is people-making education, and should be for all, barring none. This book attends to implement peace and value education in different sectors as per NEP 2020 to become a Viksit Bharat @2047. The editors are highly indebted to all the contributors of this book. We look forward to suggestions from all the readers for further improving the subject content as well as presentation of the book.

Lokanath Mishra
Rashmirekha Das
Mikael L. Chuaungo

Contents

Introduction

As India marches towards its centenary of independence in 2047, the vision of *Viksit Bharat* (Developed India) is not just about economic growth and technological advancement but also about fostering a society rooted in peace, ethics, and human values. This book, *Peace and Value Education for Viksit Bharat @2047*, explores how moral and ethical education can serve as the foundation for a progressive, inclusive, and harmonious India.

In today's fast-changing world, conflicts, social unrest, and ethical dilemmas challenge the very fabric of society. The need for peace education—focused on tolerance, non-violence, and conflict resolution—has never been greater. Simultaneously, value education, which instils honesty, empathy, responsibility, and respect for diversity, is crucial in shaping future leaders who will guide India towards sustainable and equitable development. To integrate peace and values into society effectively, school and colleges should include structured lessons on peace, ethics, and social responsibility. Programmes promoting inclusivity, volunteerism, and social service should be encouraged. Responsible use of technology to spread positive values and counter misinformation, and training youth to be ethical leaders in politics, business, and social sectors is needed.

This book delves into the philosophical, historical, and contemporary relevance of peace and value education, linking it to the broader aspirations of *Viksit Bharat.* It highlights the role of educational institutions, policymakers, communities, and technology in integrating these principles into daily life. Through insightful discussions, case studies, and practical strategies, this book serves as a roadmap for educators, students, and policymakers committed to building a morally strong and prosperous India by 2047.

The book is consisting of twenty two chapters dealing with various aspects of peace education and its implementation. *Chapter 1* written by *Lokanath Mishra* and *Sanchari Bhunia* deals with Approaches and Strategy of Peace and Value Education for Viksit Bharat@2047, *Chapter 2* is a case study of Manipur violence written by *Rachel Lhingkhovah* and *Lokanath Mishra, Chapter 3* deals with Peace and Value Education in India by *Qaisur Rahman.* Inclusive Education as a Catalyst of Peace written by *Tage Yalung* and *Prasanta Kumar Acharya* presented in *Chapter 4.* Role of School in Nurturing Peace Among Children written by *Kritika Mishra* highlighted in *Chapter 5* Similarly, Peace the Dynamic Philosophy of Egalitarian World written by *Soumya R. Panigrahi et al.* presented in *Chapter 6.* Conflict Management and Peace Education written by *Seema Saleem* and *Shruti Pandey* presented in *Chapter 7. Arun Kumar Dubey* and *Abha Dubey* jointly wrote on Education for Peace Values and Skills presented in *Chapter 8.* Global Research Trends on Peace Education in Higher Education written by *Ramakanta Pradhan, Bhaskar Gurramkonda* and *Shivakumar S.* presented in *Chapter 9.* Role of Universities in Promoting Peace Education written by *Sana Parveen* presented in *Chapter 10.* With regards to Peace Pedagogy in Formal Education written by *Akhil Kumar Rai* and *Garima Rai* presented in

Chapter 11. Educating for Global Citizenship through Peace Pedagogy written by *Suman Mazumdar* and Critical Analysis of Animated Movie Zootopia within the Purview of Peace & Value Education written by *Debolina Mukherjee* are presented in *Chapters 12* and *13* respectively. A special *Chapter 14* written by *Girish Chandra Behera* and *Pranati Priyadarshini* about Peace Pedagogy in Formal Education. Ramayana the Epic for Peaceful Existency written by *Arti Srivastava* presented in *Chapter 15.* Integrating Gandhian Educational Philosophy into Contemporary Indian Education by *Pradip Das,* Role of Sports Entertainment in Peace written by *Bimal Soreng, et al.,* Forgoing a Future of Peace through Education in India by *Bhawani Shankar Gadatia,* Students' Conflict Resolution through Ananda Parisar in the Schools by *Arnab Kumar Dutta,* Promoting Peace Education in Schools by *Suhana Begum,* Peace Pedagogy for Viksit Bharat in 2024 by *Mou Banerjee* and *Lokanath Mishra* and Cultivating Peace in the Classroom Environment by *Ankur Nandi, Tapash Das* and *Tarini Halder* are presented in *Chapter 16, 17, 18, 19, 20, 21* and *22* respectively. We the editors thank to all the contributors for their support for development of this book.

Through this book, we hope to empower individuals with the knowledge and skills needed to create a more peaceful, just, and compassionate world. Whether you are a student, teacher, or a lifelong learner, this book will help you develop a deeper sense of responsibility, ethical consciousness, and a commitment to peace in your personal and social life.

As we embark on this journey, let us remember that a truly developed nation is one that not only achieves economic and scientific progress but also upholds the highest ideals of peace, compassion, and ethical integrity.

List of Contributors

Abha Dubey (Dr.), Vice-Principal, Columbia College, Raipur (C.G.).
Email: mrs.abhadubey@gmail.com

Akhil Kumar Rai, (NCERT Doctoral Fellow of 2008), Assistant Professor-B.Ed. Jawahar Lal Nehru Smarak P.G. College, Maharajganj, U.P.
Email: raiakhil84@gmail.com

Ankur Nandi, Research Scholar, Department of Education, Kalyani University, West Bengal, India.
Email: ankurpalashdanga@gmail.com

Anupam Kumar Patel (Mr.), Research Scholar, Sambalpur University.
Email: anupam.edu@suniv.ac.in

Arnab Kumar Dutta (Dr.), Assistant Professor, Raiganj B.Ed College (Government Sponsored), Karnajora, Uttar Dinajpur, West Bengal.
Email: Rikdutta8@gmail.com

Arti Srivastav (Dr.), (ICSSR Senior Fellow, 2022-2023)
Email: arti_srvstv@yahoo.co.in

Arun Kumar Dubey (Dr.), Principal, Columbia College, Raipur (C.G.).
Email: mr.arunkumardubey@gmail.com

Bhaskar Gurramkonda, Ph.D. Research Scholar, Department of Education, Central University of Kerala, Kasargod, Kerala.
Email: bhaskargurramkondascholar@gmail.com

Bhawani Shankar Gadatia, Department of Education, Sonepur College, Sonepur, Odisha, India.
Email: bhawanigadatia@gmail.com

Bimal Soreng (Mr.), Research Scholar, Sambalpur University.
Email: bimalsoreng.edu@suniv.ac.in

Debolina Mukherjee (Dr.), Assistant Professor, Department of Education, JIS University, Agarpara, Kolkata, West Bengal.
Email: debolina.mukherjee@jisuniversity.ac.in

Garima Rai, Assistant Professor, Department of Education, Mahila P.G. College, Bahraich, U.P.
Email: garimarai1910@gmail.com

Girish Chandra Behera (Mr.), Assistant Professor in Odia (Teacher Education), Shailabala Women's Autonomous College, Cuttack.
Email: girishchandrabehera82@gmail.com

Jubraj Khamari (Prof.), Department of Education, Sambalpur University, Jyoti Vihar-768019, Burla, Sambalpur, Odisha.
Email: jubrajkhamari@suniv.ac.in

Kritika Mishra, Research Scholar, Faculty of Education, Dayal Bagh Educational Institute (Deemed University), Agra.
Email: mishrakritika88@gmail.com

Lokanath Mishra (Prof.), Head, Department of Education, Mizoram University.
Email: munumishra7@gmail.com

Mou Banerjee, Research Scholar, Department of Education, Mizoram University.
Email: psycheemon@gmail.com

Pradip Das (Dr.), Guest Faculty, Voice of World Teachers Training College, Kolkata.
Email: pradipdivyang@gmail.com

Pranati Priyadarshini (Ms.), Assistant Professor in Botany (Teacher Education), Shailabala Women's Autonomous College, Cuttack.
Email: ppriyadarshini21@gmail.com

Prasanta Kumar Acharya (Prof.), Department of Education, Rajiv Gandhi University, Arunachal Pradesh, India.
Email: prasantaacharya20@yahoo.in

Qaisur Rahman (Dr.), Assistant Professor, Deo College of Education, Vinoba Bhave University, Hazaribag-825301 Jharkhand, India.
Email: qaisur.rahman@gmail.com

Rachel Lhingkhovah (Ms.), Research Scholar, Department of Education, Mizoram University, Mizoram.
Email: Mzu230007860@Mzu.Edu.In

Ramakanta Pradhan, Ph.D. Research Scholar, Department of Education, Central University of Kerala, Kasargod, Kerala.
Email: ramakantapradhan.2301607009@cukerala.ac.in

Sana Parveen, Research Scholar, Department of Teacher Training & Non-Formal Education (IASE), Faculty of Education, Jamia Millia Islamia, New Delhi.
Email: sana74040@gmail.com

Sanchari Bhunia (Dr.), Assistant Professor, Mizoram University, Mizoram.
Email: Sanchari.bhunia@gmail.com

Seema Saleem, Assistant Professor, Amity Institute of Rehabilitation Sciences, Amity University, Noida, Uttar Pradesh.
Email: seemasaleem21@gmail.com

Shivakumar S. (Dr.), Assistant Professor in Education, Central University of Kerala, Kasargod, Kerala, India.
Email: drshivakumars@cukerala.ac.in

Shruti Pandey, Assistant Professor, Faculty of Education, Banaras Hindu University, Varanasi.
Email: shrutipandey@bhu.ac.in

Sonalita Nayak (Ms.), Research Scholar, Sambalpur University, Sambalpur.
Email: sonalitanayak2019@gmail.com

Soumya Ranjan Panigrahi (Mr.), Research Scholar, Sambalpur University, Sambalpur.
Email: soumyapanigrahi.edu@suniv.ac.in

Suhana Begum, Assistant Professor (Educational Studies), Nabakrushna Choudhary College of Teacher Education, Angul, Odisha.
Email: thatsosuhana.asra@gmail.com

Suman Mazumdar, Research Scholar, Department of Educational Studies, Jamia Millia Islamia, New Delhi.
Email: sumanmazumdar55.jmi@gmail.com

Tage Yalung, Department of Education, Rajiv Gandhi University, Arunachal Pradesh.
Email: tage.yalung@rgu.ac.in

Tapash Das (Dr.), Assistant Professor, Department of Education, Kazi Nazrul University, Asansol, West Bengal.
Email: tapash.das@knu.ac.in

Tarini Halder (Dr.), Professor, Department of Education, Kalyani University, Kalyani, Nadia, West Bengal.
Email: thalderku@gmail.com

1

Approaches and Strategies of Peace and Value Education for *Viksit Bharat* @2047

Lokanath Mishra and *Sanchari Bhunia*

> There is no way of peace, peace is the way
> If we not teach peace, somebody will teach violence to the student.
>
> – **Gandhiji**

The present world is turning into a global village; every citizen of the world wants this global village to be a place of peace based on the principle of freedom, equality, and fraternity. This global village is also a place with plural democratic society. There is an urgent need to create a culture of non-violence and tolerance in all walks of life, which may help in creating a peaceful and affectionate society. The need to make the present world a peaceful global village is being felt by educationists and they are of the view that the most effective and permanent instrument to achieve the above objective is the instrument of education. In order to understand how the environment and natural resources can facilitate peacebuilding, it is important to explain the causes that lead to environmental conflicts. Environmental conflicts are those induced by ecological factors such as the scarcity and destruction of natural resources, the transboundary movement of hazardous materials, the loss of livelihoods dependent on natural resources that may lead to demographic pressure and forced migration, and degradation resulting from climate change. Environmental resources are a nation's lifeline and must be preserved; this is possible only through active cooperation between the public, the government and the stakeholders. Peace has always been among humanity's highest values. Peace, however, is also seen as concord, or harmony and tranquility. Peace is commonly understood as the absence of conflicts and violence in society. Conflicts are pervasive in society and are held in place due to uneven distribution of socio-economic as well as political power, religious and regional differences. Conflicts among culturally or politically diverse groups cannot be wished away but management and effective resolution of conflicts could contribute significantly to the maintenance of peace and friendly relationships across these diverse groups.

Larsen (1976) stated that peace is the absence of war and conflicts which means the absence of physical violence and other forms of conflicts and states that peace is not only the absence of war but also the absence of conflicts.

McAllister (1982) has a broader meaning than the absence of war and defines it as an end to all the way of violence to ourselves and each other.

Moreillon (1990) stated that peace is not the absence of war. Peace is a dynamic process of collaboration between all states of people. This collaboration must be used for ensuring respect for liberty, independence national sovereignty, equality, respect for the law and for human rights as well as just equitable distribution of resources to meet the need of the people. According to the above statement contribution to peace does not only occur in the sector of peace-making but also peace-keeping. Peace is the development of individual and his her/his relationship with others and also cultures. Peace is the relationship between humankind and available resources on earth. It is the equitable distribution of available resources to satisfy the needs of all individuals and to maintain global equality and justice. Peace cannot be brought about by changes in human consciousness alone, belligerence and violence are so deeply anchored in social structures that they cannot be overcome solely by peoples' initiatives, but also appropriate policy measures, legal and regulatory frameworks.

Peace is enriched by a society whose cultural and spiritual values are in sync with universal human values. Indian schools are based on what are termed universal human values such as love, reciprocity, empathy and concern for others, and justice and fairness. Such values can be included in peace education for schools throughout the world. But at the same time this curriculum, being developed in India, reflects the country's multiple and diverse problems, Indian culture, its strong religious beliefs, and the country's needs especially as the curriculum moves up to higher levels of education. So, it is enriched by certain widespread Indian spiritual and cultural values as *ahimsa*, that is, non-violence and non-killing. But today the scope of peace education includes not only the causes, the nature, and the terrible consequences of war but also the study of violence in all forms. Such forms of violence include conflict, a threat to life, ethnic hatred, discrimination, prejudice, racism, injustice, genocide, poverty, violence in the home and family, destruction of the environment, and so forth. A basic aim of peace education is to save humankind from destroying a large portion or all of itself. Once we become aware of our suicidal behaviour, peace education points out to us the alternatives that can gradually slow down and stop this mad rush. The growing literature on peace education reflects a dynamic field. Harris (2004) divides peace education into five categories: international education, development education, environmental education, human rights education, and conflict resolution education. Curricula in peace education cover a range of topics, including the history and philosophy of peace education (Reardon, 1988; Burns and Aspeslagh, 1996; Harris and Morrison, 2003), the dialectic between 'negative' and 'positive' peace (Galtung, 1969; 1996), gender and militarism (Reardon, 1993; 2001), conflict resolution education (Johnson and Johnson, 2006) and the formation of peaceful values in education (Boulding, 1988; Toh and Cawagas, 1991). On nurturing cultures of peace, Sommerfelt and Vambheim (2008) write that peace requires citizens to contain their aggression, exhibit cooperative behaviour, and resolve conflicts without violence. Jenkins (2007) illuminates the difference between education about peace and education for peace. Education about peace includes modules on war and peace and leaders of peace movements, such as Gandhi and Martin Luther King. Education for peace, on the other hand, intends to nurture knowledge, values, behaviours and capacities to confront violence. Peace education as a practice in schools is attributed to Maria Montessori, John Dewey, and Paulo Freire, among other scholars, though earlier thought on education for peace can be traced back to Comenius, Erasmus and Socrates. Montessori, in her work, sought to foster peace on three inter-related levels: the individual, community and nation, and the global/cosmos. The individual level relates to person-cantred awareness of the self, whereas the community level refers to interpersonal relations, and the global level concerns cultural and environmental consciousness at the level of interaction between States and non-State actors (Montessori, 1949).

NEP-2020 envisions fostering a profound and enduring sense of pride in being Indian among learners. This pride extends beyond mere thoughts, encompassing their spirit, intellect, and actions. It aims to cultivate a holistic understanding that integrates national identity with global perspectives. Beyond national pride, the policy seeks to nurture essential knowledge, skills, values, and attitudes that promote responsible citizenship. Learners will be encouraged to uphold human rights, champion sustainable development, and adopt ethical and environment friendly lifestyles. This approach ensures that individuals are not only committed to their nation's growth but also contribute meaningfully to global progress and well-being. By instilling these qualities, the policy aspires to shape individuals into true global citizens—people who are deeply connected to their heritage while actively engaging with and contributing to the global community. This vision aligns personal growth with societal advancement, fostering an educational framework that balances national pride with international responsibility.

Peace Education serves as a foundational framework that allows schools to design programmes aimed at instilling universal values, fostering positive attitudes, and equipping students with essential skills. These programmes help learners develop a deep understanding of peace, conflict resolution, and cooperation, enabling them to become responsible and engaged global citizens. The framework is structured around several key guiding principles.

1. Promotion of Universal Values

At the core of Peace Education is the emphasis on values such as empathy, respect, tolerance, equality, justice, and non-violence. These values are essential for fostering harmonious relationships within communities and across nations. Schools play a crucial role in transmitting these ideals, ensuring that students internalize them and apply them in their daily interactions.

2. Cultivation of Enduring Attitudes

Attitudes shape the way individuals perceive and respond to the world around them. Peace Education encourages the development of a mindset that values cooperation over competition, dialogue over conflict, and understanding over prejudice. By nurturing these attitudes, students learn to approach challenges with patience, open-mindedness, and a commitment to peaceful coexistence.

3. Development of Critical Skills

For students to become active participants in promoting peace, they must be equipped with key skills, including:

- *Conflict Resolution and Mediation:* The ability to resolve disagreements constructively without resorting to aggression.
- *Communication and Active Listening:* Expressing ideas clearly while also valuing different perspectives.
- *Critical Thinking and Problem-Solving:* Analyzing complex social issues and devising effective solutions.
- *Emotional Intelligence:* Understanding and managing one's emotions while empathizing with others.

4. Encouraging Active Global Citizenship

Peace Education goes beyond theoretical knowledge by encouraging students to take responsibility for fostering peace in their communities and the world. This includes:

- Participating in social service and community engagement projects.
- Advocating for human rights and social justice.
- Promoting environmental sustainability and responsible global stewardship.

5. Recognizing Interdependence and Diversity

The framework acknowledges that the world is interconnected, and global challenges require collective action. Schools, therefore, emphasize the importance of respecting cultural diversity and promoting dialogue between different communities and nations. Understanding different perspectives fosters mutual respect and strengthens global unity.

6. Commitment to Sustainable Peace and Development

Sustainable peace is not merely the absence of conflict but the presence of justice, equality, and opportunity for all. Peace Education aligns with the principles of sustainable development, ensuring that students recognize the role of economic, social, and environmental stability in maintaining lasting peace.

1. Each member of the global society is bound by principles relating to human welfare, such as justice, liberty, responsibility, equality, dignity, security, democracy, and solidarity.
2. Each member of society is an active participant in a local community and is in turn committed to a global harmony reflective of the diversity of the human population.
3. Each member of the global society must act individually and communally toward guardianship of our world, guaranteeing the right to a sustainable future.

There are many peace education programmes for current practice around the world. Each programme has built a framework based on specific sets of beliefs and the context within which the programme runs. These peace education programmes have many divergent meanings depending on different individuals in different places (Salomon, 2002).

By embracing Peace Education, schools create an environment that nurtures responsible individuals who are not only academically competent but also socially conscious and morally grounded. This comprehensive approach ensures that students are prepared to contribute meaningfully to a more just, peaceful, and sustainable world.

Value and Peace Education for "*Viksit Bharat*"

India's vision of *Viksit Bharat* (Developed India) is not just about economic growth and technological advancements but also about fostering a society rooted in strong moral values, social harmony, and global responsibility. **Value and Peace Education** plays a crucial role in shaping responsible citizens who contribute to the nation's progress while upholding the principles of peace, justice, and sustainability.

1. The Role of Value and Peace Education in Nation-Building

A truly developed nation is one where progress is inclusive, ethical, and sustainable. Value and Peace Education ensures that individuals not only excel academically and professionally but also possess the emotional intelligence, integrity, and compassion needed to build a harmonious society. This education framework instils a sense of purpose, responsibility, and commitment to national and global well-being.

2. Core Principles of Value and Peace Education for Viksit Bharat

A. Instilling Core Human Values: For India to achieve holistic development, its citizens must be guided by values such as:

- **Integrity and Honesty** – Strengthening ethical leadership and governance.

- **Compassion and Empathy** – Encouraging social inclusion and care for the underprivileged.
- **Respect for Diversity** – Embracing India's rich cultural, religious, and linguistic diversity.
- **Social Responsibility** – Promoting civic duty and active participation in nation-building.

B. Fostering a Culture of Peace: Peace is the foundation of a prosperous society. Education systems must actively promote:

- **Non-violence and Conflict Resolution** – Teaching negotiation, dialogue, and mediation skills.
- **Human Rights Awareness** – Ensuring dignity and equality for all sections of society.
- **Emotional Intelligence and Mindfulness** – Encouraging self-awareness and resilience to handle societal challenges.
- **Community Engagement** – Strengthening grassroots participation in social initiatives.

C. Encouraging Responsible and Sustainable Development: *Viksit Bharat* is envisioned as a nation that balances economic growth with environmental and social responsibility. Value and Peace Education fosters:

- **Environmental Stewardship** – Encouraging sustainable lifestyles and conservation efforts.
- **Ethical Entrepreneurship** – Promoting business practices that align with social welfare.
- **Global Citizenship** – Preparing youth to engage with international issues such as climate change, social justice, and global peace.

3. Implementing Value and Peace Education in Schools and Institutions

- **Integrating Moral Education in Curricula** – Including

lessons on ethics, peace, and civic duties at all levels of education.

- **Experiential Learning** – Encouraging real-world problem-solving through community service, cultural exchange programmes, and peace-building activities.
- **Teacher Training Programmes** – Equipping educators with the skills to impart value-based education effectively.
- **Encouraging Dialogue and Reflection** – Creating safe spaces for discussions on social and ethical dilemmas.

4. The Vision: A Developed India with a Peaceful and Inclusive Society

For *Viksit Bharat* to become a reality, development must go hand in hand with human values and social cohesion. Through Value and Peace Education, India can cultivate a generation of individuals who not only contribute to economic and technological advancements but also uphold the principles of justice, peace, and sustainability.

There are many teaching-learning strategies that are compatible with the approaches to peace education described above. They are as follows:

1. **Exchange of Ideas:** Exchange of ideas is very important in school system to resolve the conflicts and thinking about environmental degradation. The small group discussion is a strategy that is used to enable the individual participant's voice to be heard.
2. **Teacher as Moderator:** It is a discussion technique where many groups are formed. Teacher poses a question or topic for discussion. Students of different groups may answer the question in a non-violent way.
3. **Visualization/Imagination Exercise:** The visualization exercise helps the students to use their imagination. It

allows them to imagine alternatives, to, for example, situations of conflict.

4. **Problem Solving:** It is a skill used in problem-solving. This entails "standing in the shoe of the other and walking in them for a while". This device is often used to develop empathy and tolerance.
5. **Role-playing:** This strategy is used to provide the participants with the opportunity to "feel" the situation rather than merely intellectualize about it. Role-playing also develops empathy and greater understanding for other vantage points. It can cultivate both cognitive and effective learning.
6. **Mock-up Games:** Allows students have a better feel of the situation of peacelessness and allows them to be more creative in suggesting alternatives to the situation of injustice. An example is the simulation on the distribution of wealth in "Sharing the Earth's Resources".
7. **Developing Leadership Qualities:** This activity is used to develop leadership qualities among the students. Selection of class representative will be held in a peaceful way so that conflicts among the students may not occur.
8. **Encouraging Action:** Whenever appropriate, the participants are asked to express a resolution or commitment to certain actions as a form of application of learning(s). It is an opportunity seized by the teacher to discuss the hot issue of the day. It may be an issue that is internal to the class (e.g. an ongoing conflict).
9. **Writing Quotation:** The reading of a peace-related quotation in the beginning or at the end of a lesson encourages learner to think or appreciate better the concepts learned in the session. Quotations on peace on different issues should be written on the wall of

the schools in the classrooms also. Peace activists, religious leaders, indigenous community leaders, and philosophers have said words of wisdom and inspiration that relate to peace. Let your students ponder on these quotations and speak about the impact of these ideas on them.

10. **Social Media:** Writing a word such as "war" or "peace" on the board in the beginning of a session and inviting learners to write or draw their associations with the word stimulate thinking. It is also a good springboard for the discussion of a peace-related concept in what's app, face-book and linked in. students and teachers may create a page on Facebook and post-peace related issues on it
11. **Use of Youtube:** The showing of film and/or photographs of different issues in environment in Youtubes by the teacher help create vivid images in the minds of the learners. This can be followed by a discussion on messages conveyed and learners' reactions about the inner and outer peace.
12. **Telling Stories:** Learners sometimes remember the concepts we want to share through our anecdotes and stories. Sharing your personal experiences related to the issue will help illustrate better the points you want to make. Such strategy also helps learners connect with you on a more personal basis.
13. **Participation in Co-curricular Activities:** In the school, more stress should be given so that students will participate in different co-curricular activities like essay, debate and song competitions, games and sports. In these activities, the opinion of each participant is briefly solicited.
14. **Expert Resources:** Learners are exposed to the ideas of advocates for justice and peace. The use of a third person is most helpful for very controversial topics. Students

take turn in facilitating: "What we hear, we usually forget; what we see, we usually remember; but what we do, we better understand." When given a chance to teach the subject matter, students are given the chance to comprehend better the concepts, values and skills we want to impart.

15. **Exposure Trips:** Students are given the opportunity to be touched by victims of injustice. Seeing, hearing, and encountering a victim of violence is more powerful in developing empathy and compassion among the learners. Contact opportunities also motivate better in prodding students to action.
16. **Brainstorming:** It is a method that helps people think creatively by letting many ideas flow from the students without any comment from the others. This strategy can be useful in generating many different solutions or alternatives. Evaluation of the ideas is done after the brainstorming.
17. **Case Studies:** This strategy gives the students an opportunity to know real-life situations of violence or injustice. Case studies are stories or scenarios that require and invite solutions. Students are put in the position of problem solvers who discover underlying issues, positions and interests.
18. **Peace Club:** In each school Peace Club may be established to perform these activities. The Peace Club established in each secondary school with the help of principals for the students, teacher's like-minded peace supporters from all walks of life to pursue their interests in and share their views on peace. Furthermore, it provides a platform for peace builders to inspire one another to put words into action and really make a difference in 'bringing hope and changing lives' of the disadvantaged.

Cultures can and do change over time. This gives us the encouragement to believe that there is a way forward to create a more peaceful society around and beyond the world. It all starts with each one of us. To achieve Peace at home, Peace at school, Peace in the Society and Peace in the Nation, we need to promote social integration and create a Culture of Peace. Also encourage students to promote the 'Culture of Peace': Choose patience and tolerance, Choose peace and harmony, Choose love and care, Choose acts of kindness, Choose to give first, Choose understanding and acceptance etc.

19. **Peace Parks:** In each school peace park must be established in order to sensitize the students about environmental degradation and conservation. It is formally dedicated to the protection and maintenance of biological diversity and of natural and associated cultural resources, and to the promotion of peace and cooperation.

The desired citizen who is a product of peace education is, therefore, one who: Can live in a multicultural society, respects diversity, does not compete based on differences, values or tolerates other cultures, trusts others, treats others as human beings; is not racist; can analyse the causes of intercultural disharmony objectively:

1. Is democratic in decision-making, can work in a team without conflict, seeks to understand the ideas of others, can share resources, has an open mind, thinks critically, can act assertively, respects and ensures others' rights.
2. Communicates well, and in each others' language, is an active listener.
3. Can solve problems and face challenges, particularly challenges of the multicultural society.

Fig. 1.1: Needs of Peace Education

4. Can transform conflict, and can think positively.
5. Has discovered inner peace, has a peaceful and sustainable lifestyle, can understand his/her own capacity and scope of work.
6. Is politically enlightened.
7. Is not corrupt or does not accept bribes; serves others without expectations; has civic virtues, is willing to sacrifice.
8. Has a global vision and is a global citizen; has the courage to participate in the development of the world; is environment friendly.
9. Does no harm to anybody in thoughts or deeds; respects others' feelings; is empathetic.
10. Can protect traditions, culture and values.

Peace educators have a goal—of stopping violence in the world. Students are the instruments and future citizens of the world. They should be sensitized through learning and teaching to resolve conflicts non-violently, to share limited resources equitably, and to live within the limits of sustainability to create a better world. This will become increasingly important as the 21st century unfolds with increasing human populations all seeking a better life.

REFERENCES

Auer, M. (2002). *The Strange War, Stories for a Culture of Peace, Non-violent Conflict Resolution in and Out-of-School,* UNESCO, Paris, pp. 72-73.

Begum, A. (2012). "The Concept and Perception of Peace Education in Gilgit Baltistan Pakistan: A Comparative Case Study". *The Peace and Conflict Review, 7*(1): 25-39.

Bar-Tal, D. (2002). "The Elusive Nature of Peace Education. Peace Education: The Concept, Principles, and Practices Around the World, G. Salomon and B. Nevo (Eds). London, Lawrence Erlbaum, 27-36.

Bar-Tal, D. and Rosen, Y. (2009). "Peace Education in Societies Involved in Intractable Conflicts: Direct and Indirect Models." *Review of Educational Research, 79*(2): 557-575.

Mishra, L. (2013). "Peace Education Tool for Effective Conflict Management in Secondary Schools of Odisha", *Sakarya University Journal of Education,* 3/1 ss. 69-76.

National Curriculum Framework Review (2005.). "Education for Peace". New Delhi: National Council of Educational Research and Training, p. 42.

Salomon, G. and Nevo, B. (2002). *Peace Education: The Concept, Principles, and Practices around the World.* New York, Lawrence Etlbaum.

Subramanian, D. (2016). "Teaching-Learning Approaches and Strategies in Peace Education". *IRA International Journal of Education and Multidisciplinary Studies, 3*(3). doi: http://dx.doi.org/10.21013/jems.v3.n3.p9

Zembylas, M., Charalambous, C. & Charalambous, P. (2016). "Teachers' Responses to a Peace Education Initiative". In *Peace Education in a Conflict-affected Society: An Ethnographic Journey*, pp. 77-130. Cambridge: Cambridge University Press.

https://www.cambridge.org/core/books/peace-education-in-a-conflict affected-society/teachers-responses-to-a-peace-education-initiative

2

Education for Promotion of Peace in Manipur

Rachel Lhingkhovah and *Lokanath Mishra*

Introduction

Peace Education in India is a varied approach aimed at implementing a culture of peace and non-violence. "Peace education is the learning of skills and building of attitudes that support the development of a peace-seeking minds-set". The teachings of Mahatma Gandhi and other Indian reformers like J. Krishnamurti have emphasized so much on non-violence and social justice. Gandhiji's view on peace education emphasis mainly on non-violence (*Ahimsa*) and truth (*Satya*) as core values. In India, after the assassination of Mahatma Gandhi, the foremost leader in the movement for India's Independence from British rule, in his remembrance, "Gandhi Peace Foundation", a voluntary organization was established in the year 1956 in New Delhi that studies and develops Gandhiji's thoughts and ideas on peace. It helps young scholars to study more in depth about peace by exploring different peace foundations in different parts of India. In India, institutions like the University of Madras, University of Mumbai (Mahatma Gandhi Peace Centre) and Jamia Millia Islamia (Nelson Mandela Centre for Peace and Conflicts Resolution) have established centres for peace and conflicts studies in integrating peace education into their curricula, though it is not yet widespread into mainstream curriculum. According to the national focus group on education for peace which was established as a part of the National Curriculum Framework (NCF) 2005 by the National Council of Educational Research and Training (NCERT), with the alarming increase in violence in school life, peace education was aimed to be integrated in school curriculum to initiate a culture of peace, truth and non-violence among students. It suggested that peace education subject should be integrated into existing subjects like social sciences, language and even science. Interactive and participatory teaching methods were advocated and activities like group discussion, role-playing and community project are recommended to help the learner internalize the values of peace and cooperation in the society.

Manipur, a state in North-eastern India, has faced numerous conflicts and social unrest over the years. Manipur is in the eastern frontier of India sharing border with Myanmar, Mizoram, Nagaland and Assam. The geography of the state greatly influenced relations between different communities of the state. There are four major communities residing in the state of Manipur (Meitei, Meitei Pangals, Nagas and the Kukis). Besides, there are Nepalese, and other communities from the mainstream who came mainly for commercial purposes constituting of the Marwaris, Deshwalis, Biharis, Punjabis, Tamils etc. The total population of Manipur as per Census 2011 is 25,70,390 out of which Scheduled Tribe population is 9,02,740. In the last decade, the rural population is increased by 1,45,416 and urban area is 2,58,186. The highest decadal growth rate is in rural Chandel district which constitute 23.2 per cent growth rate and Imphal East constituts 69.2 per cent growth rate and is the highest in the urban areas.The need for peace and harmony in this region is more pressing than ever. Education plays a pivotal role in fostering peace and building a harmonious society. Through value-based education, conflict resolution training, and community involvement, Manipur can achieve lasting peace and stability.

Manipur's history is marked by ethnic conflicts, insurgency, and political instability. These issues have significantly affected the socio-economic development of the state. Understanding the historical context of Manipur's conflicts is essential to appreciate the importance of promoting peace through education. In the past few months from 3 May, 2023, National and International media has covered what has happened in the state of Manipur, one of the north-east states of India. The ongoing conflicts outbursts as members of the Tribals living in Manipur initiated peaceful protests organized by the All Tribals Students Union Manipur (ATSUM) against the Manipur High Court Order on 19 April, 2023 that directed the state government to consider the inclusion of Meitei community in the Scheduled Tribe list. As a result, this has hurt the sentiments of the tribals living in the state of Manipur. In Manipur there is a significant lack of educational and employment opportunities in general. Thus, the scant educational opportunities for all, including those in the hill communities in particular, are viewed as becoming reduced if the demand for Scheduled Tribe status is accepted (Leth, 2023). What is more interesting is that the Kuki areas and community are only the targeted groups and was done with a clear intention of provoking and harming them. Churches, houses, vehicles, properties belonging only to the Kukis are vandalized. There are also several counter-blockades on different parts of the valley districts by members of Meitei Leepun that has worsened the situation on the day before of 3 May, 2023. On the other hand,

Tribals of Naga groups and their areas were left untouched, but the peaceful rally was organized by all the tribals of Manipur. This indicates that only the minority Kuki community was targeted by the Majority Meitei militants.

Despite the fact that illegal poppy farming for drug production is practised by all three primary ethnic groups in Manipur—the Kukis, Nagas, and Meiteis—the Kuki community is disproportionately portrayed as the primary culprits of this illegal activity. Manipur's Chief Minister Biren Singh, who has initiated an anti-drug campaign, has actively perpetuated this discriminatory narrative by using stigmatizing language such as "poppy cultivators" and "narco-terrorists" specifically targeting the Kuki people, despite the evidence that poppy cultivation is not exclusive to their community (Leth, 2023).

Social media platforms like twitter, Facebook, WhatsApp etc. has also spread lots of false information and propaganda, exacerbated tensions and fuelling the conflicts. During the conflicts, violent extremist Groups uses different platforms to recruit members and spread their ideologies. Some examples regarding the false allegations made during the Majority Meitei and Minority Kuki conflicts are Ayushi Chaudhary Case, the lies about the rape and murder of 37 Meitei women in Churachandpur Jantar Mantar lies, and the lies about the rape case of MBBS student which was totally false information spread so as to use their propaganda used by the Meitei community as a victim card that creates the situation very aggressive and leads to loss of many lives but was later clarified as false information by the father of the MBBS student and DGP, P. Doungel during the conflicts in Manipur (*The Indelible Trauma*: 118-121). After all the fake propaganda, misinformation and one-sided news, the impact is on the viral videos of two minority Kuki women parade naked, shaking the worldwide exasperate. The disturbing viral video showing two Kuki women being subjected to severe public humiliation finally prompted Prime Minister Narendra Modi to publicly address the ongoing violence in Manipur on July 20th. In a concise statement, he expressed his horror at the video's contents and promised that those who experienced sexual violence would receive justice. However, the credibility of this commitment remains uncertain, with questions lingering about whether his words will result in meaningful legal or protective actions (Leth, 2023).

Global rally on leaked tapes: Ethnic cleansing exposed "Save us from Manipur" organized by Students Bodies, Churachandpur District on (31 August, 2024) 11:10 AM.

The ethnic conflicts between the Meitei and the minority Kuki tribals that leads to destruction of trusts between both the communities that does not bring any productive results instead bring disaster to the society. As a result, hundreds of churches, houses are burnt down in the state capital, Imphal, which has destroyed relationship between the two groups, while the Kukis were on the defensive when the Majority Meitei Groups under the leadership of Arambai Tenggol which is a state sponsor anti-social group in Imphal. This kind of activities and conflicts is not recommended because it does not bring any positive outcome. The role of Assam Rifles at different camps at the heart of Imphal city has tremendously saved lots of Minority Kuki. Many conflicts and violence have been happened in the state of Manipur, India and being an inhabitant of Manipur, and doing doctoral research in Education, Mizoram University. The researchers have reviewed related literature on the present situation of Manipur and found that no such studies have been conducted on the above topic. The researcher is interested to take this study to examine the present education system of Manipur. Similarly, researcher is interested to study the implementation of peace education in Manipur and examine the role of Assam Rifles for mitigating violence and conflicts inside Manipur University.

Three main aspects of conflict should be addressed by peace education, according to Kotite (2012, p. 13), who reflects on the difficulties facing peace-building in the twenty-first century: the structural aspect, where education alters "societal contradictions", the behavioural aspect, where education enhances "relations and interactions", and the attitudinal aspect, where education promotes "changes in attitudes in ways that can reduce the risk of conflict and help build a sustainable peace." The formal school system may be one of the most appropriate avenues for fulfilling this mandate.

The research of Basabose and Habyarimana (2019) identifies three possible responses from students: accepting the contradictory messages, rejecting them, or struggling to make a clear decision between the curriculum content and the conflicting messages. This difficulty in handling contradictory messages poses a risk to the effectiveness of the peace education programme. The study examines the challenges faced by peace education programmes in Rwandan secondary schools, highlighting how students encounter contradictory messages from various sources, such as family and peers. The post-conflict environment in Rwanda suggests that peace education should be viewed as a peace-oriented endeavour that aims to empower individuals and foster their capacity for prevention. Given Rwanda's history, which is characterised by numerous violent conflicts, wars, and the genocide against the Tutsi (Basabose, 2006), any successful peace education programme in the nation must take into account empowering the participants and giving them a pro-peace mentality.

According to Devi (2008) conflicts in Manipur has disrupted the education of the children by denying their basic right to education. The role of the teachers becomes very important to deal with children in the conflicts zone, child-friendly trained teachers should be engaged in schools and learning centres to help "psychosocial and physical well-being" of the learner. With the help of education, children in a conflict zone can be nurtured with proper guidance and counselling. At this stage, if the children are not under proper care and guidance through education then, the outcome may lead to school dropout and may lead to anti-social organization which may doomed their life. Singha (2017) highlighted about the importance of peace education as a culture to provide basic quality education. "Peace education is an essential component of quality of good life." Peace through education will improve the livelihood of the individual, community and nature. Devi (2019) emphasis on the youth of Manipur, how youth are vulnerable in the society because they can join anti-social activities so easily in the name of the religious and communal force because of lack of understanding of humanity. So, in today's aspects of life, quality education in the school system for youth can become very essential component to save them from anti-national activities. "Peace and Integrity" should be structured in the society to erase any kind of inequality and mistrust among the different communities. With the increases in numbers of insurgency groups in Manipur during the ethnics' conflicts and communal clashes, youth are often a prey in name of protection for their land. In the ongoing conflicts between the State sponsored conflicts and the minority Kuki tribals, thousands of youth from both the community have volunteered their time, energy and life to defend for their land and own people. This has created disturbance in the education journey in the life of thousands of youth in Manipur. Conflicts have brought chaos across the state.

Objectives of the Study

1. To examine the present education system in Manipur University after the conflicts and violence.
2. To find out the implementation status of peace education in Manipur.
3. To examine the role of Assam Rifles inside Manipur University for mitigating violence and conflicts inside Manipur University.

Research Methodology

Qualitative approach was used for the study. Fifteen victims of Manipur Conflicts were identified through snow-ball samplings procedure. A self-made interview schedule was prepared to collect the information from the participants. The reliability and validity of the interview schedule was checked by split half method, and it is found 0.72 which is more reliable in nature. Data were collected through personal interview and online Focus Group Discussions (FGD) (Mishra, 2016). Consolidated criteria for reporting qualitative research (COREQ): a 32-item checklist for interviews and focus groups by Allison Tong, Peter Sainsbury, Jonathan Craig (2000) was used for collecting data. Further to examine the present education system in Manipur after the conflicts and violence researcher interviewed the administrative officers *via* telephone. Similarly, to examine the role of Assam Rifles inside Manipur University for mitigating violence and conflicts inside Manipur University administrative officers of Assam Rifle was also interviewed *via* telephone.

Result and Discussion

Present Education System in Manipur University after the Conflicts and Violence

The present education system in Manipur University after the conflicts and violence has erupted only for the Kuki community (including the teaching and non-teaching staff) inside the campus from 3 May, 2023 onwards. As per the source through online focus group discussions, since the university is central university, the students belonging to Kuki community believe that security and safety might be provided but mob of men are entering the central university (Manipur University) women hostel and looking for a particular community (Kuki community) because of the conflicts happening in different parts of the state. The women inside hostel did every possible way to protect themselves by locking the hostel gates. At the meantime, there are also videos of mobs shouting and chanting "we are looking for Kuki community inside the campus" (translated). The women belonging to Kuki community inside the campus panicked and literally hiding, running for their lives. They were ready to jump off the building and die instead of been captured in the hands of the Meitei mob, the women did not know why they are targeted. At the spot, their only last option to protect themselves from those mobs were chili powder in their hand from the kitchen to smash the face of the mob in case they attacked. The family of the students from the Kuki community back home was also very worried for their safety. The Mob includes students from Meitei community because the mob could access the hostel so easily and could recognize and detect the room of every Kuki student inside the campus. The mob forced themselves inside the hostel gates, they were shouting and lots of things also happens, doors were kicked, opened, windows were broken. The mob checked each room and bathrooms hunting only for the Kuki community inside the campus. The rooms and the belongings include academic certificates, laptops, printers are all destroyed by the mob including both men and women hostel. There were hostel security staffs and police present at the spot, but no help received by any of them, instead they were given free hand to carry out anything to this group of students. The students from Kuki community only received help by the Assam Rifles only. Since the Assam Rifles were shortage of Men powers, the Assam Rifles team took a longer time to rescue the Kuki students from their hostel to Assam Rifles camp inside the campus. The Assam Rifles play an important role in saving the lives of students from Kuki community inside Manipur University campus.

Implementation Status of Peace Education in Manipur

As per the focus group discussion (FGD) held in five colleges of Churachandpur district, there is peace and conflict resolution paper in BA political science paper in second semester but there is no Peace Education as a subject directly in the curriculum. The Rayburn College at Churachandpur district had actively organized a poetry on the topic Global Peace as mentioned by the students which was organized by English Department. The group believes that this type of activities are promoting awareness about peace among the peer's groups and to the society. The role of Evangelical Union (EU) also plays an important role in shaping the minds of the youth in the colleges. The Evangelical Union (EU) had prayer meeting every Friday and camps on spiritual growth every year. This activity has helped the students in building the peace of mind and career in the future life ahead. Lamka College and Bethany College had also organized a National seminar on Peace and Conflict Resolution. This Seminar had created a sense of responsibility among the college students in peace building in the society. The study showed that peace education components implanted in the existing curriculum were being taught through curriculum and extra curriculum activities.

In the context of Manipur, in September 2000, CFPEM (Centre for Peace Education Manipur) was established in Manipur University and is linked with the Education Department(s), SCERT (State Council for Education Research and Training) and is coordinated by Dr. Leban Serto for implementing peace education into the school curriculum and for training the teachers for peace to prepare the young minds for the overall development of peace in their day-to-day life. It was active for about a decade till 2012 in which activities were highlighted by Dr. Leban Serto. After analyzing the work on peace education, there has been a gap of about ten years from the establishment of CFPEM. The need for peace education has been recommended in his paper because of conflicts nature to prevent interviolence among the communities in Manipur and North-east India. Manipur has often experienced ethnic conflict in the state. Kipgen (2013) analyzed the conflict between the Kuki and the Naga. Land disputes, identity problem and government indifference seems to be the consequences of the ethnic conflicts that has occurred between the different communities. After 2012, CFPEM seems to be inactive and neglected and it has no reformation on school and university curriculum. According to Serto (2012), Peacemaking should be going on hand in hand, enable to communicate, continually flowing without any opposition towards quality and should not be static. Dealing with different types of struggles like overpower show of militants and goons has now become new norms during the conflicts. The need for learning to stay in harmony among different communities has now become necessary to adapt during the hard times.

The Role of Assam Rifles inside Manipur University for Mitigating Violence and Conflicts

The role of Assam Rifles inside Manipur University for mitigating violence and conflicts inside Manipur University has played an important role on the 3rd of May, 2023. As per the source through telephonic interview with Assam Rifles Officers, the minority community Kuki Tribes were targeted by the majority Meitei community inside the campus. There were lots of challenges inside the campus because of the distrust between the Kuki and Meitei community spreading across the state. Thousands of mobs were inside the campus attacking hostels and quarters inside the campus. The major challenges was evacuation challenges because of sort of manpower by the Assam Rifles. The evacuation process is slow. The Assam Rifles had evacuated thousands of students and staffs from their hostels and quarters to Assam Rifles Camps inside the Campus, later was shifted to 2nd MR and different parts of Assam Rifles Camp in the heart of Imphal City because of accommodation problem inside AR Camp inside MU Campus. Issues like crime against women was spreading across the state. There were lots of issues on responding to phone calls seeking for help from the minority Kuki tribes, by the Assam Rifles. The situation inside the campus was risky and Assam Rifles also suffered but their role and job had played an important role in saving the tribal students and staffs of Manipur University.

Conclusion

Education is a powerful tool for promoting peace in Manipur. By incorporating value-based education, teaching conflict resolution skills, and involving the community, we can build a more peaceful and harmonious society. It is essential for all stakeholders to work together to ensure the success of these initiatives and create a brighter future for the people of Manipur. At the present situation in Manipur, Education through Peace and quality education system will be the way forward to uplift the society during the conflict. Peace Education is the need of the hour to handle the situation on any type of conflicts prevailing across the state. It can act as a catalyst in addressing the root cause of ethnic conflicts and thus believe to bring resolution for future sustainable and more peaceful co-existence. The more peace and values we inculcate in our tender generation the more inclusive it will become to live in harmony with themselves, others and environment relishing their potential. Anti-social activities and conflicts are not recommended because they do not bring any positive outcome instead can led to separation and destruction. Peace Education in Manipur and North-east India is essential to promote peace among different communities living together in one region and to create more friendly and decent environment across the state. By implementing Peace Education in Manipur, it would shape a better earth to live in harmony and to uphold peace. This includes teaching the youth kindness and moral values towards the betterment of our mother earth. Last but not the least, by introducing Peace Education in Manipur will contribute to the overall growth and development with improvements in economic opportunities and quality of life. Implementing peace education in Manipur comes with its challenges, such as resistance from certain groups, lack of resources, and inadequate training for educators. To overcome these challenges, the government and NGOs should invest in teacher training, develop culturally relevant curricula, and allocate sufficient funds to peace education programmes.

REFERENCES

Basabose, J. de D. & Habyarimana, H. (2019). "Peace Education in Rwandan Secondary Schools: Coping with Contradictory Messages". *Journal of Peacebuilding & Development, 14*(2): 138-149. https://doi.org/10.1177/1542316619846825

Carter, C. (2022). "Elements and Structures of Peace Education in the United States". *Proceedings of the 2022 AERA Annual Meeting.* https://doi.org/10.3102/1881852

Census.(2011).Government of India (https://epaolive.net/download/education/2013/06/Manipur_Census_2011_Executive_Summary.pdf)

Chakrabarti, A. (16 April, 2024). *Behind India's Manipur Conflict: A Tale of Drugs, Armed Groups and Politics.* Aljazeera. (https://www.aljazeera.com/economy/2024/4/16/behind-indias-manipur-conflict-a-tale-of-drugs-armed-groups-and-politics)

Devi, N.R. (2008). "Conflict Situations and Children's Education in Manipur". *Journal of Indian Education,* NCERT, New Delhi.

Devi, O.S. (2019). "Youth and Peace Volunteering in Manipur". *International Journal of Peace Education and Development, 7*(1). https://doi.org/10.30954/2454-9525.01.2019.8

European Parliament Resolution of 13 July, 2023 on India, the Situation in Manipur [*2023/2781*(*RSP*)]. (13 July, 2023). European Parliament. (https://www.europarl.europa.eu/doceo/document/TA-9-2023-0289_EN.html)

Evidence of burnt Houses (n.d.). Google Photos. Retrieved May 2023, from https://photos.app.goo.gl/pu6W45dJs2aecp5v5

Gill, S. (2022). "Interreligious Education and Peace". *Wiener Beiträge Zur Islamforschung,* 105-123. https://doi.org/10.1007/978-3-658-36984-2_6

Googles Photos (May 2023). *Kuki Church Vandalised.* (https://photos.app.goo.gl/BFqSJB8nvb6y5V337)

Grewal, J.S., Sabharwal, N., Sharma, M.C., Singh, A., Gupta, K.M., Guru, G. & Pandey, S. (2004). *Peace Education* (1st edn.). National Council of Educational Research and Training. ISBN 81-7450-322-6

Harris, I.M. (2004). "Peace Education Theory". *Journal of Peace Education, 1*(1), 5-20. https://doi.org/10.1080/1740020032000178276

"How Fake News and Videos Inciting Violence in Manipur." (24 July, 2023). *The Economic Times* (https://m.economictimes.com/news/india/how-fake-news-and-videos-inciting-violence-in-manipur/articleshow/102065845.cms)

Imphal. (2024, October 28). "Thousands Participate in Tribal Solidarity March in Manipur". *The New Indian Express.* (https://www.newindianexpress.com/nation/northeast/2023/May/03/thousands-participate-in-tribal-solidarity-march-in-manipur-2571701.html)

Kipgen, N. (2013). "Politics of Ethnic Conflict in Manipur". *South Asia Research, 33*(*1*), 21-38. https://doi.org/10.1177/0262728013475541

Kuki Students Organisation. (2024, May). *The Indelible Trauma: The Truth behind Manipur Mayhem,* Vol.1.

Kuthar, G. (1 June, 2023). *Twitter.* (https://x.com/jeegujja/status/1664254576730701825?s=46)

Lähnemann, J. (2022). "Peace Education at the 10th World Assembly of Religions for Peace (RfP) 2019." *Peace Education and Religion: Perspectives, Pedagogy, Policies*, 357-372. https://doi.org/10.1007/978-3-658-36984-2_20

McLaughlin, C. (2022). "Building Enabling Environments in Schools as a Contribution to Peace". *Wiener Beiträge Zur Islamforschung*, 217-231. https://doi.org/10.1007/978-3-658-36984-2_12

Mishra, L. (2015). *Gandhian Views on Education for Peace.*

Mishra, L. (2022). "Practices of Peace Education Followed in the Secondary Schools of Mizoram India". *Wiener Beiträge Zur Islamforschung*, 505-517. https://doi.org/10.1007/978-3-658-36984-2_28

National Focus Group on Education for Peace (2006). National Council of Educational Research and Training.

NCERT (2007). *National Curriculum Framework 2005.*

Rajagopalan, P. (2009). "From Agenda to Action: Interpreting and Implementing the NCF Peace Education G (Volume 1)". *Educational Policy Research Series.*

Reardon, B.A. (2002). *Human Rights and the Global Campaign for Peace Education (283-284)*. Kluwer Academic Publishers. Printed in the Netherlands.

Sami Adwan (2022). "Preparing Future Teachers of Religious Education: An Approach to Peaceful and Harmonious Coexistence among the followers of different Religions". *Wiener Beiträge Zur Islamforschung,* 233-253. https://doi.org/10.1007/978-3-658-36984-2_13

Serto, L. (June 2012). *Peace Education.*

Singha, K. (2013). "Conflict, State and Education in India: A Case Study of Manipur". *American Journal of Educational Research, 1*(6), 181-193. https://doi.org/10.12691/education-1-6-3

Singha, Th. A. (2017). "Classical Opportunities for Culture of Peace Education" in *Peace Education* (pp. 22-25).

Suri, K. (2013). "Establishing Peace through Peace Education in the Schools of conflict-hit Jammu and Kashmir". *Global Academic Research Journal, 1*(2): 40-46.

Thomson, G. (2022). "The Relevance of Religions to Peace Education". *Wiener Beiträge Zur Islamforschung,* 67-85. https://doi.org/10.1007/978-3-658-36984-2_4

Tong, A., Sainsbury, P. & Craig, J. (2007). "Consolidated Criteria for Reporting Qualitative Research (COREQ): A 32-item Checklist for Interviews and Focus Groups." *International Journal for Quality in Health Care, 19*(6), 349-357. https://doi.org/10.1093/intqhc/mzm042

Zubair, M. (20 July, 2023). *Twitter.* (https://x.com/zoo_bear/status/1681796429571043328?s=46) (2023a, May). Google Photos. (https://photos.app.goo.gl/rXfiJLi8KJq83omM7) (2023b, May 22). Google Photos. (https://photos.app.goo.gl/h7mpooBaEAzPagVx8)

3

Peace and Value Education in India

Qaisur Rahman

Introduction

Education system is expected to create the necessary human capital and knowledge workers who will bring the country to greater heights. In this regard, a holistic education programme is needed which can equip students with both the hard and soft skills required as well as human values. However, the main emphasis on education today lies in acquiring large amounts of information passing examinations and securing qualifications for future employment. This chapter highlights the implementation of a programme called the education in human values. This programme seeks to improve the teaching-learning environment that will foster character building through the incorporation of basic universal values thus contributing towards academic excellence. The stress of an ever-increasing workload and a working environment dominated by social problems will continue to make a teacher's profession more difficult and less satisfying. With so many external influences, demands and constraints, it can be easy to lose hold of the values that make up a civilized society. This education in human values programme seeks to help teachers, parents and children to focus on the basic positive values that underlie all aspects of a moral society. This is done through what is called a triple role for education between teachers, parents and students meaning that all three groups play key roles in reversing current trends and in reaching towards the goal of truly successful value based education respectively. Peace education is the kind of method which helps in obtaining wisdom experience. It helps to develop attitudes skills and behaviour to live in oneness with each other. This concept basically apprehended from philosophical ideals. Peace education helps to nurture the values of non-violence, love, trust, respect towards human and all living organisms on our planet. It is a performance which leads towards peaceful socialization. By this kind of practice men could enshrine values. Highlighting peace education in schools is very much necessary. It begins first with an honest will-power to engage educators in the process of learning through which it is an essential and effective mean to modify them individually and collectively. The students must be competent to form and maintain peace. Peace education system is, therefore, enthusiasm to critical thinking and preparing students to act on their convictions. Peace education or the values related with peace is the ultimate goal of education which should be converted into immediate goals of education. These goals of education could be implemented in curriculum. Curriculum developer must observe these areas and consider them as a vital part of a curriculum by which practices of peace could be inculcated effectively. They must concern regarding peace when they are constructing or developing curriculum. This type of curriculum must provide a peaceful group to peaceful society which leads towards a peaceful planet. Human values are things that have an intrinsic worth in usefulness or importance to the possessor principles, standards or qualities considered worth-while or desirable. Human values constitute an important aspect of self-concept and serve as guiding principles for an individual. Human values are the virtues that guide us to take into account the human element when one interacts with other human beings. There are many positive dispositions that create bonds of the humanity between people and thus have value for all of us as human beings. They are our strong positive feelings for the human essence of the other. It's both what we expect others to do and what we aim to give to other human beings. These human values have the effect of bonding, comforting, reassuring, and procuring serenity. Human values are the foundation for any viable life within society they build space for a drive a movement towards one another which leads to peace. Human values thus the needs are universal they are shared by all human beings whatever their religion, their nationality, their culture and personal history. By nature they induce consideration for others. We can relate the human values to the three levels of consciousness—the conscious mind, the sub-conscious mind and the super conscious mind. One must realize that we are not just a body but we also have a mind which is very important in the learning process. The human values integrated learning concept starts with the interaction with the environment. Students have to study mathematics, sciences, languages and other subjects so as to prepare themselves for their careers in life. But at the same time, human values are integrated into all subjects so as to bring about peace and calmness of the mind which will prepare the learner for the journey within and that is education. When the conscious mind is raised towards the super-conscious mind then knowledge and wisdom will be drawn out from the education.

Human Values

The following is the basic principle of the human values integrated instructions:

(i) Human values are an integral part of all subjects and activities in the school and in the home. In fact human values are an integral part of our life.

(ii) The five human values of truth, right conduct, peace, love and non-violence are one and cannot be separated. If one value disappears then all the values will disappear.

(iii) Human values cannot be taught they have to be brought out from within the learner. It has been a mistake in the past where teachers have been teaching morality ethics, values and good character as subjects. Learners can memorize them and can pass examinations but they fail to put them into practice in their daily life. There seems to be a general decline in morality throughout the world. Transformation of the person cannot take place by mere teaching but can be achieved through self-realization when the values come out from within the learner. In such cases, there is a direct experience of the human values in the life of the learner.

(iv) In real life everything is interrelated. Thus, a good learning experience is to have an integrated approach. In our daily life we do not just have one value throughout the day. For example, right conduct cannot be there alone but it is found that all the five human values are inter-related and exist at the same time. Thus, it would be a mistake to teach one value at a time. In the same way, mathematics should not be taught as a separate subject as in real life science exists along side by side in all the subjects.

(v) Human values integrated instruction gives the learner the ability to solve problems from various perspectives by giving varied interrelated experiences.

(vi) Human values integrated instruction opens up a wider worldview for both the teacher and learner making the learning process much more interesting. The education in human values is a multi-cultural, multi-faith and self-development programme designed for children and young people all over the world. However, education in human values takes a holistic approach to educating the child and recognizes five values as an integral part of the human being. These values are recognized by all major religions adopt a multi-faith approach allow and encourage each child to follow his faith and are simply conducive to application in diverse cultural conditions. The function of most of the basic values is to make it possible for every human to realize or maintain the highest universal core values of life with love and happiness. Respect is one of the most important human values for establishing relations of peace and yet it remains elusive. Its understanding varies according to age of child, teenager and adult to one's education and surrounding culture. It is better understood when combined with other values. The disposition that is deeper than civility very close to consideration and approaching appreciation. Indeed to respect someone, one must be able to appreciate some of his human qualities even if one does not appreciate his opinions or past behaviour. The value system is an enduring organization of beliefs concerning preferable modes of conduct along a continuous importance. Thus, the importance of different values co-varies with the importance of others in the value system.

Significance Role of Value Education

Values are conscious and unconscious preferences, beliefs and attitudes which are accepted by the majority of members of society and are socially regulated. Values are standards to evaluate and judge. Values reflect one's personal attitude and judgements, decisions and choices behaviour and relationships dreams and vision. Education is a sub-system of society. Education and society both are interrelated or interdependent because both mutually influence each other, i.e. complimentary. Without education how we can build an ideal society and without society we can organize education system systematically that means both are needed to understand. Education helps individuals to learn how to live, how to behave, how to organize everything in their lives, so it is an agent which brings change in society or we can say in one line education is a social change agent. Human society is a set of connections of human relations interactions and interdependences. The interaction of persons takes place under such circumstances that such a course of interaction may be called a system. Social system refers to the orderly collection of parts or components of society particularly human interactions. Every individual in the practice of interaction influences each other. There is a significant lapse on the concept of human development and nation building process. With so many external influences, demands and constraints, it can be easy to lose hold of the values that make up a civilized society. The best way to address these issues is to impart value based ethical education that is incorporated in the academic curriculum just the way it was being practised in the ancient time. Where the education system was value based then education would help in the improvement of human character and recognition of their inner purity. The curriculum instructional materials and technology methods should be directed to inculcate values of humanism, socialism, national integration as well as ethical and moral values in general education. Life-long learning should aim at the pursuit of excellence and the attainment of quality life. Therefore, value oriented education is essential for balanced personality and harmonious society. It helps a person in unfolding his personality by bringing it forth and revealing the potentials and qualities in him.

Concept and Meaning of Peace

Education for peace is a conceptual framework from which schools may devise a programme comprising the transmission of universal values and enduring attitudes and the development of skills which enable our students to become active global citizens. The implementation of this conceptual framework recognizes the practice of peaceful relations at all levels—personal, familial, inter-cultural and global. It entails a process of knowledge acquisition and skill building which affects the behaviour of individuals and groups and provides a model for the formal and informal curriculum of the school. Education for peace is a process and condition which permeates all aspects of school life with implications for learner's teachers and administrators and it extends beyond the school to society as a whole.

Definition of the Peace Education

According to **Albert Einstein,** "Peace is not merely the absence of war but the presence of justice of law and of order". Peace education is an attempt to respond to problems of conflict and violence of scale ranging from the global and national to the local and personal.

According to **John Dewey,** "Peace education is grounded in active citizenship preparing learners for participation in a democracy through problem posing and problem solving education and a commitment to transformative action in our societies."

Peace of mind, serenity and calmness are descriptions of a disposition free from the effects of stress. In some cultures, inner peace is considered a state of consciousness or enlightenment that may be cultivated by various forms of training such as prayer, meditation, yoga. Many spiritual practices refer to this peace as an experience of knowing oneself. Finding inner peace is often associated with traditions and religious practices.

Concept of Education System in Indian Context

Education is a sub-system of society. Education and society both are interrelated or interdependent because both mutually influence each other, i.e. complimentary. Without education how we can build an ideal society and without society we can organize education system systematically that means both are needed to understand. Human society is a set of connections of human relations, interactions and interdependences. The interaction of persons takes place under such circumstances that of interaction may be called a system. System refers to the logical arrangements of parts. Social system refers to the orderly collection of parts or components of society particularly human interactions. Every individual in the practice of interaction influences each other. Social system refers to any kind of social grouping from a group of two friends to a large complex society. It is extensively used in sociology because it makes us to think of the way in which social units fit together into a whole and the basic similarities among all forms of social interaction.

Significance Role of Life Skill Education

Life skills are the abilities that help to promote psychosocial competence and general well-being of individuals. To enhance the efficiency of prospective pre-service teachers and to convert them into individuals with high potential teacher education programme should be reformed giving due importance to life skill education. Imparting life skills can empower prospective teachers to take positive action promotes healthy and positive social relationships. It also entails being able to establish productive interpersonal relationships. The teacher education curriculum should encompass life skill education to impart diversity of skills among prospective teachers thereby to build an open and flexible mind not only to adapt to diverse classroom situations but also to develop life skills of their students in real teaching situations. Life skill education as a full-fledged subject is necessary to enhance the efficiency and well-being of prospective teachers. Life skills help individuals to deal with rapid changes brought about by modernization. The life skills include creativity, critical thinking, problem solving and decision making, the ability to communicate and collaborate along with personal and social responsibility that contributes to become both a good citizen as well as a successful person. Life skill training equips people with the social and interpersonal skills that enable them to meet the challenges of daily life in an effective way. The life skills approach aims at assisting children to gain new ways of learning as well as control over their behaviour and to take informed decisions that can lead to gain positive values in life. Teaching life skills to young people prevents maladjustment and enhances human potential in discovering personal capacities like discussion debate and brain-storming respectively. Professional training in imparting life skill education for practicing teachers is the need of the hour. It has been felt that life skills education bridges the gap between basic functioning and capabilities in students. It strengthens the ability of an individual to meet the needs and demands of the present society and helps in dealing with the above issues in a manner to get desired behaviour changes. Imparting life skill training through inculcating life skill education will help youth to overcome such difficulties in life. This focuses on the importance of life skills education in curriculum, i.e. developing social-emotional and thinking skills in students as they are the important building blocks for a dynamic citizen who can cope up with future challenges and survive well.

Current Status of Skill Development in India

Teaching is a profession requiring specialization in terms of knowledge and skills. There exists a wide gap between theory and the knowledge and skills of teaching required in the actual classroom curriculum transaction. India has gradually evolved as a fast developing modern economy due to the abundance of qualified capable, motivated and flexible human capital. The term skills development is used to describe a wider array of institutions and activities influencing employment and earnings. When referring to the preparation of youth and adults for employment, a subtle shift in understanding occurs. Attention extends to informal learning on the job structured apprenticeships and other enterprise-based training along with government and non-governmental training programmes besides technical and vocational education. Skills development is a much broader concept more diverse hence more difficult to monitor. Despite the utmost important and attention given to education and training there is still a shortage of skilled manpower in India to address the mounting needs and demands of the economy. In the current scenario, the government is dedicatedly striving to initiate and achieve formal and informal skill development of the working population *via* education, vocational education or skill training and other upcoming learning methods the education research and innovations contribution to the field of youth and adult education for skills development. It is in line with the skills acquired in formal education to prepare youth and adults for the world of work ranging from informal learning on the job apprenticeship and enterprise based training to learning off the job in government and non-governmental training institutions. It also highlights livelihood programmes run by government under different programmes. The objective is to look into the current policies supporting skills development. The aim is to collect information learned from past policy interventions how higher education institutes can contribute in successful skill development of the country.

Education for Problem Solving Curriculum

Indigenous Knowledge Systems (IKS) are seldom reflected as a dynamic outcome of situated processes of continuing knowledge generation and innovation in response to changing socio-cultural and ecological conditions. We believe that the plurality of knowledge allows continuing critical projects to represent subject knowledge's reflect on learning across plural epistemic dispositions in a changing world. Alongside this evidence of adaptive knowledge transformation most indigenous knowledge practices have receded in rural areas and have in many cases been lost to urban indigenous populations due to exposure to Western livelihood systems and practices. In this way, current urban indigenous generations have suffered a double blow as a result of the lack of exposure to their knowledge heritage along with the experiential cultural capital to be able to successfully access the abstractions of modern scientific curriculum knowledge. Indigenous knowledge is approached as an adaptive and responsive sphere of meaning making and innovation that has been marginalized by continuing colonial modernity and an associated urbanization. The impacts of Westernized curriculum have played out as a double blow impeding many learners from relating knowledge to the world they live in and achieving their potential in the subject. This enabled us to contemplate a re-appropriation of heritage practices amongst teachers, their learners and parents as urban custodians of indigenous knowledge and to work with this as situated heritage practices for working with the modern scientific knowledge in the school curriculum to contemplate future sustainability. Mother Tongue re-appropriation is thus proposed as a starting point for a research collaboration to enhance epistemological access to decontextualized scientific knowledge in the curriculum and for exploring how this might be achieved in ways that open up a third space of empowering socio-cultural innovation through Education for Sustainable Development (ESD). The proposed integrating dialectical pedagogy is being undertaken by learners through engagement with parents and community elders as custodians of indigenous knowledge to generate knowledge practices that relate to contemporary environmental issues. These are being taken into a deliberative engagement with the curriculum that enables contextualized access for indigenous learners and reciprocal of knowledge in formal education processes. Reflecting on situated reflexive learning processes in this open-ended way it is possible to reframe curriculum encounters with subject so that learners might pose problems and engage with the scientific knowledge from within expansive cultural practices and propositions for engaged meaning making with the common goals in mind. This curriculum process raises contradictions that might provoke learning towards explanatory insights that resonate with the social realities of the modern world and emerging risk.

Problems and Challenges for Curriculum Development

Not only in India but in other countries of the world as well education is regarded as an imperative area that leads to growth and development of the individuals. One is able to sustain his living in an adequate manner when he is well educated and informative. The aims and objectives of any society or nation can be achieved when the education system is well-developed. Teacher education and curriculum development are considered as imperative areas for the development of the education system. Teachers have an important role to play towards society. It is essential for them to be efficient, skilled, resourceful, conscientious and diligent in the performance of job duties. Teacher education refers to the policies and procedures that are designed to equip the prospective teachers with the knowledge attitude and behaviour that is essential to perform one's job duties well within the classroom settings, schools and external to the educational institutions. Curriculum development is a problem solving process and it involves the consideration of the needs and problems for the upgrading of the programmes and the implementation of solutions and alternatives for learners and their frameworks. Education is the key for development of any nation and it depends upon the quality of teachers. Information awareness, commitment, quality, professionalism and motivation of teachers are the factors responsible for quality education and learner achievement. Well-organized and less genius teacher education programmes are required in the present world. Teacher education programmes have to be critiqued, studied, reformed and reoriented in the present existence. Curriculum development is concerned with the development of content and material that would facilitate the learning of students. It is vital to formulate appropriate measures and procedures that would enhance teacher education and curriculum development. The curriculum should include space for learning beyond subject boundaries so that children and young people can make connections between different areas of learning. Interdisciplinary studies based upon groupings of experiences and outcomes from within and across curriculum areas can provide relevant challenging and enjoyable learning experiences and stimulating contexts to meet the varied needs of children and young people. The students should be provided relevant information and knowledge that would not only enhance their academic concepts but also inculcate the traits of morality ethics norms and values within them.

Discussion

The human values integrated learning concept obtained through intuition has gained wide acceptance around the world. The students and teachers have benefited greatly from this unique method of teaching and learning experience. The nation needs heroes who can bring their country to greater heights. What we witness today is that current approaches to education only address at most one or two aspects of personality in the teachings. These techniques are not adequate in bringing out the potential latent in each child. In most education system, individuals are treated merely as action agents unable to bring out the divine potential within a child. By adopting the human values approach with the right teaching techniques it has been proven that it is possible to create a balanced individual and society. The good education system with the education in human values can make it a reality. Human values play a very leading role in present educational institutions. Human values take precedence over social values. Human values are now withering very fast for which we humans are most responsible. The value based education should be emphasized ranging from school to university level of education. Human value is generally known to be a moral standard of human behaviour. Therefore, human values should be preserved and protected. Human values may be treated as keys to the solution of the global problems. Already some universities prescribed human values and moral values syllabus to improve the humanity of the students. It is a great achievement to present society and educational institutions.

The skill is the learned ability to carry out the task with pre-determined results often within a given amount of time, energy or both. In other words, the abilities that one possesses. Skills can often be divided into domain general and domain specific skills. Skill usually requires certain environmental stimuli and situations to assess the level of skill being shown and used. India has gradually evolved as the developing modern economy due to the abundance of qualified capable motivated and flexible human capital. However, there is a need to further develop and empower the human capital to ensure that country is standing tough and tall in global competitiveness. The term skills development is used to describe the wider array of institutions and activities influencing employment and earnings. When referring to the preparation of youth and adults for employment a shift in understanding occurs. The results begin to shift from talking about education to development of skills. The informal learning on the job structured apprenticeships and other enterprise based training along with government and non-governmental training programmes besides technical and vocational education. Skills development is much broader concept more diverse, hence more difficult to monitor. Despite the utmost important and attention given to education and training there is still shortage of skilled manpower in India to address the mounting needs and demands of the economy. In the current scenario, the government is dedicatedly to initiate and achieve formal or informal skill development of the working population *via* education, i.e. vocational education or skill training and other upcoming learning methods. The peace education's purpose is to introduce amplify, condense and positioned the outset of the thinking of the students regarding the concept of peace. There are many approaches to peace education has lot of thoughts that basically depends on ideology, realistic experience and good passions. Peace is the kind of internal and external mental satisfaction that effect life directly. This might be on educating our next offspring with the skills attitudes sights and values and behavioural structures that would help them to make and sustain peace in the era of 21st century.

Conclusion

All humans are ideal social animals, their successful life leading is largely dependent on their successful social relations. The use of co-operative learning so, therefore, educates the pupils with various competencies needed to construct and carry on positive peace. The important factors which is essential to be accomplished at different levels of educational institutions to organize peace education in educational institutions. It helps to secure pupils from the generally opponents for several years.

REFERENCES

Amabile, T.M. (1983). "The Social Psychology of Creativity and Componential Conceptualization". *Journal of Personality and Social Psychology, 45*(2): 357-377.

Bereiter, C., and Scardamalia, M., (2008): *Toward Research Based Innovation in Innovating to Learn Learning to Innovate,* OECD, Paris, pp. 67-88.

Brown, A.L. (1994). *The Advancement of Learning: Educational Researcher, 23*(8): 554-562.

Darling-Hammond, L. and Baratz Snowden, J. (2007). "A Good Teacher in Every Classroom Preparing the Highly Qualified Teachers Our Children Deserve". *Educational Horizons, 85*(2): 111-132.

Deutsch, M. (1949). "A Theory of Co-Operation and Competition." *Human Relations, 2*: 129-152.

Galtung, J. (1996). *Peace by Peaceful Means: Peace and Conflict, Development and Civilization,* PRIO: International Peace Research Institute of Oslo and Sage Publication.

Herrington, J. and Oliver, R. (2000). "Instructional Design of Frameworks for Authentic Learning Environment". *Educational Technology Research and Development, 48*(3): 23-48.

Hicks, D. (1985). *Education for Peace: Issues Dilemmas and Alternatives.* Lancaster: St. Martin's College. London.

Inderpreet, K.C. (2015). "Innovative and Best Practices in Teaching", *Learning and Evaluation, 4*(10): 155-159.

Johnson D.W. and Johnson, F. (2009). *Joining Together: Group Theory and Group Skills*: (9th edn.). Boston: Allyn and Bacon.

Johnson, D.W. and Johnson, R. (1996-b). "Cooperative Learning and Traditional American Values". *NASSP Bulletin, 80*(579): 11-18.

Karpagam, S. and Ananthasayanam, R. (2012). "Soft Skills in Teacher Education Programme". *Education Tracks*, p. 11.

Kreidler, W.J. (1995). *Teaching Conflict Resolution Through Children's Literature*, New York: Scholastic.

Mazumdar, A. (1998). *Developing Values Education for the New Millennium Through a Cross-cultural Approach: (SSEHV). Theory and Practice.*

Naga Subramani, P.C. (2011). *Effective Teaching and Learning*, Laxmi Book Publication, Solapur.

Narayan, R.S. (2006). *A Textbook on Professional Ethics and Human Values*, New Age International Pvt. Ltd., New Delhi.

Norman, R. (1998). *The Moral Philosophy: An Introduction to Ethics*, Oxford University Press, Oxford.

Padmanabhan, J. and Manjula, R.P. (2007). "Approach and Problem Solving Ability in Science". *Journal of Community Guidance and Research, 28*(1): 56-70.

Pradeep, K. and Raman, C. (2013). *Human Values and Professional Ethics*, Paramount Publishing House, Hyderabad.

Qaisur, R. (2021). "Educational Quality and Sustainable Development of Students Learning and teaching through Skills Development in India". *Journal of Education and Development, 11*(22): 8-22.

Qaisur, R. (2021). "Role of Developing Perception and Professional Ethics towards Personal Values among Secondary School Students". *Journal of Education and Development, 11*(22): 74-85.

Qaisur, R. (2021). "Significance Role of Value Education: Its Importance and Need at Present Education System in India". *Journal of Education and Development, 11*(22): 113-122.

Qaisur, R. (2023). "Need of Human Values in Educational Institutions for Social Development of Students". *Journal of Education and Development, 13*(26): 74-84.

Rank, J., Pace, V.L. and Frese, M. (2004). "Three Avenues for Future Research on Creativity Innovation, and Initiative". *Applied Psychology, 53*(4): 518-528.

Tapia, G. (2009). *The Importance of Human Values in the Education in the Presence of the Globalization Challenges*. Penguin Ltd.

Tripathi, A.N. (2008). *Human Values,* New Age International Pvt. Ltd. New Delhi.

4

Inclusive Education as a Catalyst of Peace

Tage Yalung and *Prasanta Kumar Acharya*

Introduction

The world is a diverse place enriched with a rich diversity of people belonging to a wide range of nationalities, cultures, beliefs, identities, abilities, and social and economic backgrounds. While the rich diversity adds to the strength and beauty, it also presents challenges in fostering understanding and harmony among the different groups. There has been an alarming report of increasing disruptions of peace worldwide due to existing differences. One of the pressing issues today thereby is the need to promote peace education to ensure a way— away from any conflicts, and transition from discord to dialogue. While no doubt education serves a fundamental role as a driving force of change, Inclusive Education, a powerful social cohesion tool, can play a primary role in navigating the challenges and functioning as a catalyst for peace. Grounded in the principle that "education is a fundamental human right" and "social justice for all". The concept of inclusive education signifies a major paradigm shift (Kuhn, 1997; Vad'urová & Pančocha, 2023). It ensures an equitable and accessible education for all, irrespective of their abilities, disabilities, or any differences in formal, non-formal, and informal settings. It ensures a fair chance for all to come, learn, and grow together side by side, benefiting all (UNESCO, 2019).

Inclusive Education and Social Equity

1. **Access to Quality Education:** Inclusive education ensures that every child from diverse backgrounds has the same equitable opportunities. It fosters a supportive learning environment (Ainscow & Miles, 2008; Hasan, Halder & Debnath, 2018), provides the students with differentiated instruction to ensure each student can effectively access the curriculum (Tomlinson, 2014), and advocates for equal access to teaching-learning resources (Booth & Ainscow, 2016).
2. **Upliftment of the Marginalized Section of Society:** A marginalized section of society refers to the group of people in society that are sidelined and face limitations to their access to rights, opportunities, and resources. These include people from various castes, genders, classes, disabilities, religious minorities, language speaking etc. They are highly prone to facing exclusion. Inclusive education serves as a means to equity, access, and social justice (Lindsay, 2003), and elevates marginalized communities (Hasan *et al.*, 2018).
3. **Empowerment and Self-esteem:** Inclusive education reinforces the idea of belonging and equal rights (Ainscow & Miles, 2008). It equips an individual with the essential tools and supports requisite to function and participate fully in society (Uchem, Ngwa, & Asogwa, 2014). It contributes to the development of a skilled

workforce and future leaders who are likely to advocate for equity and social justice.

Inclusive Education and Social Integration

1. **Promotes Diversity:** Breaking the barriers of social isolation—inclusive education brings learners from diverse backgrounds together into mainstream classrooms (Ballard, 1997). This exposure develops positive relationships among peers from diverse backgrounds and a deeper understanding, and appreciation for diversity.
2. **Improved Learning Outcome:** Studies indicate that inclusive education not only benefits and improves the overall learning outcomes of the marginalized but also of every learner as they are interfaced with a positive, diverse, and supportive learning environment.
3. **Long-term Social Benefits:** Inclusive education contributes to long-term social benefits by developing a sense of empathy, understanding, and acceptance in individuals (UNESCO, 2020). This fosters a positive outlook and cooperation in learners. The benefit extends beyond empowering individuals to build a more inclusive and harmonious society that promotes social cohesion and peace.

Role of Inclusive Education in Peace Building

1. **Promotes Social Cohesion:** The integration of learners from diverse backgrounds, provides opportunities to instil a sense of understanding, acceptance, support, respect for one another's differences, and value for diversity. These also help in dismantling stereotypes and diminishing prejudices, leading to greater social cohesion in the long-term.

2. **Addresses Root Causes of Conflict:** Deprivation and disparity in any form are the root causes of conflict, leading to tension and violence. Inclusive education addresses these root causes (Smith & Vaux, 2003). It fosters values such as support, inclusion, justice, and equity, which are essential for building a peaceful society (UNESCO, 2016).
3. **Cultivates a Culture of Peace:** Inclusive education instils conflict-resolving skills and the values of respect, collaboration, and non-violence. This contributes to the cultivation of future generations of peacebuilders who will ensure and promote the peaceful coexistence of all. One take away is the success story of Rwanda, a country that had a gruesome history of genocide. The country witnessed a developmental step towards peace with the promotion of inclusive education (Uchem *et al.*, 2014).
4. **Supports Peacebuilding in Post-Conflict Settings:** Inclusive Education can play a key role in reconciliation and healing in post-conflict societies. It can prevent the re-emergence of hostilities by promoting a shared vision of peace and by building a democratic and inclusive society where voices are heard and conflicts are resolved through dialogue.

Conclusion

Driven by the principles of access, equity, social justice, inclusion, cohesion, positive outcomes, and empowerment of all, Inclusive Education plays a crucial role in society and in addressing the root causes of conflicts in societies that disrupt peace. Inclusive education is unquestionably a critical strategy for addressing discrimination in any form that results in conflict and indeed is a viable approach to achieving sustainable, peaceful coexistence. It aids in the creation of a more equitable, prosperous, and peaceful world. And due to the very nature of inclusive education that involves 'educating all', it instils values that promote peace in learners. The urgent need, therefore, is; in the reconsideration of inclusive education and a proper implementation and investment in inclusive education, by addressing any barriers to inclusive education to yield significant returns in terms of 'peace' for society in the future.

REFERENCES

Ainscow, M. & Miles, S. (2008). "Making Education for All Inclusive: Where Next?", *Prospects, 38*(1): 15-34. https://doi.org/10.1007/s11125-008-9036-0

Ballard, K. (1997). "Researching Disability and Inclusive Education: Participation, Construction and Interpretation". *International Journal of Inclusive Education, 1*(3): 243-256.

Booth, T. & Ainscow, M. (2016). *The Index for Inclusion: A Guide to School Development led by Inclusive Values.* Centre for Studies on Inclusive Education.

Hasan, M., Halder, U.K. & Debnath, D. (2018). "Inclusive Education and Education for All". *International Journal of Research and Analytical, 5*(3): 605-608.

Kuhn, T.S. (1997). *The Structure of Scientific Revolutions* (Vol. 962). Chicago: University of Chicago Press.

Lindsay, G. (2003). "Inclusive Education: A Critical Perspective". *British Journal of Special Education, 30*(1): 3-12.

Smith, A. & Vaux, T. (2003). *Education, Conflict and International Development.*

Tomlinson, C.A. (2014). *The Differentiated Classroom: Responding to the Needs of All Learners* (2nd edn.). ASCD.

Uchem, R.N., Ngwa, E.S. & Asogwa, U.D. (2014). *Inclusive Education and Sustainable Peace in Africa.*

UNESCO. (2016). *Education for People and Planet: Creating Sustainable Futures for All.* Global Education Monitoring Report. UNESCO.

UNICEF (2019). *Inclusive Education.* UNICEF. https://www.unicef.org/education/inclusive-education

UNESCO (2020). *Global Education Monitoring Report 2020: Inclusion and Education: All Means All.* UNESCO. https://www.unesco.org/gem-report

Vad'urová, H. & Pančocha, K. (2023). "Inclusive Education in the Czech Republic: A Scoping Review of a Paradigm Shift". *European Journal of Education, 58*(2): 245.

5

Role of School in Nurturing Peace among Children

Kritika Mishra

Introduction

Recently almost every individual is struggling with persistent inequalities, hate speech, violence conflicts and discrimination at different places and levels. Education has a vital role in developing a culture of peace in individuals as well as in society (United Nations, 1999). So, there is a strong need to address peace education within school because school serves as an agency for socialization and formal learning, and it is a school responsibility to create a culture of peace, i.e. to develop attitude, skills, values and knowledge to maintain peace. If children feel safe and have peaceful environment within school, then they learn the value of promoting peace. In the school, classroom works as a laboratory where transformational ideas, knowledge are received and nurtured. With the support of teachers socially responsible initiatives are designed to cultivate values among children. School curriculum should be designed in such a way where all topics of the subjects are interrelated and leads towards peaceful and happy life.Teacher serves as influencer in the society because students imitate them. Teacher's creativity and school climate determine the implementation of peace education (Kartadinata *et al.*, 2018). If a teacher is peaceful then she/he can promote peace. If it is not so then he can not teach because their behaviour is contrary to what they teach (UNESCO, 2005). Teacher should not use harsh words and violent behaviour within the school and society. Teacher should teach the basic principles of peace education and its effect on the human life with the synchronization in the society. Teacher can design an ample activity to support the creation of peaceful school climate. Building peaceful environment within the school is the responsibility of school stakeholders. Sometimes in the school surroundings students fight turns into violence because they do not know how to resolve the issue in constructive way. School is the best place for inculcation of peace. Thus, Peace Education plays a significant role in the education system.

Peace Education

Peace Education is a powerful tool for preventing and resolving social division and intolerance and promoting peace building, social cohesion and sustainable development. Peace Education facilitates peace and harmony in the society. Peace education is the most appropriate strategy to promote a culture of Peace. Peace education is not just limited to the teaching of prevention of war, conflicts and how to resolve it rather it is the learning of development of insight among learners to respect the diversityand inculcation of values that are relevant for local and global context. Peace education is an urgent necessity for developing an understanding of resolving conflicts. According to Fountain (1999: 1) peace education refers as the process of promoting the knowledge, skills, attitudes and values needed to bring about behavioural changes that will enable children, youth and adults to prevent conflict and violence, both overt and structural transform conflict peacefully; and to create the conditions conducive to peace, whether at an intrapersonal, interpersonal, intergroup, national, or international level. Peace education is a lifelong learning process. Initially it start from family then moving towards school, higher education institutions and workplace. Peace education empowers learner to utilize their creative and non-violence means and deliver message to the society that every problem will be handled by Peace. It is not just what we educate for but also how we show in our action, words and behaviour and create a culture of peace and should practice in our daily life.

The objectives of Peace Education are:

1. To shape the character of the children with love, care, well-being, empathy and respects for others.
2. Inculcation of values—social, moral, cultural, human, spiritual and aesthetic.
3. To develop competencies through which they become citizen of peace and peace messenger.
4. To increase social competence and social connectedness among children.
5. To decrease aggression, disrupted disorder and behaviour of the children.

In the education system excessive focus is on Academic achievement, advancement and unfortunately neglecting the dimension of human authenticity. Education system is failed when it is unable to equip the children with ability to live peacefully. Kartadinata *et al.* (2016) showed that building a safe and peaceful classroom climate has not become the vision and mission of the teachers because they put more emphasis on mastering the subject matter. Nurturing peace through education is a complex process and it requires comprehensive, multifaceted approach involving curriculum design, teachers' training etc. Human rights and multiculturism should be integrated with the school subject. In the subjects like social science teaching and learning, focus should be on understanding of past, present and future and telling the stories of wars and conclude that all wars are the powerful tool to destroy mankind and peace is the only way to save mankind and universe. There is a negative correlation between violence and academic growth. A study by Fusco and Fantuzzo (2009) revealed that violence contributes to lack of attention span, problematic behaviour and academic decline. Sternberg *et al.* (2006) showed violence increased personal problems, deviant behaviour and sometimes it can cause trauma. The content of peace education should be in the form of noble peace award story and daily life events and skills that occurs within classroom and outside, that are able to students to become agents of peace in their lives (McLeod & Reynolds, 2010). In the curriculum, the peace education is introduced as a subject in which meaning, objectives, theories and principles are taught in the school but sometimes fail to impart peace in their behaviour. In the curriculum, all the topics are directed to lead a peaceful and happy life but the learning process about is has not been real in the classroom (Kartadinata, Setiadi & Ilfiandra, 2018). So, there is a need to focus on pedagogical approaches that helps to inculcate peace among children.

Pedagogical Approach for Peace Education

Peace education pedagogy is an art of teaching peace education within the school, and it is not merely learning about the peace and war but developing an insight about learning to live peaceful citizen of the society. Peace education pedagogy is the process of developing attitude among children to serve as a peace-loving citizen of the society, having positive mindset, learn conflict resolution skills and anger management skills. The pedagogical approach to peace should be holistic, humanistic, participatory, cooperative and experiential. In peace education pedagogy teacher should use collaborative, cooperative learning and experiential learning as these methodologies focus on learning together, learn from experience of our own as well as of others, sharing and caring which constitute to the foundation of Peace. The focus should be on—How to learn rather than being informative and rote learning. Virginia Cawagas (2007) has identified four key pedagogical principles in peace education, i.e. holism, value formation, dialogue, critical empowerment. Holism shows all issues are interrelated and multidimensional. so it focuses on development of holistic approach. A holistic vision involves looking at past, present and future and at micro, macro level. To accomplish this whole school approach should be incorporated in the education system which laid emphasis on developing insight among children to see holistic view of the things not just the parts. Secondly, peace education should focus on inculcation of values because values are the base of peace education, and thirdly, dialogue is a key component of peace education pedagogy, because it laid emphasis on how to expressive ourself. He suggested some tools for dialogue as small group discussions, role play and guest lectures etc. The last is critical empowerment, i.e. development of deeper understanding of problems and take action to resolve the actions.

Following points should be considered for peace education pedagogy:

- Focus should be on self-initiative and participatory approach.
- Imparting peace through religious activities and media.

- Organizes conferences, seminars, talk, on peace in school as well as in public domain.
- Motivate learners to promote peace.
- Conduction of peace education programme.
- Incorporate peace education as basic teachers training certification.

Strategies to Promote Peace within School

School is the place where children learn knowledge, skills which refine their behaviour and ultimately make them as the responsible citizen of the society. A child reflects what he/she has learnt from their school, family, and society. It is a prime duty of the school to provide secure and peaceful environment to them. To promote peace, these are some strategies that should incorporate within school:

Mindful Learning: Mindset plays significant role in the life because all the wars, hatred and conflicts begin in our mind. A calm mindset always thinks about the conflict resolution and try to avoid the situation where conflicts might take place. "Mindfulness is a way of training our minds through intentional awareness so one can stay in a more peaceful and compassionate state" (Srinivasan, 2014: 27). In the school the focus should be on mindful learning which develop insight among children for openness and to be live in the present moment. "Mindfulness teach learner to how to focus their attention back after losing focus and again maintain their attention" (Hanh, 2011). "Mindfulness can help learners to get rid of distractions, negativity, fear, anger and anxiety" (Hassed & Chambers, 2014). It helps in increasing personal well-being and develop the tools to work for social justice. It helps in reducing stress and enhance our ability to recognize and manage emotions, gives emotional stability.

Conflict Resolution Programme: Conflicts are natural, necessary and important in our life. As we all have different thought process, perception, so disagreement occurs at most of the places which results in conflicts. It can have both positive and negative aspects. In the positive aspect sometimes, it means to encourage initiative, creativity and in the negative aspect it leads towards violence. Conflict resolution programme focus on developing critical skills and ability among individual to deal effectively with conflicts. Skills which are essential for conflict resolution are effective listening, perspective taking, emotional awareness and emotional control. Effective listening is the first step of communication. By active listening and responding to another person ultimately improves understanding. Perspective taking is the most important skill. When children learn to take the perspective of another, they can increase their ability to empathize with another person. In the school system, the focus should be on development of empathy by narrating stories of peace and war and create a scenario where they learn how to put oneself into someone else's shoe then only, one can unlikely judge another one in unfair means. The more we empathize with someone then there is lesser chance of conflict.

Anger Management: Anger is a natural emotion but we all should learn the art to manage it. In the school, the Anger management workshop should be organized so that children learn to express their anger in form which does not involve into violence.

There are four steps of anger management:

1. *Admit it:* When you feel angry admit it to yourself.
2. *Explore it:* Firstly, identify what made you angry and try to understand the situation.
3. *Express it:* Find the way to calm yourself, take deep breath and walk and try to express in normal way.

4. *Drop it:* If possible, try to drop it and be calm in the situation.

Learning to Live Together: School is the place where diversity is seen, i.e. children are coming from different religion, culture, caste, class, language, social economic status. It is the schools' responsibility to bring all children at one level and teach them to respect the diversity among them, accept each other and learning to live together. In the school, main festivals of every religion should be celebrated to indulge everyone with one another by accepting the rituals that develops the feeling of belongingness with each other.

Raising Awareness to Settle Dispute without Resorting to Violence: This is the basic thing which school should teach their children. It is school's duty to raising awareness about the dispute settlement without violence by showing the role play, drama that conclude that violence is not only the solution of any problem there are always better alternative to solve the issue.

To achieve all these, there is a strong need to build competencies among children such as Active listening, collaborative and team-work, self-awareness, sensitivity to gender, religious and cultural differences and openness to others, mediation and negotiation, interpersonal and intercultural communication, critical thinking, nurturing values, respect, empathy and responsibility, reconciliation and forgiveness (UNESCO Arigatou International, 2008).

Conclusion

Peace will be achieved when all citizens are aware and understand the local and global issues and learn conflict resolution skills, anger management skills, mindfulness, respect for diversity. Children plays incredible role in creating peaceful world. They can work as a messenger of peace. They should feel empowered to make positive changes to the world, find innovative ways to resolve the conflicts, understanding and practicing equalities, freedom and justice. Building a peaceful environment within the school should be the prime duty of school stakeholders where optimal development of the children take place and children get the freedom of expression, learn sharing and caring and respect the individuality of one another. Teacher plays significant role in character formation of their children so the prominent figure in the school is teacher whose behaviour really means to their children so teacher should organize group assignment, field trip, celebration of national and international festivals, guidance and counselling services collaborative and cooperative learning methods are the best way to nurture peace among children.

REFERENCES

Arigatou Foundation. (2008). *Learning to Live Together*. An Intercultural and Interfaith Programme for Ethics Education. Geneva, ATAR Roto Presse SA. https://ethicseducationforchildren.org/images/zdocs/Learning-toLive-Together-En.pdf

Cawagas, V. (2007). "Pedagogical principles in educating for a culture of peace", in S.H. Toh & V. Cawagas (Eds.) *Cultivating Wisdom, Harvesting Peace*. Brisbane, Queensland: Multi-Faith Centre, Griffith University.

Fountain, S. (1999). "Peace Education in UNICEF". *Working Paper.* New York, UNICEF. https://www.unicef.org/education/files/PeaceEducation.pdf

Fusco, R.A. & Fantuzzo, J.W. (2009). "Domestic Violence Crimes and Children: A Population-Based Investigation of Direct Sensory Exposure and the Nature of Involvement". *Children and Youth Services Review*, 31(2), 249-256.

Hanh, T.N. (2011). *Planting Seeds: Practicing Mindfulness with Children.* Berkeley, CA: Parallax Press.

Hassed, C. & Chambers, R. (2014). *Mindful Learning: Reduce Stress and Improve Brain Performance for Effective Learning*. Boulder, CO: Shamhala Publications Inc.

Kartadinata, S., Setiadi, R. & Ilfiandra (2018). *Pedagogi Pendidikan Kedamaian: Rujukan Pengembangan Sekolah Aman dan Damai.* UPI Press.

Kartadinata, S., Setiadi, R. & Ilfiandra (2016). Pengembangan Model Pedagogi Kedamaian Untuk Membangun Budaya Damai Pada Jalur Pendidikan formal. Laporan penelitian unggulan P.T. Bandung: LPPM Universitas Pendidikan Indonesia.

Kim, J., Talbot, N.L. & Cicchetti, D. (2009). "Childhood Abuse and Current Interpersonal Conflict: The Role of Shame". *Child Abuse and Neglect, 33*(6), 362-371.

McLeod, J. & Reynolds, R. (2010). *Peaceful Pedagogy, Teaching Human Rights through the Curriculum.* UK: Newcastle University.

Sternberg, K.J., Lamb, M.E., Guterman, E. & Abbott, C.B. (2006). "Effect of Early and Later Family Violence on Children's Behaviour Problems and Depression: A Longitudinal, Multi-Informant Perspective". *Child Abuse and Neglected, 30*(2).

Srinivasan, M. (2014). *Teach, Breathe, Learn: Mindfulness in and out of the Classroom.* Berkeley, CA: Parallax Press.

UNESCO (2005). *Peace Education: Framework for Teacher Education.* New Delhi: Safdarjung Enclave.

6

Peace the Dynamic Philosophy of Egalitarian World

Soumya Ranjan Panigrahi, Bimal Soreng, Sonalita Nayak, Anupam Kumar Patel and *Jubraj Khamari*

Introduction

What is Peace?

Silence and space are the meaning of peace for an individual in a crowded bus, but for a man in jail peace meaning roaming around freely in the crowded market with friends. It is very clear that the meaning of peace varies from individual to individual and also depend upon the situation. But the most generalized meaning of peace can be written as a state of calmness, security and freedom from the inner conflicts as well as from the outer world. Peace is itself a life long process and also a fundamental need of every living species.

The Western philosophy explained peace as a state of harmony within the soul and the state that can be acquired through justice. There absence of war, battles and conflicts and presence of rule of law are some of the pathways to achieve peace. Individual and its relationship with the society also determine the state of peacefulness, hence peace is also a social contact, in which individuals collectively agree to form a set of laws and govern themselves. Hence, we can see that the Western aspect of peace is more concerned with the individual relationship with the surrounding and with himself.

However, the eastern philosophy gave a specific emphasis to inner harmony, the concept of divinity in all living beings and there interconnections. The central Hindu philosophy of peace revolves around the concept of *ahimsa* that is non-violence which was emphasized by the Vedas as well as great saints like Mahatma Gandhiji. It gave importance to the idea of *dharma,* i.e. one's duty, it states that if an individual performs his duty with true devotion and righteousness he will achieve peace. Buddha's view on peace is *Nirvana* or the liberation that can only be achieved by non-attachment to the worldly things, and absence of desires will lead to peace.

Why Peace is Necessary for All Living Beings

Peace will ensure security, security will ensure freedom, freedom will ensure growth and growth will ensure progress for the individual as well as for the society. Peace is one of the fundamental needs of all living beings in this world and it is rightly said that "threat to peace anywhere is a threat to humanity everywhere". In the current world, there is enormous growth of technology and the same technology is a beautiful tool that work towards betterment of lives of millions but it also can be used as a tool to cause severe damage to the world in the form of wars. Peace is necessary to guide the technological developments towards a positive side. Social issues like gender inequality, social discrimination, racial discrimination, persecution of religious minorities etc. can be reduced drastically by the development of peace in the society and peace can be achieved through proper education that will make people aware of the reality and develop tolerance in them. However, there is a need of global cooperation among the leaders of the world to deal with this issue and to spread peace.

Philosophies of the World and the Idea of Peace

In the ancient world there were development of various religious philosophy took place and all of them preach the idea of peace in there own ways. The reason for the development and acceptance of religious philosophy across the world is that they guide the individual to be a socialize person and teach them the most accurate way to live in the society and work for its betterment. We can take examples from *Bible* itself the word of Christ "Oh god they don't know what they are doing please forgive them." It shows the sense of tolerance and non-violence which is the pathway to peace. The same goes with Hindu and Islamic as well as Buddhist philosophy.

The philosophy of peace varies with the change in the parent philosophy hence we will try to extract the philosophical meaning of peace in various philosophies in this world.

Vedic Philosophy

Vedic philosophy, which forms the foundation of Hindu thought, places a significant emphasis on the concept of peace, known as "*Shanti*". Peace in Vedic philosophy is not merely the absence of conflict but is viewed as a harmonious state of existence, encompassing the self, society, nature, and the cosmos. This holistic understanding of peace is deeply intertwined with the principles of *Dharma* (moral order), *Rita* (cosmic order), and *Satya* (truth).

Shanti (*Peace*)

- Shanti is a central concept in Vedic philosophy, representing peace at various levels: personal, societal, and universal. It is often invoked in Vedic chants and prayers, like the Shanti Mantras, which seek peace in all realms—physical, mental, and spiritual.

- The phrase "Om Shanti Shanti Shanti" is commonly recited to invoke peace in the body, mind, and environment, reflecting a comprehensive desire for tranquility.

Dharma (Righteousness)

- *Dharma* is the moral law that governs individual's conduct and is considered essential for maintaining order and peace in society. It is believed that when individuals and societies adhere to *Dharma*, peace naturally ensues.
- The Vedic texts emphasize that peace can be achieved through righteous living, fulfilling one's duties, and maintaining harmony with the natural and cosmic laws.

Rita (Cosmic Order)

- *Rita* represents the natural and cosmic order that governs the universe. It is the principle of harmony and balance that ensures the smooth functioning of the cosmos.
- Peace, in this context, is seen as the result of aligning human actions with *Rita*, thereby maintaining balance in nature and society.

Ahimsa (Non-violence)

- *Ahimsa*, or non-violence, is a core value in Vedic philosophy that contributes to peace. It teaches restraint from causing harm to others, whether through thoughts, words, or actions.
- By practicing *Ahimsa*, individuals contribute to a peaceful existence, both within themselves and in the world around them.

Peace in Vedic philosophy is a multifaceted concept that encompasses inner tranquility, social harmony, and cosmic balance. It is deeply connected to living in accordance with *Dharma*, practicing non-violence, truthfulness, and maintaining harmony with the natural and cosmic orders. The pursuit of peace is seen as a spiritual endeavour, essential for individual well-being and the sustenance of the universe.

Biblical Philosophy

In Biblical philosophy, peace is a profound and multidimensional concept that permeates both the Old and New Testaments. It is closely tied to the notions of righteousness, justice, and the relationship between humanity and God. The Hebrew word for peace, "Shalom", and the Greek word "Eirene" are central to understanding the Biblical view of peace, which extends beyond mere absence of conflict to encompass wholeness, harmony, and well-being.

Shalom (*Peace in the Old Testament*)

- *Shalom* is a Hebrew word that signifies peace, completeness, welfare, and tranquility. It is a state of holistic well-being that includes health, prosperity, security, and spiritual fulfilment.
- In the Old Testament, *Shalom* is often associated with God's covenant with His people. It is seen as a divine gift, resulting from living in accordance with God's commandments and maintaining a right relationship with Him.
- *Shalom* also represents the ideal state of harmony within the community and between nations. The prophetic visions of peace in the Old Testament, such as in Isaiah's vision of the wolf dwelling with the lamb (Isaiah 11: 6-9), reflect the ultimate realization of Shalom in the Messianic age.

Eirene (Peace in the New Testament)

- *Eirene* is the Greek equivalent of *Shalom* and is frequently mentioned in the New Testament. It encompasses not only the absence of conflict but also a state of inner peace that comes from reconciliation with God through Jesus Christ.
- In the New Testament, Jesus is often referred to as the "Prince of Peace" (Isaiah 9:6) and His mission is described as bringing peace to the world, not through worldly power, but through self-sacrifice, forgiveness, and love.
- The peace that Jesus offers is a peace that transcends understanding (Philippians 4:7), rooted in a restored relationship with God, leading to inner tranquility and harmony in human relationships.

Peace as Reconciliation with God

- Biblical peace is deeply connected to the idea of reconciliation with God. Sin is seen as the source of discord and strife, separating humanity from God and disrupting peace.
- Through the life, death, and resurrection of Jesus Christ, Christians believe that reconciliation with God is made possible, restoring peace between humanity and the divine (Romans 5:1).
- This reconciliation also extends to human relationships, encouraging forgiveness, love, and the pursuit of peace with others (Matthew 5:9).

Peace as a Fruit of the Spirit

- In Galatians 5:22-23, peace is listed as one of the fruits of the Holy Spirit. This indicates that peace is a virtue cultivated through the indwelling of the Holy Spirit, leading believers to live in harmony with others and experience inner tranquility.

- This peace is not dependent on external circumstances but is a result of living in alignment with God's will and experiencing His presence in one's life.

Peace in the Community

- The *Bible* emphasizes the importance of peace within the community of believers. The early Christian communities were exhorted to live in peace with one another, to seek reconciliation, and to avoid division and conflict (Romans 12:18, Ephesians 4:3).
- This communal peace is seen as a reflection of God's kingdom on earth, where justice, mercy, and love prevail.

Peace in Biblical philosophy is a comprehensive concept that encompasses personal, communal, and eschatological dimensions. It is rooted in a right relationship with God, which brings about inner tranquility and harmony in human relationships. Biblical peace is not just the absence of conflict but the presence of righteousness, justice, and the fullness of life as intended by God. The ultimate realization of peace is seen in the future hope of God's kingdom, where perfect peace will reign eternally.

Islamic Philosophy

Peace in Islamic philosophy is a fundamental concept deeply rooted in the teachings of the *Qur'an* and the *Hadith* (sayings and actions of the Prophet Muhammad). The Arabic word for peace, "Salaam", shares the same linguistic root as "Islam", highlighting the importance of peace in the religion. Peace in Islam is understood as a comprehensive state of harmony that includes inner peace, social justice, and a peaceful relationship with the divine.

Salaam (*Peace*)

- *Salaam* is the Arabic term for peace, and it is one of the names of God in Islam: "As-Salaam", meaning "The Source of Peace" (*Qur'an* 59:23). This emphasizes that peace is not only a divine attribute but also a goal for human beings to strive toward.
- Muslims greet each other with "As-Salaamu Alaikum", meaning "Peace be upon you", which reflects the desire for peace in all interactions and relationships.

Islam as a Path to Peace

- The very word "Islam" is derived from the root "S-L-M", which means peace, submission, and safety. Islam teaches that true peace is achieved through submission to the will of God (Allah). By following God's guidance, believers can find inner peace and contribute to peace in the world.
- The *Qur'an* describes Islam as a way of life that promotes justice, compassion, and mercy, which are essential for creating a peaceful society.

Inner Peace (*Sakinah*)

- *Sakinah* refers to a state of inner tranquility and calmness granted by God. This inner peace is achieved through faith, prayer, and remembrance of God (*dhikr*). The *Qur'an* states, "Verily, in the remembrance of Allah do hearts find rest" (*Qur'an* 13:28).
- Inner peace in Islam is closely linked to spiritual well-being and is seen as a foundation for external peace in one's relationships and community.

Justice (*Adl*) *and Peace*

- In Islamic philosophy, peace is intrinsically linked to justice (*Adl*). The *Qur'an* emphasizes that peace cannot exist without justice, and Muslims are encouraged to stand up for justice, even if it is against themselves or their kin (*Qur'an* 4:135).

- Social justice is a key component of peace, and Islam advocates for the fair treatment of all individuals, the protection of the rights of the oppressed, and the distribution of wealth to ensure that everyone's basic needs are met.

Forgiveness (Afw) and Reconciliation

- Islam strongly encourages forgiveness and reconciliation as means to achieve peace. The *Qur'an* and *Hadith* frequently urge believers to forgive others, control their anger, and seek reconciliation in times of conflict (*Qur'an* 41: 34).
- The Prophet Muhammad is reported to have said, "The strong man is not the one who is good at wrestling, but the one who controls himself in a fit of rage" (Sahih al-Bukhari). This highlights the importance of self-control and forgiveness in maintaining peace.

Peace in Islamic philosophy is a multifaceted concept encompassing inner tranquility, social justice, and harmony with the divine. It is deeply connected to the principles of justice, forgiveness, and communal responsibility. Islam teaches that true peace can only be achieved through submission to God's will, living a righteous life, and actively working towards justice and reconciliation in society. The pursuit of peace is seen as both a spiritual and practical endeavour, essential for the well-being of individuals and the world as a whole.

Buddhist Philosophy

Peace in Buddhist Philosophy is a central theme, closely tied to the concepts of suffering (*dukkha*), mindfulness, compassion, and enlightenment. Unlike some other traditions, where peace is often viewed as an external or social condition. Buddhism emphasizes inner peace as the foundation for all other forms of peace. The ultimate goal in Buddhism is to achieve *Nirvana*, a state of complete liberation and peace beyond all sufferings and desire.

Inner Peace (Citta-Santi)

- Inner peace is considered the most essential form of peace in Buddhism. It is achieved through the cultivation of mindfulness (*Sati*), wisdom (*Prajna*), and ethical conduct (*Sila*).
- The practice of meditation (*Bhavana*) is central to developing inner peace. Through meditation, individuals learn to quiet the mind, observe their thoughts and emotions without attachment, and gradually eliminate mental disturbances like greed, hatred, and delusion.
- The Buddha taught that inner peace is not dependent on external circumstances but is achieved by understanding the true nature of reality and overcoming the root causes of suffering.

The Four Noble Truths and Peace

- The Four Noble Truths form the foundation of Buddhist philosophy and offer a path to achieving peace:

   1. **The Truth of Suffering (*Dukkha*):** Life is inherently filled with suffering.
   2. **The Truth of the Cause of Suffering (*Samudaya*):** Suffering arises from desire, attachment, and ignorance.
   3. **The Truth of the Cessation of Suffering (*Nirodha*):** Suffering can be overcome and peace can be attained.

4. **The Truth of the Path to the Cessation of Suffering (*Magga*):** The Eightfold Path leads to the end of suffering and the attainment of peace.

- By following the Eightfold Path, which includes right understanding, right intention, right speech, right action, right livelihood, right effort, right mindfulness, and right concentration, individuals can achieve inner peace and ultimately attain *Nirvana*.

Compassion (Karuna) and Loving-Kindness (Metta)

- Compassion and loving-kindness are essential qualities for cultivating peace in Buddhism. *Karuna* is the desire to alleviate the suffering of others, while *Metta* is the unconditional love and goodwill extended to all beings.
- The practice of *Metta Bhavana*, or loving-kindness meditation, involves generating feelings of goodwill and peace towards oneself, loved ones, strangers, and even adversaries. This practice is intended to foster a peaceful heart and contribute to a more peaceful world.
- The Buddha emphasized that true peace comes from extending compassion and kindness to all beings, breaking the cycle of violence and retaliation.

Interconnectedness and Dependent Origination (Pratityasamutpada)

- Buddhism teaches that all phenomena are interconnected and interdependent. This principle, known as *Pratityasamutpada*, suggests that nothing exists in isolation; everything arises in dependence on conditions.
- Understanding this interconnectedness leads to a deeper sense of empathy and responsibility toward others, as one's actions inevitably affect the broader web of life.
- This insight encourages a peaceful approach to life, as individuals recognize that harming others ultimately

harms themselves, and helping others contributes to their own peace and well-being.

The Middle Way (Madhyama Pratipada)

- The Middle Way is a key principle in Buddhism, advocating for a balanced approach to life, avoiding the extremes of self-indulgence and self-mortification.
- This balanced approach fosters peace by promoting moderation, contentment, and wisdom, helping individuals avoid the turmoil that comes from extreme behaviours or views.
- The Middle Way is also applied to conflict resolution, encouraging peaceful solutions that consider the well-being of all parties involved.

Non-violence (Ahimsa)

- Non-violence is a fundamental ethical principle in Buddhism. The Buddha taught that violence only leads to more suffering and that true peace can only be achieved through non-harming (*Ahimsa*).
- Buddhists are encouraged to practice non-violence in thought, word, and deed, promoting peace in their interactions with others and in the world at large.
- The first precept of Buddhism, "Do not harm living beings", underscores the importance of cultivating peace and avoiding actions that cause suffering.

Peace in Buddhist philosophy is a profound and multi-layered concept that encompasses inner tranquility, ethical living, compassion, and the ultimate liberation from suffering. Buddhism teaches that true peace begins within, through the cultivation of mindfulness, wisdom, and compassion. By following the Middle Way, practicing non-violence, and understanding the interconnectedness of all life, individuals can contribute to a peaceful world. The ultimate expression of peace in Buddhism is the attainment of *Nirvana*, where all suffering ceases, and perfect peace is realized.

Gandhian Philosophy

Peace in Gandhian philosophy is a central concept that is deeply intertwined with non-violence (*Ahimsa*), truth (*Satya*), and the pursuit of justice. Mahatma Gandhi, one of the most influential leaders of the 20th century, developed a unique approach to peace that emphasized the importance of moral integrity, personal responsibility, and active engagement in social and political life to bring about change. His ideas have had a profound impact on movements for civil rights and social justice around the world.

Ahimsa (*Non-violence*)

- *Ahimsa*, or non-violence, is the cornerstone of Gandhian philosophy. Gandhi believed that true peace could only be achieved through non-violent means. *Ahimsa*, for him, was not just a tactic but a way of life, an active force that could transform individuals and societies.
- Gandhi's interpretation of *Ahimsa* extended beyond physical non-violence to include non-violence in thought, speech, and action. He argued that harbouring ill-will or hatred towards others was as harmful as physical violence.
- Non-violence, according to Gandhi, was the most powerful weapon available to oppressed people in their struggle for justice and freedom. He famously led India's independence movement through non-violent resistance, including civil disobedience, non-cooperation, and peaceful protests.

Satya (*Truth*)

- Truth, or *Satya*, is another fundamental principle in Gandhian philosophy. Gandhi equated truth with God, asserting that living truthfully was essential for achieving peace.
- He believed that truth and non-violence were inseparable and that adherence to truth would naturally lead one to practice non-violence. For Gandhi, seeking the truth required courage, integrity, and a willingness to confront injustice without resorting to violence.
- In the pursuit of truth, Gandhi advocated for "Satyagraha", a form of non-violent resistance where individuals hold firmly to the truth and resist oppression without aggression. *Satyagraha* became the moral and ethical foundation of his political activism.

Satyagraha (*Non-violent Resistance*)

- *Satyagraha*, often translated as "soul force" or "truth force", is Gandhi's method of non-violent resistance. It is a proactive approach to achieving peace and justice through the power of truth and non-violence.
- *Satyagraha* involves civil disobedience, non-cooperation with unjust laws, and peaceful protest as means to bring about social and political change. It is based on the belief that unjust systems can be reformed through the moral power of non-violence and the willingness to endure suffering for a righteous cause.
- Gandhi used *Satyagraha* extensively during India's struggle for independence from British colonial rule, advocating for peaceful non-cooperation with the British authorities. His approach inspired many other movements for civil rights and social justice globally.

Sarvodaya (Welfare of All)

- *Sarvodaya*, meaning "the welfare of all", is another key principle in Gandhian philosophy. Gandhi envisioned a society where the well-being of every individual is ensured, and the benefits of social progress are shared equally among all members of society.
- *Sarvodaya* emphasizes social and economic equality, the upliftment of the poor and marginalized, and the elimination of social injustices. Gandhi believed that true peace could only be achieved when everyone's needs were met, and social harmony prevailed.
- This principle led Gandhi to advocate for the development of self-reliant, sustainable communities, and to oppose exploitation, inequality, and materialism.

Trusteeship

- Gandhi's concept of trusteeship is based on the idea that wealth and resources should be used for the benefit of society as a whole, rather than being concentrated in the hands of a few. He believed that those who possess wealth should act as trustees, using their resources to promote the welfare of others.
- Trusteeship is a model of ethical capitalism that seeks to balance individual rights with social responsibilities. Gandhi argued that this approach would lead to a more just and peaceful society, where the gap between the rich and poor is minimized.

Spiritual Peace

- For Gandhi, peace was not just a social or political goal but also a deeply spiritual one. He believed that true peace begins within the individual and is rooted in a spiritual connection to truth and non-violence.
- Gandhi practised regular meditation, prayer, and

self-discipline as means to cultivate inner peace. He saw personal spiritual development as essential for contributing to peace in the broader world.

Peace in Gandhian philosophy is a holistic concept that encompasses non-violence, truth, justice, self-reliance, and social harmony. Gandhi's approach to peace is deeply ethical and spiritual, emphasizing the importance of individual responsibility and moral integrity. Through the principles of *Ahimsa, Satya, Satyagraha*, and *Sarvodaya*, Gandhi sought to create a society where peace is not merely the absence of conflict but the presence of justice, equality, and human dignity. His ideas continue to inspire movements for peace and social justice worldwide.

Conclusion

Peace is a dynamic philosophy of human existence, it is what makes us different from all other living organism of the world but in the 21st generation of science and technology the emotion of peace is getting volatile. The way of living and competitive environment develops intolerance, greed and self-centric behaviour which causes enormous harm to the global peace and harmony. Is it possible to bring back the idea of peace, forgiveness and tolerance back into the world? The answer is yes and this change can be bring by the collective efforts of parents and teachers along with the support of the socio-political leaders. The education system needs to be transformed in such a way that these noble ideas can get drilled into the mind of the young generation, our future and the world will become the lands of god.

REFERENCES

Adolf, A. (2009). "Peace: A World History." *Polity.*

Adedeji, A.M. (2013). "Justice, Equality and Peace: The Necessary Tripod for National Development." *Greener Journal of Social Sciences, 3*(1), 33-38.

Alfred, T. (1999). *Peace, Power, Righteousness.*

Armstrong, C. (2014). *Global Justice between Minimalism and Egalitarianism.*

Christensen, K. (2009). *Non-violence, Peace, and Justice: A Philosophical Introduction.* Broadview Press.

Christensen, K. (2005). *The Transformation of Peace* (Vol. 110). Basingstoke: Palgrave Macmillan.

Frankman, M. (2004). *World Democratic Federalism: Peace and Justice Indivisible.* Springer.

Galtung, J. (2007). "Introduction: Peace by Peaceful Conflict Transformation—the TRANSCEND Approach." In *Handbook of Peace and Conflict Studies* (pp. 14-32). Routledge.

Gilabert, P. (2012). *From Global Poverty to Global Equality: A Philosophical Exploration.* Oxford University Press.

Murphy, C.N. (2016). "Egalitarian Social Movements and New World Orders." In *Evolutionary Interpretations of World Politics* (pp. 262-284). Routledge.

Richmond, O.P. (2022). "Emancipatory Peace." In *The Palgrave Encyclopedia of Peace and Conflict Studies* (pp. 333-349). Cham: Springer International Publishing.

Rivera, J.D. (2009). *Handbook on Building Cultures of Peace.* Spinger Science and Business Media.

Rothbard, M.N. (2000). *Egalitarianism as a Revolt Against Nature and Other Essays.* Ludwig von Mises Institute.

7

Conflict Management and Peace Education in School Curriculum

Seema Saleem and *Shruti Pandey*

Introduction

Peace education, as an integral component of school curricula, aims to impart the values, knowledge, and skills necessary for harmonious living with oneself, others, and the environment. Its primary goal is to cultivate a culture of respect and peaceful coexistence, moving beyond merely eliminating conflict or war. By embedding peace education within educational frameworks, educators equip students with essential tools for resolving conflicts peacefully and contributing to a more just and sustainable society. This approach not only transforms individual communities but also fosters global citizenship by encouraging students to engage with and understand diverse perspectives.

Incorporating conflict management into educational settings is vital for maintaining a harmonious learning environment. It involves proactively identifying, addressing, and resolving conflicts in a constructive manner, which is especially important in diverse school environments where students come from varied backgrounds. Effective conflict management helps preserve relationships and promotes collaboration, allowing students to develop crucial social-emotional skills. Through conflict management training integrated into the curriculum, students learn to handle disagreements respectfully and productively, leading to a more positive school climate and enhancing overall academic performance.

Conflict management skills encompass techniques such as active listening, effective communication, empathy, and problem-solving. These skills enable students to express their feelings, understand differing viewpoints, and collaboratively work towards solutions. Implementing various models of conflict management, such as mediation programmes and school-wide approaches, can effectively teach these skills. Prioritizing conflict management training for both educators and students fosters a supportive environment that encourages positive interactions and minimizes the escalation of conflicts, ultimately contributing to a more cohesive and effective educational experience.

Modern schools face a range of challenges that impact the overall educational experience. Interpersonal conflicts among students, such as bullying, social exclusion, and peer disagreements, are prevalent issues that can disrupt the learning environment. These conflicts often stem from a variety of sources, including differences in cultural backgrounds, socio-economic status, and individual personalities. The presence of such conflicts can lead to a hostile or uncomfortable atmosphere that affects students' academic performance, emotional well-being, and social interactions.

Additionally, teachers and school staff frequently encounter difficulties in managing and resolving conflicts effectively. Traditional disciplinary methods may not always address the underlying issues or teach students how to resolve disputes constructively. This can lead to recurring problems, increased stress among staff, and a negative impact on the school's overall climate. The inability to address conflicts proactively can result in a cycle where unresolved issues contribute to further discord and academic disengagement.

Integrating conflict management skills into school curricula provides a proactive approach to addressing these challenges. Early conflict resolution training equips students with practical tools and strategies to handle disputes constructively. Key benefits of this approach include:

1. **Development of Essential Interpersonal Skills:** Conflict resolution training helps students develop crucial skills such as empathy, active listening, negotiation, and effective communication. These skills enable students to understand different perspectives, express their own views respectfully, and collaborate to find mutually acceptable solutions.
2. **Reduction in Conflict Escalation:** By learning how to address conflicts early and constructively, students are less likely to allow disputes to escalate into more serious issues. This proactive approach can reduce incidents of bullying, violence, and classroom disruptions, creating a more positive and focused learning environment.
3. **Improved School Climate:** When students are equipped to manage conflicts effectively, the overall school climate improves. A positive and supportive environment fosters better relationships among students and between students and teachers. This can lead to increased student engagement, higher academic achievement, and a more harmonious school community.
4. **Enhanced Emotional and Social Development:** Learning to resolve conflicts constructively contributes to students' emotional intelligence and social development.

It helps them navigate complex social situations, build healthy relationships, and develop resilience in the face of challenges.

5. **Preparation for Future Challenges:** Conflict management skills are valuable beyond the school setting. By learning these skills early, students are better prepared to handle conflicts in their future personal and professional lives. This preparation contributes to their overall success and ability to contribute positively to society.
6. **Empowerment and Responsibility:** Conflict resolution training empowers students to take responsibility for their actions and interactions. It encourages them to be proactive in seeking solutions and fosters a sense of accountability for maintaining a respectful and inclusive environment.

Incorporating conflict management skills into school curricula not only addresses immediate issues but also fosters a culture of respect and cooperation. By investing in these skills, schools can create a more positive and supportive learning environment, ultimately contributing to the development of well-rounded, empathetic individuals who are equipped to handle future challenges effectively.

Developing a Conflict Management Curriculum

Creating a conflict management curriculum involves several key components to ensure it is comprehensive, engaging, and effective. The curriculum should be designed to define what students should know and be able to do by the conclusion of the programme. Objectives may include understanding the nature of conflict, developing negotiation skills, and acquiring the ability to mediate disputes. These goals can provide a clear framework for the curriculum, ensuring that students gain essential conflict management skills.

Criteria for assessing students' achievement of the desired outcomes should be established. This assessment may involve practical demonstrations of conflict resolution techniques, role-playing exercises, and reflective writing assignments. These measures should serve to evaluate students' proficiency and progress in applying conflict management principles. Assessments should be designed to ensure that students can effectively demonstrate their skills in real-world scenarios and reflect on their learning experiences. The curriculum can begin with foundational concepts, including the causes of conflict, various types of conflict (such as interpersonal and intragroup), and the impact of unresolved conflict. Instruction should cover specific strategies and skills, such as active listening, empathy, assertiveness, and problem-solving. Real-life scenarios can be used to illustrate the application of these techniques. Interactive activities should be incorporated to allow students to practice conflict resolution in a controlled environment. Role-playing exercises should enable students to experience different perspectives and experiment with various resolution strategies. Additionally, programmes can be developed to train students as peer mediators, enhancing practical application while fostering leadership and responsibility.

The curriculum should employ videos, case studies, and digital tools to enhance learning and offer diverse perspectives on conflict management. Teamwork can be encouraged through group discussions, collaborative problem-solving tasks, and group projects related to conflict resolution. Opportunities for individual reflection should be provided, utilizing journals, essays, or personal action plans to help students assess their experiences and growth in handling conflicts. These varied learning methods should aim to engage students and deepen their understanding of conflict management. Lessons in conflict management should be linked with other academic subjects, such as social studies, language, arts, and health education. For example, literature can be utilized to explore themes of conflict, while social studies can provide historical context for conflict resolution strategies. This interdisciplinary approach should enrich students' understanding by connecting conflict management principles with broader educational content. Ongoing assessments can be used to gauge students' understanding and development of conflict management skills throughout the course. This may include quizzes, class discussions, and practical exercises. Final projects or presentations should be required to demonstrate students' ability to apply conflict management techniques to complex scenarios. Constructive feedback shall be provided to help students improve and refine their skills, ensuring they develop proficiency in conflict resolution.

To ensure the conflict management curriculum is both relevant and effective, it should be aligned with educational standards and frameworks. This alignment may integrate conflict management into broader educational objectives and ensure consistency with other areas of learning. The curriculum should examine national and state educational standards related to social-emotional learning, character education, and interpersonal skills. It should identify how conflict management fits within these standards and contributes to their achievement. The curriculum shall be aligned with specific goals and priorities set by the school or district, ensuring it supports broader educational initiatives and addresses the unique needs of the school community.

Many educational systems may incorporate Social Emotional Learning (SEL) frameworks that emphasize skills such as self-awareness, self-management, social awareness, relationship skills, and responsible decision-making. The conflict management curriculum should be designed to complement these SEL competencies. It should map out how conflict management skills align with SEL standards and integrate them into existing SEL programmes. This approach shall create a cohesive strategy for developing students' social and emotional skills. The curriculum should be tailored to reflect the specific challenges and cultural context of the student population. It should address real-life issues and scenarios pertinent to students' experiences. The focus should be on practical skills and strategies that students can immediately apply in their daily lives. The curriculum should provide actionable solutions and tools for effectively resolving conflicts, ensuring its relevance and practicality.

Educators should receive the necessary training and resources to effectively teach conflict management skills. This may include professional development workshops, teaching materials, and ongoing support. Collaboration among educators should be encouraged to share best practices, experiences, and resources related to conflict management. This approach shall help maintain consistency and quality in the implementation of the curriculum.

Strategies for Integrating Conflict Management into Existing Curricula

Integrating conflict management into existing curricula shall require a strategic cross-curricular approach. Educators from different subject areas should collaborate to develop interdisciplinary lessons that incorporate conflict management themes. For instance, social studies teachers may work with language arts instructors to explore historical conflicts and literary themes of resolution. The curriculum should be designed to create thematic units where conflict management is a central theme. In these units, conflict resolution skills may be integrated into the study of various subjects, such as exploring conflicts in literature, history, and current events.

Project-based learning may be employed to facilitate real-world application of conflict management skills. Students might engage in projects that require teamwork, negotiation, and problem-solving, thereby practicing conflict resolution in context. Consistent messaging about conflict management should be reinforced across subjects. Educators should use common language and principles related to conflict resolution, ensuring that students receive a cohesive learning experience. Conflict management may be effectively infused into core subjects to reinforce its importance and applicability. In language arts, conflict resolution themes may be explored through literature, drama, and creative writing. Students should analyze conflicts within texts, role-play scenarios, and write about resolution strategies. In social studies, the curriculum should examine historical and contemporary conflicts, studying conflict resolution strategies employed in different contexts. Students may evaluate the effectiveness of these strategies and discuss their relevance to current issues. Although less obvious, conflict resolution skills may be applied in science and mathematics through collaborative problem-solving tasks and group experiments. Students should learn to navigate disagreements in scientific inquiry and mathematical reasoning. Health education should include conflict management as part of emotional well-being and interpersonal relationships. Lessons should cover the impact of unresolved conflict on mental health and provide strategies for managing conflicts in personal and social contexts.

Effective implementation of conflict management in schools shall hinge on robust professional development programmes. Continuous professional development should be provided to keep educators updated on new conflict resolution strategies and research. This may include refresher courses, online modules, and access to resources for sustained learning. Professional development should emphasize practical application of conflict management skills. Educators may participate in simulations and role-playing exercises to practice conflict resolution techniques and receive feedback on their effectiveness.

Creating a supportive environment for educators should be crucial to the successful integration of conflict management. Schools shall establish collaborative networks where educators can share experiences, strategies, and resources related to conflict management. Regular meetings and forums should facilitate the exchange of best practices and support among staff. School administrators should actively support conflict management initiatives by providing necessary resources, allocating time for professional development, and recognizing educators' efforts in implementing these programmes. A mentorship system may be developed where experienced educators guide and support their colleagues in implementing conflict management strategies. Peer support should help build confidence and competence in handling conflicts effectively. Educators should have access to a variety of resources, including teaching materials, toolkits, and digital platforms, to assist in the integration of conflict management into their curricula. Ensuring that these resources are readily available should facilitate the smooth adoption of conflict resolution practices.

Practical Classroom Activities and Exercises

To effectively teach conflict management skills, practical classroom activities and exercises should be crucial. These interactive exercises should be designed to engage students actively and help them apply conflict resolution principles in a supportive environment. Teachers may present students with realistic conflict scenarios that require resolution. Students should work in groups to analyze the situations, discuss possible solutions, and present their proposed resolutions. These scenarios should help students practice critical thinking and collaborative problem-solving. Structured debates and discussions may be used to help students practice articulating their viewpoints, listening to others, and negotiating mutually acceptable outcomes. Topics for debate should be selected to reflect relevant and age-appropriate issues, encouraging students to engage in constructive dialogue. Classrooms may be organized into different stations, each focusing on a specific conflict resolution skill, such as active listening, empathy, or negotiation. Students should rotate through the stations, engaging in activities that reinforce each skill and reflecting on their learning.

Teachers should present problem-solving challenges that require students to work collaboratively to address conflicts. These challenges should be designed to foster teamwork and apply conflict resolution techniques in a practical context. Role-playing scenarios and simulation games may be integral to helping students experience and practice conflict resolution skills in a controlled setting. Strategies may include: Students should participate in role-playing exercises where they assume various roles in conflict situations. They may practice negotiating and resolving disputes from different perspectives, gaining insight into the experiences and viewpoints of others. Interactive simulation games should be employed to create complex scenarios that mimic real-life conflicts. Students should work through these simulations, applying conflict resolution strategies and reflecting on their effectiveness.

Special workshops may be organized where students engage in simulations and role-playing activities focused on specific conflict resolution techniques. These workshops should provide an opportunity for in-depth practice and feedback. To foster a sense of responsibility and leadership, students should be encouraged to participate in and lead mediation programmes.

Students may receive training to become peer mediators, learning techniques for facilitating discussions and resolving conflicts among their peers. This programme should help students develop leadership skills and practical experience in conflict management. Student-led mediation committees may be established to handle disputes within the school. These committees should provide a structured way for students to apply their mediation training and contribute to a positive school environment. Clubs dedicated to conflict resolution may be created, where students can further develop their skills, organize events, and promote conflict management within the school community. Peer mediation and leadership opportunities should be provided to enhance student engagement and practical application of conflict management skills. Students should be trained to mediate conflicts among their classmates. They may work alongside teachers and counsellors to support their peers in resolving disputes amicably and constructively. Students should be given leadership roles in conflict management initiatives, such as leading workshops, organizing events, or presenting at school assemblies. These opportunities should help build confidence and reinforce the importance of conflict resolution. Students should be encouraged to provide feedback on conflict management programmes and suggest improvements. Involvement in programme development and evaluation may give students a sense of ownership and contribute to the effectiveness of the initiatives.

The effectiveness of conflict management programmes should be assessed through evaluations of programme implementation and outcomes. This may involve analyzing data on programme participation, resolution rates, and changes in conflict behaviour. Assessments should include evaluating students' performance in conflict resolution exercises, role-playing scenarios, and real-life applications of conflict management skills. This should help determine how well students are applying the techniques they have learned. Longitudinal studies may be conducted to track the impact of conflict management programmes over time. This may involve assessing changes in students' conflict resolution skills, behaviour, and overall school climate.

Gathering feedback from all stakeholders should be essential to understanding the impact and effectiveness of conflict management programmes. Surveys should be administered to gather students' perspectives on the conflict management curriculum, including their experiences, challenges, and perceived benefits. This feedback should be used to make improvements and address any issues. Teachers should provide evaluations of the conflict management programme, including their observations of student progress, the effectiveness of classroom activities, and the integration of conflict resolution skills into their teaching. Parents may be invited to provide feedback on their observations of their children's conflict management skills and the overall impact of the programme on their children's behaviour and interpersonal relationships. Focus groups with students, teachers, and parents should be organized to facilitate in-depth discussions about the conflict management programme. These discussions should provide valuable insights into programme effectiveness and areas for improvement. By implementing these practical activities, involving students in conflict management initiatives, and conducting thorough assessments and evaluations, schools should be well-positioned to foster a positive and effective conflict resolution culture.

Conclusion

The integration of conflict management education into school curricula offers significant long-term benefits for students and the broader school community. Educating students in conflict management not only enhances their behaviour and academic performance but also fosters a positive school culture and community. Effective conflict resolution skills lead to improved interpersonal interactions, reduced behavioural issues, and increased academic engagement, as students learn to manage disputes constructively rather than allowing them to disrupt their learning. This education also contributes to a supportive and cohesive school environment, where mutual respect and understanding are prioritized, thereby strengthening the overall sense of community. By fostering improved behaviour, academic performance, and a positive school culture, conflict management education plays a crucial role in creating a conducive learning environment. Continued support and innovation in this field will ensure that conflict management practices evolve to meet the changing needs of students, ultimately contributing to a more harmonious and effective educational experience.

Innovations may include the integration of digital tools and platforms for virtual conflict resolution training, as well as the development of new methodologies informed by research in social-emotional learning and neuroscience. Potential areas for growth include expanding conflict management programmes to include more diverse perspectives and incorporating advanced techniques for mediating complex disputes. Schools will benefit from staying abreast of these developments to continually enhance their conflict management practices.

REFERENCES

Bhuttah, T.M., Sarwat, S., Farid, F., Qi, Z. & Bibi, A. (2020). "Integration of Peace Education: The Role of Values, School Curriculum and Teachers in Inculcating Peace Education". *Pal Arch's Journal of Archaeology of Egypt/Egyptology, 17*(7), 69-92. Retrieved from https://archives.palarch.nl/index.php/jae/article/download/5300/5215/10220

"Conflict Resolution in Schools/Programmes, Principles & Benefits". (n.d.). Retrieved from https://study.com/academy/lesson/principles-of-conflict-management-in-schools.html

IntechOpen. (2020). "School Conflicts: Causes and Management Strategies in Education". Retrieved from https://www.intechopen.com/chapters/74550

"Managing and Resolving Conflicts Effectively". (n.d.). Retrieved from https://www.creducation.net/resources/resolving_conflicts/files/day1.html

National Council of Educational Research and Training. (2006). *National Curriculum Framework 2005: Position Paper—National Focus Group on Education for Peace. NCERT.* Retrieved from https://ncert.nic.in/positionpaper/education_for_peace.pdf

Office of Justice Programmes. (n.d.). "Conflict Management in Schools". Retrieved from https://www.ojp.gov/pdffiles1/Digitization/149714NCJRS.pdf

Safety Solutions Training Ltd. (n.d.). "Conflict Management for Teachers". Retrieved from https://www.safetysolutionstraining.co.uk/personal-safety-training/conflict-management-techniques-for-teachers/

8

Education for Peace Values and Skills

Arun Kumar Dubey and *Abha Dubey*

Introduction

The need for peace education in this contemporary world is very crucial for establishing a society which ensures equality and equity for all without any discrimination based on caste, creed, religion and gender. Everyone lives his life with wisdom of virtuousness and righteousness. This very quality of righteous and virtuous conduct leads to the peaceful coexistence of all the living beings on the Earth without having any feeling of viciousness and denial of any kind of violence, injustice, biasness, inequality, disparity and prejudices. This view resembles the philosophical ideals of Indian culture founded on the Feeling of "Vasudaiva Kutumbakam" (Raina & Kumar, 2023) reflecting integrity and coherence of the universe and value of concern and togetherness (Galtung, 1969). This ideal of Integrity and entirety is only possible by training the young minds at the very outset to their journey of life and throughout their learning experience. Education is the key to create awareness among the learners for achieving the goal of Peace Education.

Understanding Peace

Peace can be defined in variety of ways, the narrow meaning of peace is the absence of war, violence, argument, quarrel, dispute over any issue between individual and group and between countries (Srinivasan, 2016). The threat to peace exists in society in the forms of social degradation, discrimination, oppression, exploitation, poverty, injustice, and so on. Eliminating these threats can be defined as peace. According to *Oxford Dictionary* 'Peace' refers to:

1a. Freedom from, or cessation of, world of hostilities; that condition of a nation or community in which it is not at war with another.
1b. A ratification or treaty of peace between two powers previously at war.
2. Freedom from civil commotion and disorder; public order and security.
3. Freedom from disturbance or perturbation.

The Wider Concept of Peace is feeling harmony in the mind. It is a state one can achieve through establishing harmonious inter- and intra-personal relation with the environment (Grewal *et al.*, 2004). Peace advocates the love, respect and care for all. It believes in integrity in disparity. It provides sound background to every being to lead a sustainable life without turbulence and disharmony. This state of mind can be achieved through developing a belief of sharing, caring, empathy, tolerance, understanding and love.

Understanding Violence

Let's think of all the ways of disrupting and hurting human and non-human resources causing unrest, threats, fear, apprehension, anxiety, dejection and physical injury and ailments. This problem sometimes causing severe damage in the life of people. Violence is defined as harming people mentally, physically and verbally. If somebody inclines to injured people leading to mental harm which causes severe damage in the personality of individuals. Mental harm is unnoticeable but have severe consequences. Sometimes, it causes panic attacks, anxiety, tension, fear and psychological disruption. Verbal harm is associated with hurting others with harsh words which lays the foundation of enmity and grudges against each other. Physical harms define as applying physical force to harm others, can be easily identified and perceptible. Physical harms are commonly occurred between individuals, different groups, organisations, communities and countries. The meagre conflicts, if triggers from individual to culture and to nations will cause huge destruction and devastation for the humanity.

UNESCO (2005) explains violence or absence of peace has several manifestations in the form of fight between:

- Individuals (fight between two individuals),
- Groups (clashes of gangs),
- Communities (caste conflicts and communal violence),
- Nations (war between two countries), and
- Cultures (world wars and contemporary Russia and Ukraine strife).

As the conflicts are scaled up from individual to cultures, destructions are also scaled up in sync with long-term impact and implications. To Gandhiji, exploitation was the most familiar and practical form of violence on an individual by the state, a group, another individual, or by machines; on women by men; and on one nation by another (NCERT, 2006).

Concept of Peace Education

Peace Education refers to the kind of education which inculcates values and attitudes within children for establishing peace at every aspect of life and ensures peaceful coexistence of all living and non-living beings (Tandon, 2014). Peace Education is informative about how to understand social and cultural context and should be incorporated with spiritual values and also teaches the students about various local and global contexts with the ideas of sustainable development. Peace Education strives for eradicating violent social structure from the society by promoting equality and equity so that everyone enjoys the equal share of natural resources and lead a happy life. Peace education also advocates that peace is not merely absence of war but it is love, care and tolerance. Peace Education is defined at many ways as there is no universally accepted definition.

- Peace Education is an attempt to respond to problems of conflict and violence on scales ranging from the global and national to the local and personal. It is about exploring ways of creating more just and sustainable futures (Laing, 1978).
- Peace Education is holistic. It embraces the physical, emotional, intellectual, and social growth of children within a framework deeply rooted in traditional human values. It is based on a philosophy that teaches love, compassion, trust, fairness, co-operation and reverence for the human family and all lives on our beautiful planet (Schmidt and Friedman, 1988).

Nature of Peace Education

Peace Education creates awareness of importance of peace for sustaining a blissful life. Peace Education exhorts:

1. Peace is needed in every dimension of life in an interconnected way. A human being requires mental

peace, spiritual peace, psychological peace, social, economic and ecological peace.

2. The human values like love, freedom, truth, compassion and solidarity are the foundation of peace.
3. Peace needs the practice of values such as love, truth, justice, equality, tolerance, harmony, humility, togetherness, and self-control.
4. Peace for self and peace with others are strengthening factors to establish peaceful environment.
5. Peace is not only the absence of violence but build the capacity to live together with harmony.
6. Peace denies the exploitation and injustice of every kind.
7. Peace advocates equality and equity in social, economic, cultural, education, vocational development.
8. Feeling of International cooperation and understanding helps in creating just international society.
9. Self-peace is required to promote peace in the society and the world.

Objectives of Peace Education

The Fundamental Duties (Article 51A) enshrined in the Constitution of India expressed the objectives that needed to promote peace education. They are as follows:

(a) To promote harmony and the spirit of common brotherhood amongst all the people of India transcending religious, linguistic and regional or sectional diversities; to renounce practices derogatory to the dignity of women;

(b) To value and preserve the rich heritage of our composite culture;

(c) To protect and improve the natural environment including forests, lakes, reserves, wildlife and to have compassion for living creatures; and

(d) To safeguard public property and abjure violence.

Some objectives can be applied for inculcating peace values after carefully study of various policies and literature. They are mentioned below:

1. To inculcate the feeling among students to understand the importance and needs of peace.
2. To establish reciprocal relationship with their peers and with their family members.
3. To equip them with tools and techniques to maintain peaceful life in their immediate environment.
4. To establish cordial relationship with the all living and non-living beings of the mother earth.
5. To develop sense of respect and gratitude towards life.
6. To develop ethical, moral, social, professional, emotional, spiritual values among students for leading happy and contented life.
7. To develop positive attitude towards different aspects of life.
8. To develop feeling of nationalism and sense of internationalism among students.
9. To develop feeling of brotherhood and solidarity.
10. To develop sense of equality and equity among students.
11. To inculcate the importance of inner peace and creating peaceful relationship with others.

Need and Essentiality of Peace Education

Peace Education imparts knowledge and understanding of essentiality of peace in the life of human being for their survival and to attain highest goals. It is our fundamental needs that ensures secure living. It gives training to maintain and manage our own emotions and the emotion of the others. Peace education is necessary to maintain just society and harness values and virtue of life for maintaining cordial and mutual relationship at social, national and international level for sharing resources, developing education, maintaining peace, promoting cultural harmony, avoiding wars and conflicts, promote health and medicines, science and technology for common cause of spreading goodness. "Hence, Peace Education empowers individuals to choose the path of peace rather than path of violence; and enables them to be peacemakers rather than the consumers of peace."

1. Fundamental Needs,
2. Psychological Needs,
3. Emotional Needs,
4. Social Needs,
5. National and International Needs,
6. Needs for Sustainability and Happiness, and
7. Spiritual Needs.

Fig. 8.1: Needs of Peace Education

Values to be Developed in Students

Values are something that we consider important and be acceptable by the members of the society. Values are to be considered as precious, dear and estimable. Value is an emotional attitude formed by the belief system developed over a period of time according to the preferences that are made at various situations and circumstances of life.

Values to be developed for inculcating Peace among students (Nario-Galace & Castro, 2011).

1. Physical Values

Healthy mind resides in healthy body. Physical Health helps in securing success in life. Without health no one can accomplish the task at hand. It enables an individual to restore harmonious development of the personality and establish good relationship with the fellow beings.

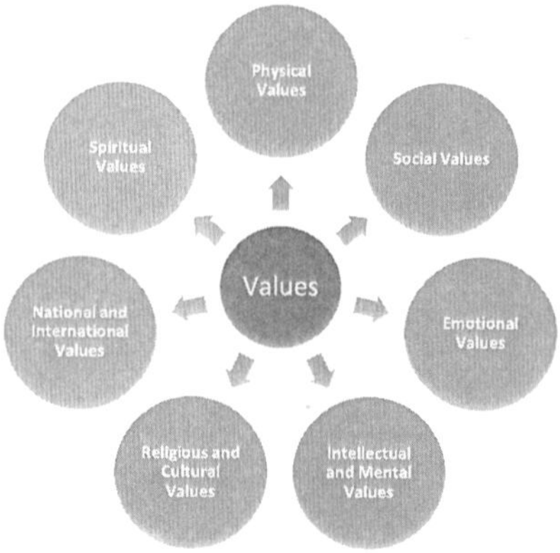

Fig. 8.2: Values to be Developed for Peace Education

2. Social Values

Social Values are the values which teaches about the way and means to acquire a reputable place in the society by following the norms and standards of the society. It helps a person to imbibe the qualities of co-operation, brotherhood, integrity, respect, solidarity, empathy, love and mutual understanding so that every member of the society thrives well in the society.

3. Emotional Values

Emotional values helps in understanding one's own emotion and the emotions of the others. This value helps in maintaining and managing his/her emotion in various situations and helps in maintaining the peace and composure of the mind. It helps in transforming individual as flexible, problem solving, empathy, perseverance, independent, original and be able to establish inter- and intra-personal relationship.

4. Intellectual and Mental Values

Intellectual and Mental values enable the individual to segregate right and wrong, good and bad and helps in making right decision promptly to settle the problems at hand and achieve predetermined aim of life.

5. Religious and Cultural Values

The foundation of every religion is to follow virtues of life. It gives us the strength to live a happy and contented life. It teaches respect for each religion and strong belief in the religion where he/she was born. Every religion's fundamental concept is the development of human values of love, truth, justice, equality etc.

6. National and International Values

Feeling of nationalism and strong faith in one's own nation reveals that the growth and development of the country, maintain just and order society, follow the rules and regulations, respect to constitution and democratic values is our prime duty. While our action towards the entire world for dealing with global problems like environmental issues and terrorism. NEP 2020 also emphasises for internalisation of education and exploration from local to global for the common cause of peace, values, elimination of poverty, handles the environmental problems and peaceful coexistence by understanding the different cultures and beliefs of other countries.

7. Spiritual Values

Kevern (2012) suggests that spirituality concerns questions of values and meanings that are fundamental in the search for meaning in life (Hussey, 2009). Spirituality is always viewed as morally or aesthetically valuable. Spirituality helps in searching meaning in life and add beauty to the life. It helps in understanding self and establish cordial relation with the self and the others.

Approaches to Develop Values and Skills for Establishing Peace

As peace education and education for peace are different terminology but both indicates the need of establishing peace by inculcating the virtue of peace among students who will be responsible for creating such kind of society in which everyone has the right to lead a beautiful life and society in itself transformed as the toast of life. According to *Bramha Kumaris*, the eternal virtues that are needed to create an environment for sustainable life are as follows:

1. Contentment
2. Love
3. Power
4. Peace
5. Knowledge
6. Purity
7. Bliss.

These are the assets of life. We all drive to gain eternal happiness, peace and blissful life. This can be achieved through seeking knowledge. Everyone is chasing after money and power. These two are interdependent and complement each other. Both these aspects cast paramount influence in the life of human beings. They may fill the life, if followed by virtue with comfort, luxury, ease and cosiness and causing turbulences, dejection, desolation and violence if having the foundation of hatred, treachery, deceit and betrayal. Various approaches and methodologies for peace education are needed for inculcation of peace in a natural way among children. Following are the different approaches for inculcating peace values within students:

1. Pedagogical Approach (NCERT, 2006)

The pedagogical approach focusses on the real transaction of the peace related components present in every topic to the students. Teacher should not merely concern with the completion of subjects but to develop feelings and attitudes among students so that they are enabled to reflect, share, care, and collaborate with each other. There are some measures adopted by a teacher during teaching and learning, which are as follows:

1. To develop positive attitude among students towards the aims and objectives of Education which is the holistic development of the personality.
2. To create in them the importance of cooperation and help in our life.
3. To develop creativity and originality within students.
4. To provide democratic environment in which students are free to share their feelings to teachers and with their peers.
5. To opt child cantred methodology like creative, child-centred, largely experiential, and participatory learning. These methods develop in them the virtues of discipline,

cooperation, help, and learning by doing and positive attitude towards manual help.

6. Teachers should organise contextual activities on history, cultures, politics and civilisation etc.
7. Teachers should demonstrate the ways to peacefully solve the conflicts, disagreements and arriving at peaceful solution.
8. Teachers should create an opportunity for students to develop sense of inquiry, asking questions and discovering values and be able to apply them.
9. Teacher should develop understanding of the importance of peace among students through examples, questions, stories, anecdotes, games, experiments, discussions, dialogues, value clarification, examples, analogies, metaphors, role-play, and simulation.

2. Impressionistic Approach

Teachers are the role model for their disciples. Teachers demonstrate their values and perception of life by their action that cast huge impression on the mind of children. They shape the personality of the students and thus be the builder of the nation.

The Role of teachers to transform a child as a peacemaker and as an advocate of peace are as follows:

1. The sole aim of teacher is to make students as good human being.
2. Teachers develop in learners the art of identifying their innate abilities and harness them not only for the self but for the society.
3. Creating democratic classroom and positive climate is of paramount importance.
4. Teacher discipline students by his impressionistic personality, his autocratic behaviour and his method

of discipline by scolding and slapping teaches students violence as a problem solver.

5. Opt various values that teaches how to create peaceful climate, resolve tension and establish inter- and intra-personal relationship.
6. Teachers develop among students to critically evaluate their behaviour, attitudes before making any judgement towards any situation, events and persons.
7. Teachers should promote empathy and compassion to understand others' perspectives and experiences.
8. Creating awareness about human rights and responsibilities.
9. Developing the feeling of "*Vasudhaiv Kutumbakam*", a sense of global brotherhood and responsibilities and interconnectedness.

3. Natural Approach

Natural approach of teaching Peace Education is the continuous process where students learn gradually during their educational journey. At various levels of education different techniques to be adopted to let the students learn reflexively the values of peace. Primary stage is to be considered the ideal time to build the foundation on which students identify the importance of Peace Education instinctively and develop as peace-oriented person. The play-way method and demonstration of the values that inculcate peace-oriented persons are hygiene of self, cleanliness, respect. Feeling of gratitude, honesty, truthfulness, sharing, cooperation, tolerance, regularity and punctuality. These values can be taught by the storytelling and by role play, games and simulation.

In the secondary and higher stage of schooling, students are enabled to think rationally and they are made aware of different cultures, abstract concepts and comparative studies of different religions. They learn the art of understanding self and basic human virtues by *Yoga* and meditation. Teachers should develop effective communication and negotiation, critical thinking and problem-solving skills for conflict resolution.

4. Activities Approach (NCERT, 2006)

Activities approach follow the principle of learning by doing and learning by experience. Teachers should devise various activities according to the grade, level, and interest of the students. Activities are to be based on the specific subjects for giving the better understanding of the concepts of peace. Different strategies are to be applied during teaching-learning for inculcation of positive attitude among students are questions, stories, anecdotes, games experiments, discussions, dialogues, value clarification, examples, analogies, metaphors, role-play and simulation are helpful in promoting peace through.

Teacher should create a climate where peace culture is developed easily and students by engaging activities automatically. Some activities are listed as follows:

1. Demonstrate children the ways to respect elders, how to say thank you, when to say sorry and apologise.
2. Demonstrate how sharing, love and care emanates happiness.
3. Conduct prayers along with sharing thought of the days with explanation.
4. Celebrating various days of national importance.
5. Cultural activities showing different cultures, dance forms of India.
6. Debates, seminars, conferences on recent trends and history of Bharat.
7. Time is the greatest healing source, explain.
8. Explain the word Secular and Freedom in different perspectives.

9. Research activities on impact of population on economic status of country.
10. Science is the boon or curse.
11. The contribution of Indian mathematicians and scientists for the development of country, give your views.
12. Role Play on Environment.

A Study at Nakshatra School Kids Academy

An analytical study was conducted at Nakshatra School Kids Academy in which various activities were analysed and suggestions were given to principal for developing skills which are essential for creating positive attitude towards every aspect of life and help in creating peace within and with their peers and developing inclusive environment which helps holistic development of the child. Students engage in skill building activities like emotional development, social development, cognitive abilities, gross motor communication skill etc.

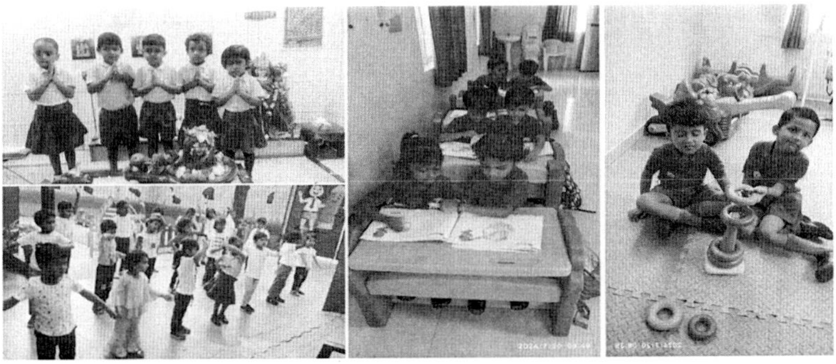

Fig. 8.3: Students engaged in different activities

1. Emotional Skill

Every child has different emotion when they cry, we give them hug and lot of love and try to convert their mind and encourage to laugh and play. Newly admitted children need lots of care, support and love. Teachers are asked to care them as their own children and help them to manage these initial days and make them enjoy every moment of school.

2. Social Skill

Social skills are developed by organising group activities, communicating with teachers and other students, sharing things like sharing tiffin, toys and helping each other etc. Morning prayer, assembly, celebrating festivals and other days were celebrated with kids for developing values and ethics among students. If they engage in squabble and stiff resolving the issues by love and asking them to shake hands and hug each other.

3. Cognitive Skill

Storytelling, puzzles, educational games, drawing, painting, display movies for kids, singing, dancing are different ways to develop cognitive skills among students. They are engaged in little tasks as puzzle solving for developing problem solving skills.

4. Gross Skill

Regular physical exercise of students to increase their gross motor skills like running, climbing, hip-hop, kicking, balancing, jumping etc. It helps to coordinate and control students movement.

Conclusion

Peace education is not just about preventing conflict but about creating a proactive, inclusive, and empathetic society. It equips individuals with the necessary skills to contribute to a peaceful and sustainable world. Given the current global challenges, peace education is indeed the need of the era. Peace education is increasingly recognized as essential in today's world due to various global and local conflicts, social tensions, and the need for promoting understanding and coexistence among diverse populations.

REFERENCES

Bramha Kumari (n.d.). *The Soul's Journey: Rediscovering Our Seven Core Values.* https://www.brahmakumaris.com/blog/self-development/the-souls-journey-rediscovering-our-seven-core-values/

Das, M. (2020). "Peace Education for Various Stages/Groups of People: A Brief Discussion". *International Journal of Advances in Engineering and Management (IJAEM), 2*(5), 631-636.

Galtung, J. (1969). "Violence, Peace, and Peace Research". *Journal of Peace Research, 6*(3), 167-191. DOI: 10.1177/002234336900600301

Galtung, J. (1996). "Peace and Conflict Research in the Age of the Cholera: Ten Pointers to the Future of Peace Studies". *International Journal of Peace Studies, 1*(1), 25-36.

Grewal, J.S., Sabharwal, N., Sharma, M.C., Singh, A., Gupta, K.M., Guru, G., Pandey, S. (2004). *Peace Education.* New Delhi: NCERT.

Hornby, A.S. (1995). *Oxford Advanced Learner's Dictionary of Current English* [by] A.S. Hornby; editor Jonathan Crowther. Oxford, England: Oxford University Press.

Hussey, T. (2009). "Nursing and Spirituality". *Nursing Philosophy, 10*(2), 71-80.

Kevern, P. (2012). "Who can give 'spiritual care'. The Management of Spirituality Sensitive Interactions between Nurses and Patients". *Journal of Nursing Management, 20*, 981.

Nario-Galace, J. & Castro, L. (2011). "Peace Education: A Pathway to a Culture of Peace". Center for Peace Education.

NCERT (2006). "Education for Peace Position Paper National Focus Group". National Council of Educational Research and Training, Delhi. Retrieved from: http://www.ncert.nic.in/new_ncert/ncert/rightside/links/pdf/focus_group/education_for_peace .pdf

Raina, S.K. & Kumar, R. (2023). "Vasudhaiva Kutumbakam—One Earth, One Family, One Future: India's Mantra for a Healthy and Prosperous Earth as the G20 Leader". *Journal of Family Medicine and Primary Care, 12*(2), 191-193, DOI: 10.4103/jfmpc.jfmpc_254_23

Schmidt, F. & Friedman, A. (1988). *Peacemaking Skills for Little Kids.* Peace Education Foundation.

Srinivasan, P. (2016). *Education for Peace: Introduction of Peace Education.* United States: Lulu Publications.

Tandon, M. (2014). "Non-violence and Peace Education—Role of Teachers and Teacher Education". *International Journal of Peace, Education and Development. 2*(2&3): 117-123.

UNCEB (2017). *Leaving No One Behind: Equality and Non-Discrimination at the Heart of Sustainable Development: A Shared United Nations Systems Framework for Action.* United Nations System Chief Executives Board for Coordination.

UNESCO (2005). *Peace Education Framework of Teacher Education.* New Delhi.

Younis, A.S. & Akhter, N. (2023). "Peace Education: A Pathway to the Culture of Peace". *Research on Humanities and Social Sciences, 13*(9).

9

Global Research Trends on Peace Education in Higher Education

Ramakanta Pradhan, Bhaskar Gurramkonda and *Shivakumar S.*

Introduction

The 21st century has brought significant advancements in science, technology, and knowledge, alongside shifts in societal values, ethics, and philosophies. However, challenges such as climate change, pandemics, migration, resource scarcity, racism, xenophobia, gender-based violence, poverty, and polarization continue to hinder global peace and stability (Sharma, 2013; UNESCO, 2024). In response, peace education has emerged as a crucial tool for fostering peace and ensuring human survival in this era (Capistrano *et al.*, 2022).

Education, particularly at the university level, plays a vital role in promoting peace by teaching students to maintain peace at interpersonal, intergroup, and international levels (Johnson & Johnson, 2010; Purwanto *et al.*, 2023). Higher education institutions are essential in integrating peace education into curricula, research, and community engagement. This integration is not just an academic pursuit but a moral imperative, addressing the root causes of conflict—social injustice, inequality, and discrimination—by fostering empathy, respect, and understanding (Bajaj, 2008).

The role of higher education extends beyond economic development, contributing to the stability of political, social, and educational systems (Sharma, 2019; Trinh, 2023). Peace education goes beyond traditional learning, teaching both about peace and for peace, and fostering critical thinking skills (Wulf, 1974). Over the past fifty years, various strategies have supported peace, including education for sustainability, global citizenship, conflict resolution, democracy, and human rights (Bhat & Jamatia, 2022). Though not always labelled as "peace education", these approaches align with its objectives and effectively instal peace values in students and communities (Rivera-Lozada *et al.*, 2021; UNESCO, 2024).

While extensive research exists on peace education and related fields, there is a notable gap in bibliometric studies focusing on peace education at the higher education level. To address this, a bibliometric analysis was conducted using Biblioshiny software to explore global research trends, patterns, themes, and contributions from various countries, organizations, and journals. This analysis is crucial for evaluating the production of valuable scientific literature for policymakers, scientists, and other stakeholders.

Objectives of the Study

The main objective of this study is to analyse the publications of Peace Education in higher education research reported and indexed in the Scopus database and present them in tabular form and diagrams. In particular, the study aims to find:

- Bibliometric data of Peace Education in higher education.
- Distribution of publication year-wise.
- Distribution of publication country-wise.
- Document-wise distribution of publications.
- Most cited publications in peace education in higher education.
- Publications growth and average citations.
- Most cited countries.
- Author impact and source impact.
- Collaborative network of documents published on peace education in higher education.
- Frequently occurred author keywords with thematic map.

Methodology

Article Selection

In the current study, the researcher searched the article on peace education in higher education between 2014 and 2024 using the Scopus database. For bibliometric analysis, only English-language publications are selected. The keywords "Peace AND in AND higher AND education" were utilised to search the articles. The researcher assessed 113 publications that matched these keywords in the initial phase of August 2024. The following keywords are used during the selection process on the Scopus website for these papers:

TITLE-ABS KEY (peace AND in AND higher AND education) AND PUBYEAR > 2013 AND PUBYEAR < 2025 AND (LIMIT-TO (SUBJAREA, "SOCI") OR LIMIT-

TO (SUBJAREA, "ARTS") OR LIMIT-TO (SUBJAREA, "PSYC") OR LIMIT-TO (SUBJAREA, "MULT")) AND (LIMIT-TO (EXACTKEYWORD, "Higher Education") OR LIMIT-TO (EXACTKEYWORD, "Education") OR LIMIT-TO (EXACTKEYWORD, "Peace Education") OR LIMIT-TO (EXACTKEYWORD, "Peace") OR LIMIT-TO (EXACTKEYWORD, "Human") OR LIMIT-TO (EXACTKEYWORD, "Sustainability") OR LIMIT-TO (EXACTKEYWORD, "Sustainable Development") OR LIMIT-TO (EXACTKEYWORD, "Peace Building") OR LIMIT-TO (EXACTKEYWORD, "Peace Studies") OR LIMIT-TO (EXACTKEYWORD, "Peace Process") OR LIMIT-TO (EXACTKEYWORD, "Peacekeeping") OR LIMIT-TO (EXACTKEYWORD, "Peace Building") OR LIMIT-TO (EXACTKEYWORD, "Education For Peace") AND (LIMIT-TO (DOCTYPE, "ar") AND (LIMIT-TO (LANGUAGE, "English")) AND (LIMIT-TO (SRCTYPE, "j"))

Data Coding and Analysis

The R program provides a bibliometric study by visualising different metrics from published publications, including the most cited articles, the most prolific authors, and frequently used keywords. First, metadata is obtained from Scopus by applying relevant keywords and downloading the data in CSV format. In R Studio, start by installing the bibliometrix package with install. packages ("bibliometrix"). Once the package is installed, load it using the library (bibliometrix). Then, initiate the bibliometric analysis programme with biblioshiny (), which will open in a browser window. Import the Scopus metadata in the "load data" section to proceed with the analysis.

Results

Findings

After exporting the metadata to biblioshiny, the initial interface of the software displays the main information of all the articles, which are now ready for analysis. The primary details regarding the documents to be analysed using bibliometric methods are shown in Fig. 9.1.

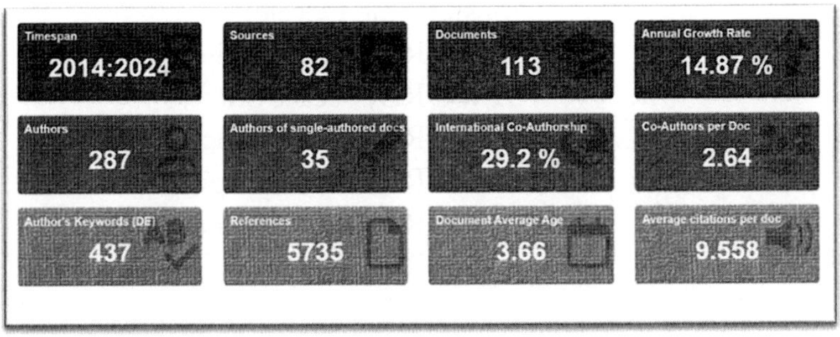

Fig. 9.1.

From Figure 9.1, the primary information shows that the bibliometric analysis was conducted on published documents from 2014 to 2024, comprising a total of 113 documents sourced from 82 Scopus-indexed journals. On average, these documents have received 9.558 citations each.

Article Distribution Year-wise

This study shows the distribution of publications year-wise on Scopus. The year of the article's first publication marks the beginning of data distribution, which lasts until the article is ready for print. The annual number of published papers distributed as seen in Figure 9.2.

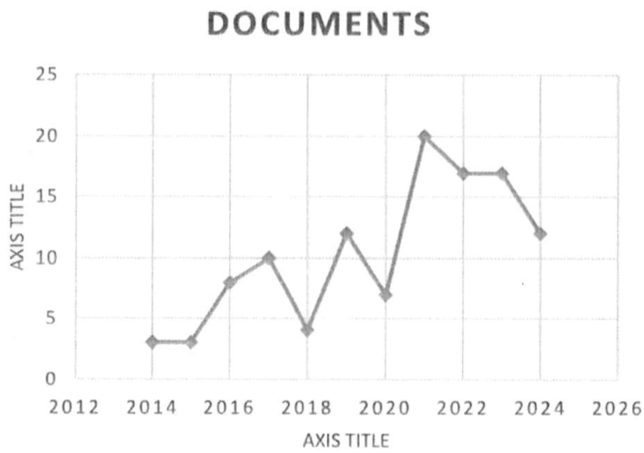

Fig. 9.2.

Figure 9.2 illustrates the annual distribution of articles in Scopus-indexed journals and proceedings. Research on peace education in higher education began in 2014 with 3 articles. The number of publications started to increase in 2016, yielding 8 articles. The research activity reached its peak in 2021, with 20 papers published on Peace Education in higher education.

Distribution of Articles by Country

Every year, many countries conduct research in Peace Education; yet, when considering output, the author's country of origin ranks among the top 10. The results are acquired in the diagram when research published by Scopus is highlighted or presented based on the country where the study was conducted.

The top 10 countries that conduct research and publish in the field are depicted in Fig. 9.3. With 21 studies, the United Kingdom is the nation with the most research conducted, as seen from Fig. 9.3. With 19 articles, Spain and the USA are at second position. Next, with 16 items, are South Korea and China, Indonesia, Colombia, India, and other countries, with 13, 12, 10, and so on.

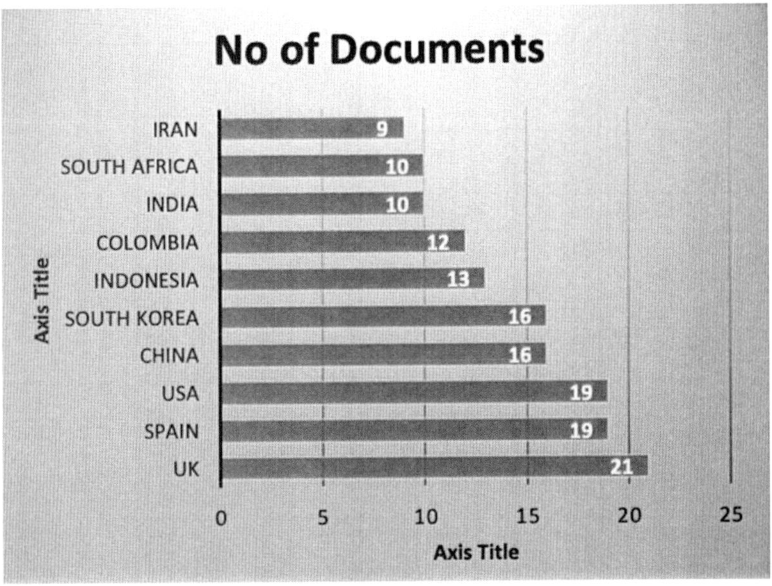
No of Documents
IRAN
SOUTH AFRICA
INDIA
COLOMBIA
INDONESIA
SOUTH KOREA
CHINA
USA
SPAIN
UK
9
10
10
12
13
16
16
19
19
21
Axis Title
0
5
10
15
20
25
Axis Title

Fig. 9.3.

Document Country-wise
21
19
16
13
12
10
9
Powered by Bing

Fig. 9.4.

Table 9.1: Sources-wise Impact

Sources	No. of Documents	h-Index	g-index	m-index	TC	NP	PY_Start
Journal of Peace Education	10	4	5	0.364	35	10	2014
Sustainability (Switzerland)	08	4	8	0.800	218	8	2020
International Journal of Sustainability in Higher Education	05	5	5	0.625	134	5	2017
Teaching in Higher Education	03	2	3	0.500	23	3	2021
Cogent Education	02	1	1	0.250	1	2	2021
Globalisation, Societies and Education	02	2	2	0.222	27	2	2016
Higher Education	02	1	2	0.250	20	2	2021
International Journal of Educational Development	02	1	2	0.167	6	2	2019
International Review of Education	02	2	2	0.222	25	2	2016
Journal of Religion and Health	02	1	1	0.500	3	1	2023

The top ten publications that the researchers recommend for peace education in higher education are listed in Table 9.2. With ten publications worldwide, the researcher discovered that the (*Journal of Peace Education*) was her top choice. With 218 citations, the *Sustainability* (Switzerland) Journal was discovered to be highly cited. It was followed by the *Journal of Peace Education* (35 Citations) and (*The International Journal of Sustainability in Higher Education*) (218 Citations). Concerning its h-index (05), min-index (0.625), and g-index (5) values, *The International Journal of Sustainability in Higher Education* held the top spot. Remarkably, a few recently established journals are performing better within the top 10.

Table 9.2: Most cited publications on peace education indexed in the Scopus database

Title	Year	Cited By
Freire P., Pedagogy of the Oppressed	1970	09
Violence, Peace, and Peace Research	1969	07
Peace Education: International Perspectives	2016	05
interpretation of Peace in History and Culture	2012	05
Transforming our World: The 2030 Agenda for Sustainable Development	2015	05
Pedagogies of Resistance and Critical Peace Education Praxis	2015	04
The Forms of Capital. Handbook of Theory and Research for the Sociology of Education. JG Richardson	1986	04
Peace Education Research in the Twenty-First Century: Three Concepts Facing Crisis or Opportunity?	2015	04
Education for a Culture of Peace in a Gender Perspective	2001	04

The document "Freire P., Pedagogy of the Oppressed", published in 1970, has received the most citations (09). It is followed in order by Violence, Peace, and Peace Research, published in 1969, with 07 citations. Then come the following five citations from the above table: "Peace Education: International Perspectives", "Interpretation of Peace in History and Culture", and "Transforming Our World: The 2030 Agenda for Sustainable Development", published in 2016, 2012, and 2015.

The most productive countries in terms of citations on peace education are displayed in Table 9.3. The country with the most citations (163) was Spain at the top of the list. The other productive nations were the United Kingdom (each work receiving 80 citations), Brazil (95 citations), Korea (95 citations), and Lithuania (161 citations). India ranked ninth with 37 citations, while Afghanistan ranked tenth with 25 citations.

Table 9.3: Most cited Countries

Country	Citation	Average Citation per year
Spain	163	32.60
Lithuania	161	161.00
Korea	95	11.90
Brazil	80	40.00
United Kingdom	80	7.30
Portugal	60	60.00
Israel	59	14.80
USA	58	5.80
India	37	12.30
Afghanistan	25	25.00

Table 9.4: Author Impact

Author Name	h-index	g-index	m-index	TC	NP	PY_Start
Kester K	5	7	0.625	95	7	2017
Abbas T	1	1	0.125	15	1	2017
Abdullah Ma	1	1	0.125	24	1	2017
Abu Moghli M	1	1	0.250	8	1	2021
Abura M	1	1	0.333	7	1	2022
Afriyanto	1	1	0.167	1	1	2019
Aggestam Pontoppidan C	1	1	0.333	22	1	2022
Aguirre S	1	1	0.167	4	1	2019
Ahmed A	1	2	0.143	5	2	2018
Ahmed Zs	1	1	0.200	5	1	2020

Table 9.5: Most Frequent Authors Keywords

Keywords	Occurrence
Higher education	15
Female	11
Human	11
Adult	8
Student	8
Education	7
Sustainable Development Goal	7
Learning	6
Sustainability	5
Peacekeeping	4

Word Clouds (Authors Keywords)

Based on their publications, citations, and h-index, the top 10 productive authors are displayed in Table 9.4. All the authors have authored 17 papers, accounting for 15.04 per cent of the total publications produced globally during the period under review, with 186 citations. Based on the number of publications, Kester K. ranked highest on the list with five publications. Kester K. outperforms all of the authors combined, with 95 citations, in the category of highest citation count. Kester K. served as the most outstanding g-index value, which is outstanding (7).

Table 9.5 and Figure 9.5 show that the authors' most frequently used keyword is higher education, appearing 15 times overall. Other frequently occurring keywords include adult and student (8 times), female and human (11 times), education and sustainable development goal (7 times), learning (6 times), sustainability (5 times), and peacekeeping (4 times). The larger the keyword size in Figure 9.5, the more times it appears, and *vice versa*.

Fig. 9.5

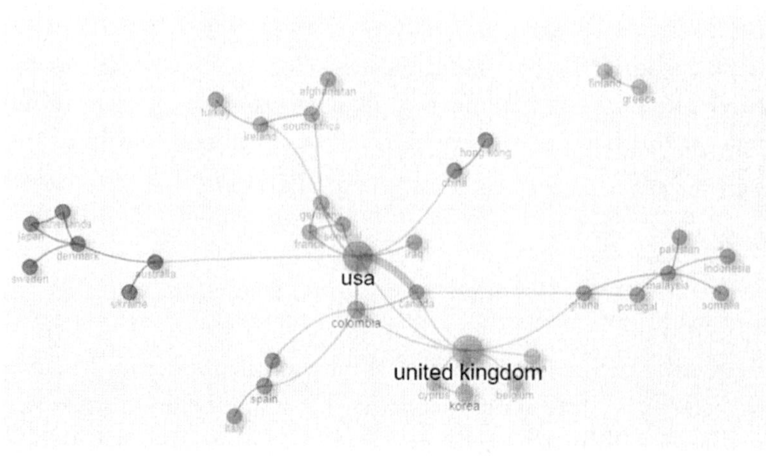

Fig. 9.6: Collaborative network of documents published on e-waste management.

Figure 9.6 shows a collaborative network of documents published on peace education. The network contains eight coloured clusters. The United States, France, Germany, Colombia, Iraq, Canada, and Senegal are included in the blue-coloured cluster network; the United Kingdom, Korea, Cyprus, Belgium, and Kenya are included in the pink-coloured cluster; and Sweden, Denmark, Australia, Japan, and the Netherlands are included in the red-coloured network. Similarly, the green colour cluster includes Ghana, Portugal, Malaysia, Pakistan, and Indonesia. Afghanistan, South Africa, Ireland, and Turkey are included in the purple-coloured cluster. Grey colour cover Finland and Greece, Maroon colour in China, Hong Kong. Keyword clusters are referred to as themes, and two-dimensional diagrams can be created by utilizing the density and centrality of these clusters to identify and map themes.

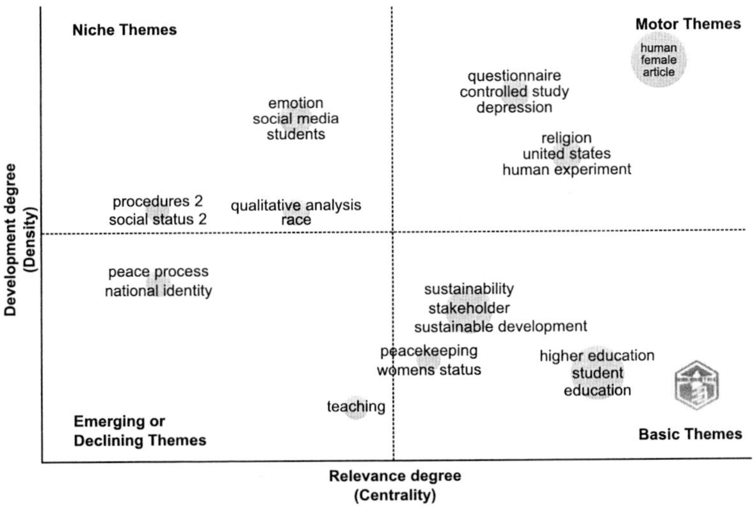

Fig. 9.7: Thematic Map

Fig 9.7, thematic map analyses themes according to the quadrant in which they are placed: firstly, the upper-right quadrant: motor themes; secondly, the lower-right quadrant:

basic themes. Thirdly, the lower-left quadrant: niche themes; and fourth, the upper-left quadrant: emergent or declining themes. Thematic Map.

Conclusion

The current study analysed the worldwide patterns in peace education research output published in the higher education sector between 2014 and 2024. The number of publications is seen to be increasing steadily. According to the study, journals with a high citation count, such as (*The International Journal of Sustainability in Higher Education*), *Sustainability* (Switzerland) and the (*Journal of Peace Education*), are the best medium for publishing peace-education research articles. With the most citations (163), Spain was first on the list, followed by Lithuania (161), Korea (95), and the United Kingdom (18). Kester K. was a productive author of peace education in higher education. *Sustainability, Journal of Peace Education*, and (*International Journal of Sustainability in Higher Education*) are the journals that are highly recommended for publication. Higher education appears 15 times at the top author's keyword list, followed by humans 11 times occurrence, Students 8 times and peacekeeping 4 times. The documents covered focused more on sustainability, peacekeeping, peace management, and higher education.

REFERENCES

Aria, M. & Cuccurullo, C. (2017). "Bibliometrix: An R-tool for Comprehensive Science Mapping Analysis", *Journal of Informetrics, 11*(4): pp. 959-975, Elsevier.

Bajaj, M. (Ed.). (2008). *Encyclopedia of Peace Education*. Information Age Publishing.

Capistrano, D., Sloan, S., Symonds, J., Samonova, E., Sugrue, C. & Devine, D. (2022). "Assessing Experiences with Violence and Peace in Primary Schools in Sierra Leone". *Journal of Aggression, Conflict and Peace Research, 14*(3): 231-243. https://doi.org/10.1108/JACPR-09-2021-0633

Johnson, D.W. & Johnson, R.T. (2010). "Peace Education in the Classroom: Creating Effective Peace Education Programmes", in *Handbook on Peace Education* (pp. 223-240). Psychology Press.

Manzoor Bhat, R. & Laxmi Jamatia, P. (2022). "Importance and Necessity of Peace Education in the School Curriculum for Fostering International Perspective". *International Journal of Educational Review, Law and Social Sciences (IJERLAS)*, *2*(5), 613-620. https://doi.org/10.54443/ijerlas.v2i5.341

Purwanto, Y., Suprapto, Munaf, D.R., Albana, H., Marifataini, L., Siregar, I. & Sumarni. (2023). "The Peace Education Concept and Practice at Universities: A Systematic Review". *Cogent Education, 10*(2): 2260724. https://doi.org/10.1080/2331186X.2023.2260724

Rivera-Lozada, I.C., Collazos-Ardila, R. & Rivera-Lozada, O. (2021). "Peacebuilding Education: A Complex Perspective". *Cogent Education, 8*(1): 1905228. https://doi.org/10.1080/2331186X.2021.1905228

Sharma, A. (2013). "Education for Peace: Transforming the Culture of Violence". *Space and Culture, India, 1*(1): 58-68. https://doi.org/10.20896/saci.v1i1.15

Sharma, G.S. (2019). "Peace Education: Why Need of Today's Education?" *Pramana Research Journal, 9*(7). https://pramanaresearch.org/

Trinh, N.T.H. (2023). "Higher Education and Its Role for National Development. A Research Agenda with Bibliometric Analysis". *Interchange, 54*(2): 125-143. https://doi.org/10.1007/s10780-023-09493-9

UNESCO (2024). *Peace Education in the 21st Century: An Essential Strategy for Building Lasting Peace—UNESCO Digital Library.* United Nations Educational Scientific and Cultural Organisation. https://unesdoc.unesco.org/ark:/48223/pf0000388385

Wulf, C. (1974). *Handbook on Peace Education* (pp. XI, 378). International Peace Research Association, Education Committee/: Frankfurt am Main; Oslo. https://doi.org/10.25656/01:1511

10

Role of Universities in Promoting Peace Education

Sana Parveen

Introduction

Background and Rationale

In a community marked by violence and division, often peace education is growing as a vital component in cultivating a mindset that fosters empathy and collaboration. Universities, as scientific and technological hubs, have the potential to play a substantial role in this particular field. They are particularly equipped to include peace education into their curricula, impact the principles of society, and help with conflict resolution and mitigation. Peace education takes a holistic approach that includes lessons on the functioning of democracy, human rights, peaceful conflict resolution, establishing an equitable economic and social system, gender equality, sustainable development, safe cultural practices, and techniques for fostering peace and protecting one's privacy.

Pursuant to the United Nations Education Agency, the ultimate objective of peace education is to strengthen comprehension competencies, views, and convictions. The purpose is to promote peaceful conflict resolution while developing ideal circumstances for peace at all degrees of challenges, including interpersonal in nature, intergroup interaction, national, and international relationships, through behaviour modification. The essential terms in the definition are the strategy of spreading knowledge, skills, attitudes, and beliefs in order to prevent, dedicate, and develop peace at all tiers.

As a result, this research seeks to chronicle the concept and practice of peace education in universities through reviewing literature published by reliable resources in the recent past. In this systematic review, the term "concept" refers to the fundamental principles underlying the research findings and serves as the guiding framework for the investigation and analysis. On the other hand, "practice" denotes to actual implementation and real-world implementations of the study's peace education principles, investigating how these ideas are executed and incorporated within educational settings as stated in the literature.

Peace requires aligning with life itself, devoid of fear and resentment. Peace evokes sentiments of security, serenity, and tranquility. While typically viewed as a worldwide issue, attaining peace inside each country is critical to global harmony. Peace education aims to disintegrate violent power struggles. It stimulates negotiations and collaboration at both individual and community levels.

A few publications examine peace education in universities as they clarify the contribution of higher education in promoting peace education. Merely a few investigations using mixed methods done by Shehi *et al.* (2018) demonstrated the two university curriculum and responses from students show an elevated focus on human-focused and relationship-focused peace-related topics. Fortunately, an investigation examining the idea and practice of peace education based on qualitative analysis continues unexplored. Additionally, John's (2018) identifies Peace Education as "a counter force and restorative process" (p. 54). Another researcher pointed out that peace and conflict education have been appealing as a method for stimulating inclusive knowledge in universities and organizations over the past several decades.

Objectives

The key objective of this systematic review is to analyse a conceptual premise and practical implementations of peace education within universities. This review seeks to:

- Recognizing the conceptual foundations for peace education in higher education.
- Examine the strategies and practices adopted by universities to promote peace education.
- Identify challenges faced and suggest improvements for more effective implementation.

Scope and Methodology

This review comprises peer-reviewed journal papers, institutional reports, and pertinent educational literature published during the last 20 years. The research papers were chosen based on their relevance to university-based peace education programmes, theoretical frameworks, and practical implications. To guarantee thorough coverage, the review approach included systematic literature searches, screenings, and evaluations of the literature.

Conceptual Dimensions of Peace Education

Defining Peace Education

The conceptual framework of 'peace' is multifaceted. It is typically defined as a condition without dispute, disruption, or animosity. Peace may also refer to any interaction among individuals marked by dignity, justice, and compassion. Peace education encompasses a range of activities and curricula designed to promote understanding, tolerance, and conflict resolution. Historically, it has evolved from a focus on conflict resolution to include broader themes of social justice, human rights, and global citizenship.

Peace Education, by R.D. Laing (1978), aspires to confront conflicts and violence at all stages, ranging from international and national to local and individual. It seeks to investigate methods for creating more equitable and sustainable futures. Key theoretical frameworks guiding peace education include:

- **Transformative Learning Theory:** Emphasizes personal and social change through critical reflection.
- **Conflict Resolution Theories:** Focus on methods for resolving disputes and building harmonious relationships.
- **Global Citizenship Education:** Aims to cultivate awareness and responsibility for global issues.

Role of Universities Developing Peace Education

Enacted by the United Nations General Assembly in 2015, the 2030 Agenda for Sustainable Development underscores the inseparable connection among security, peace, and sustainability. Universities and colleges play critical roles in achieving peace across the globe and implementing the sustainable development agenda. There is no unanimity on the term, which has been defined in several ways. Gandhi associated truth with non-violence. To attain this condition of 'peace', particularly in today's conflict-ridden globe, it is widely acknowledged that peace education is a critical component that will teach humanity to avoid violence and live in a harmonious society/world. It is being recognized as "an intellectual enterprise devoted to the study of peace and the bringing about a state of peace in human society."

Peace education encourages educators to provide instruction for young people on how to be peaceful. Educators may foster harmonious relationships by including peace education topics in their curriculum. The duty of educators is not just to teach pupils about peace but also to advocate for it that how they can easily apply this in daily life. According to Bretherton *et al.* (2003), "a teacher who tries to pass on the culture of peace without doing anything, including the act of peace, might be considered hypocrite" (p. 3). An educator who proclaims peace but fails to exhibit what they have taught is a charlatan. As an outcome of this approach, promoting peace principles becomes irrelevant for learners. Teachers who exemplify peaceful attitudes in confrontation with their pupils can effectively conduct peace education.

Iceland is the world's most peaceful nation for an unprecedented 16th consecutive year, according to the 2023 Global Peace Index (GPI), published annually by the Institute for Economics and Peace (IEP), which was followed by Denmark, Ireland, New Zealand, and Austria. On the contrary, Afghanistan is the least peaceful country. India is ranked 126th out of the 163 nations covered by the IEP.

What needs to be done to solidify the notions of peace? Peace is more significant now than ever before. It is all our responsibility to foster a sense of peace and facilitate discussions regarding the importance of this topic in developing countries, especially in India.

Implementing peace education in the university educational system can serve as an effective strategy for cultivating peace as well as generating peace in communities. Universities contribute to peace education through several means:

- **Curricular Integration**: Mahatma Gandhi, an ardent promoter of peace and non-violence, stated, "If we are to teach real peace in this world...we shall have to begin with the children." Incorporating peace education into diverse disciplines, such as international relations, social sciences, and humanities. Textbooks should incorporate captivating genuine texts that revolve around topics such as social cohesion, interfaith communication, cross-cultural comprehension, democracy, human rights, inclusiveness, and diversity.
- **Institutional Mission:** Colleges and universities, as research and development centres, are essential elements of this collaborative system. Their involvement expands across universities to encompass collaborations with governing bodies, international organizations, and other entities. This joint synergy increases the efficiency of peace-promoting measures, leading to a more comprehensive and enduring effect, aligning university missions with principles of peace, justice, and social responsibility.
- **Research and Programmes:** In 2004, the Nelson Mandela Centre for Peace and Conflict Resolution was established in Jamia Millia Islamia in New Delhi, purporting to be one of the very first centres for peace education and conflict studies at an Indian university. The University Grants Commission, the top organisation in charge of higher education, has considered implementing peace and conflict resolution studies in an organised manner in the 2007 to 2012

plan. The Commission fostered research in the field of human rights and provided funding for universities to start programmes in the field of peace.

Practical Dimensions of Peace Education

Implementation Strategies

Implementing peace education at the university level in India provides an excellent opportunity to cultivate a culture of communication, compassion, and conflict resolution among generations of students and professionals. As India negotiates its complicated socio-political terrain, universities are crucial in moulding the values and skills required for a nation with fewer conflicts. Successful peace education programmes often involve:

- **Collaborations and Partnerships:** Collaborations and partnerships with local communities, NGOs, and international organisation are critical in peace education to increase programme relevance and effect. Engaging local communities enables peace education programmes to be adjusted to unique area conflicts and cultural dynamics, ensuring that the curriculum is both relevant and actionable. NGOs provide significant field experience and practical insights into conflict resolution and peace building, facilitating the integration of real-world applications into educational frameworks. Partnerships with foreign organizations can give global perspectives and access to international standards and resources, promoting a better knowledge of global peace challenges and encouraging cross-cultural interaction.
- **Resource Allocation:** Investing in faculty development allows educators to accumulate the skills and knowledge

they require to effectively incorporate peace education, including conflict resolution, human rights, and social justice in their curriculum. Allocating resources to curriculum design enables the establishment of extensive and inclusive peace education programmes that accommodate the varied demands of various student groups. Furthermore, student support services like counselling, mentorship, and community participation initiatives are vital in developing students' emotional intelligence, empathy, and critical thinking skills by promoting resources to these specific areas.

- **Student Engagement:** Student engagement is a vital aspect of peace education because it allows students to actively participate in their learning and contribute to the goal of peace and social justice. Encouraging student engagement in workshops, seminars, and service-learning activities helps students to participate in peace education in a hands-on and experiential manner. Workshops and seminars give an opportunity for students to investigate complicated problems concerning peace and conflict. Service-learning options, such as working with local community organizations or taking part in peace-building efforts, allow students to apply theoretical principles to real-world situations, promoting a better knowledge of the intricacies of peace education.

Challenges and Barriers

Implementing peace education at the university level in India involves numerous challenges and barriers. One of the major challenges is a lack of competence and interest among students and educators. Many universities lack the resources and facilities to properly execute peace education programmes. Furthermore, the curriculum is sometimes overburdened, leaving inadequate space for the inclusion of peace education. Challenges include:

- **Lack of Skills and Awareness:** Many students and educators are unaware of the significance and relevance of Peace Education, resulting in a lack of enthusiasm and involvement.
- **Insufficient Funds and Facilities:** Universities in India frequently lack the resources required to efficiently run Peace Education programmes, such as skilled professors, curricular materials, and infrastructure.
- **Curriculum Constraints:** The curriculum is sometimes overloaded, offering inadequate space for Peace Education, which is frequently considered a modification instead of an essential component of the curriculum.
- **Societal and Cultural Barriers:** Peace Education may be considered a Western notion, and its implementation could be constrained by societal and cultural constraints, such as a preference for academic performance over social and emotional learning.
- **Policy and Administrative Barriers:** The absence of assistance from university officials and policymakers may impede the implementation of Peace Education.

Implications of Peace Education

- **Securing External Funding:** Securing external income is critical for furthering the development of peace education initiatives, which need significant resources to be implemented properly. To do this, it is critical to pursue both funding and strategic collaborations. Grants from government agencies, private foundations, and international organizations can offer the financial assistance required for programme creation and implementation.

- **Advocacy and Awareness:** Advocacy and awareness are critical to building awareness of peace education in universities. By efficiently raising awareness among university officials and stakeholders, highlight the essential role of peace education in creating a more inclusive, compassionate, and collaborative academic environment. Emphasizing the positive outcomes of peace education, such as its ability to improve conflict resolution skills, foster multicultural understanding, and contribute to overall student well-being, may help make a persuasive argument for its inclusion in curriculum. With presentations, seminars, and targeted messaging, stakeholders may see the practical influence of peace education on campus culture and community.

Discussion

Synthesis of Conceptual and Practical Insights

The review underlines the substantial relationship between theoretical frameworks and actual implementations of peace education in universities. Effective peace education involves a strong theoretical basis as well as inventive and adaptive practical approaches. Successful programmes highlight the need of incorporating peace education into both specialised and general curriculum, focusing on experiential learning and community participation.

Future Recommendations

Future researches should concentrate on:

- **Longitudinal Researches:** Longitudinal Researches look on how peace education affects students' career and personal life over time.

- **Comparative Analysis:** Examining Peace Education techniques at various institutions and cultural environments.
- **Innovative Practices:** Developing innovative educational approaches and technology to improve Peace Education outcomes.

Conclusion

Universities play a critical role towards enhancing peace education by combining theoretical frameworks and practical implications. Universities and colleges can foster peace and contribute to global conflict resolution by implementing specialised programmes, innovative teaching techniques, and strategic alliances that include peace education principles and parameters that help educators as well as students from all age groups. As problems continue, continuing research and adherence to good practices will be critical to optimizing the effectiveness of Peace Education in universities.

REFERENCES

Barash, P. David, (2000). *Approaches to Peace*, Oxford University Press, New York.

Bashir, S., Akbar, R.A. (2021). "Determining the Effect of Peace Education on Knowledge and Attitude of Prospective Teachers: An Experimental Study", *Bulletin of Education and Research*.

Bhargava, R. (2017). "Value Education: Need of the Hour in Indian Education System". *International Journal of Indian Psychology*, *4*(1), 43-49.

Charles, K. & Selvi A. (2012). *Peace and Value Education*, Neelkamal Publication Pvt. Ltd., Hyderabad.

Cuga, Candra *et al.* (2019). *The Effectiveness of Peace Education Learning Models Toward Students' Understanding of Peace Loving and Anti-Violence*. Atlantis Press.

Government of India (1986). *Report of National Policy on Education,* New Delhi, MHRD, Government of India.

Gupta, S. & Saxena, A. (2018). "Challenges and Opportunities in Implementing Value Education Programmes in Indian Colleges". *Journal of Educational Sciences, 6*(2): 45-56.

NCERT (2006). *National Curriculum Framework 2005, Position Report Focus Group of Education for Peace*, New Delhi, N.C.E.R.T.

Rajendrakumar, M.P. (2024). "Role of Teacher for Peace Education". *The International Journal of Indian Psychology, 2*(2).

UNESCO Office, New Delhi. (2005). Peace education: framework for teacher education. UNESCO Digital Library. https://unesdoc.unesco.org/ark:/48223/pf0000150262

Yemenici, A. (2016). "Peace Education: Training for an Evolved Consciousness of Non-violence". *All Azimuth: A Journal of Foreign Policy and Peace, 5*(1), 5-25.

11

Peace Pedagogy in Formal Education

Akhil Kumar Rai and *Garima Rai*

Peace Pedagogy in formal education refers to the teaching practices, curriculum, and strategies aimed at cultivating a culture of peace among students. This approach goes beyond merely teaching about peace; it actively integrates the principles of peace, non-violence, conflict resolution, and social justice into the educational experience. People of various ages can get peace education in official and informal contexts. There are programmes in place at the local, national, and worldwide levels as well as during and after conflicts. Through peace education programmes, several societal groups are frequently brought together to foster public discourse. These groups generally include civil society organizations, educational institutions, tribal leaders, and the media. However, because Peace Education encompasses so many topics, the main factors influencing efforts are context and culture, along with the goals and scope of the programmes. Thus, peacebuilding and peace education are inextricably interwoven. One of the main focuses of the UN's peacebuilding efforts is education.

Key Elements of Peace Pedagogy

Here are some key features and elements of peace education—

A. Curriculum Integration

1. **Human Rights Education:** Human Rights Education (HRE) is a critical component of peace pedagogy, aiming to empower students with the knowledge, skills, and values necessary to uphold and promote human rights.
   - (a) **Understanding Rights and Responsibilities**: Students learn about the Universal Declaration of Human Rights (UDHR) and other international human rights frameworks. They explore the rights and responsibilities that come with being a global citizen, fostering a sense of duty towards protecting the rights of others.
   - (b) **Critical Analysis of Human Rights Issues**: Through case studies, discussions, and debates, students critically examine historical and contemporary human rights issues. This includes understanding the root causes of human rights violations and exploring ways to prevent them.
   - (c) **Empathy and Solidarity**: HRE encourages students to empathize with those whose rights have been violated, promoting a sense of global solidarity. This helps students understand the impact of human rights abuses on individuals and communities.
   - (d) **Active Participation**: Students are encouraged to take action in support of human rights, whether through school-based initiatives, community projects, or by participating in broader social movements. This active participation fosters a sense of agency and responsibility.

(e) **Cultural and Social Awareness**: HRE also emphasizes the importance of understanding and respecting cultural diversity. Students learn how cultural, social, and economic factors influence the perception and realization of human rights around the world.

(f) **Promoting Social Justice**: A key aspect of HRE is its focus on social justice. Students are taught to recognize and challenge systemic inequalities and injustices that lead to human rights violations. This includes discussions on gender equality, racial justice, economic disparities, and other social issues.

(g) **Developing a Rights-based Approach**: Students are encouraged to adopt a rights-based approach in their thinking and decision-making processes. This means considering how their actions and the actions of others align with human rights principles.

Hence, Integrating Human Rights Education into the curriculum is essential for fostering a culture of respect, dignity, and justice in schools and beyond. It helps students become informed, compassionate, and active participants in their communities, committed to building a more equitable and peaceful world.

2. **Conflict Resolution:** Conflict resolution is a fundamental aspect of Peace Pedagogy that equips students with the skills and strategies to manage and resolve conflicts peacefully. By integrating conflict resolution into the curriculum, schools can help students develop the ability to handle disputes constructively, both in their personal lives and in broader societal contexts.

(a) **Understanding Conflict:** Students are taught to recognize the nature of conflict, including its causes, types, and potential outcomes. This understanding helps them approach conflicts not as inherently negative, but as opportunities for growth and positive change.

(b) **Communication Skills:** Effective communication is key to resolving conflicts. Students learn active listening, clear expression of thoughts and feelings, and non-verbal communication skills. These skills help them convey their perspectives without escalating tensions and understand others' viewpoints more empathetically.

(c) **Emotional Intelligence:** Conflict resolution education emphasizes the development of emotional intelligence, including self-awareness, self-regulation, and empathy. Students learn to manage their emotions during conflicts and respond in ways that de-escalate situations.

(d) **Problem-Solving Techniques:** Students are introduced to problem-solving strategies that help them find mutually acceptable solutions to conflicts. This includes brainstorming, negotiating, and compromising. They are encouraged to focus on interests rather than positions, fostering win-win outcomes.

(e) **Mediation and Peer Mediation:** Mediation, a process where a neutral third party helps those in conflict find a resolution, is often taught as a valuable conflict resolution tool. Some schools implement peer mediation programmes, where trained students help mediate conflicts among their peers, promoting a culture of peer-led resolution.

(f) **Understanding Power Dynamics:** Students learn about the role of power in conflicts, including how power imbalances can influence the course and outcome of disputes. This understanding helps them navigate conflicts more equitably and sensitively, particularly in diverse and multicultural settings.

(g) **Practicing Non-violence:** A key principle of conflict resolution in Peace Pedagogy is non-violence. Students are taught to reject physical, verbal, and psychological violence as means of resolving disputes. Instead, they are encouraged to use peaceful methods rooted in dialogue, respect, and understanding.

(h) **Role-Playing and Simulations:** Role-playing and simulation exercises are commonly used to practice conflict resolution skills in a safe and controlled environment. These activities allow students to apply what they have learned to real-life scenarios, helping them build confidence in their ability to resolve conflicts peacefully.

(i) **Reflective Practice:** After conflict resolution activities or real-life conflict situations, students are encouraged to reflect on the process, the outcomes, and what they learned. This reflection helps reinforce the skills and principles of peaceful conflict resolution and encourages continual improvement.

So, integrating conflict resolution into the curriculum empowers students with the tools they need to navigate disputes constructively, reducing the potential for violence and promoting a more peaceful school environment. These skills are essential for building a culture of peace that extends beyond the classroom into all areas of life.

3. **Social Justice:** Social justice is a cornerstone of Peace Pedagogy that focuses on addressing and challenging inequalities, promoting fairness, and ensuring that all individuals have access to the same opportunities and rights. By integrating social justice into the curriculum, education becomes a powerful tool for fostering a more equitable and inclusive society.

   (a) **Understanding Inequality and Injustice:** Students are introduced to the concepts of social justice, inequality, and injustice. They explore how these issues manifest in various forms, such as economic disparity, racism, sexism, and other forms of discrimination and marginalization.

   (b) **Critical Examination of Power and Privilege:** The curriculum encourages students to critically examine power structures and how privilege operates in society. They learn to recognize their own positions within these structures and understand how privilege can affect access to resources, opportunities, and justice.

   (c) **Promoting Equity and Inclusion:** Social justice education emphasizes the importance of equity, ensuring that everyone has access to the resources and opportunities they need to succeed. Students learn about inclusive practices that value diversity and actively work to dismantle barriers that prevent marginalized groups from achieving equality.

   (d) **Advocacy and Activism:** Students are encouraged to become advocates for social justice in their communities. This can involve participating in or organizing campaigns, raising awareness about social issues, and supporting initiatives that promote justice and equity. Activism is seen as a practical application of their learning.

(e) **Analyzing Historical and Contemporary Issues:** The curriculum often includes an analysis of historical and contemporary social justice movements, helping students understand the ongoing struggles for civil rights, gender equality, environmental justice, and other critical issues. This historical perspective provides context for current events and challenges.

(f) **Ethical and Moral Reasoning:** Students engage in discussions about ethics and morality, particularly as they relate to social justice issues. They explore questions of fairness, responsibility, and what it means to live in a just society, helping them develop a strong moral compass.

(g) **Empathy and Solidarity:** Social justice education fosters empathy by encouraging students to see the world from the perspective of those who are marginalized or oppressed. This empathy is linked to a sense of solidarity, where students feel connected to and responsible for the well-being of others, especially those who are disadvantaged.

(h) **Civic Engagement:** The curriculum promotes active citizenship, encouraging students to participate in democratic processes and community engagement. This involvement is aimed at bringing about social change, whether through voting, volunteering, or participating in local government and community organizations.

(i) **Challenging Stereotypes and Bias:** Students learn to recognize and challenge stereotypes, biases, and prejudices that contribute to social injustice.

This includes examining their own attitudes and behaviours, as well as those prevalent in society, media, and institutions.

(j) **Building a Just Community:** Schools that integrate social justice into their curricula often work towards building a school community that reflects these values. This includes creating policies and practices that ensure all students, regardless of their background, feel respected, supported, and valued. In this way, integrating social justice into the curriculum helps students develop a deep understanding of fairness and equity, empowering them to challenge injustice and contribute to a more peaceful and just world. This education not only shapes their worldview but also equips them with the tools to actively participate in creating a society where everyone can thrive.

B. Critical Thinking

Critical thinking is a vital component of Peace Pedagogy that empowers students to analyze, evaluate, and reflect on complex issues related to peace, conflict, and social justice. It encourages students to question assumptions, consider multiple perspectives, and make informed decisions that contribute to a more peaceful and just world.

1. **Analyzing Conflicts and Peace Issues:** Students are taught to critically analyze conflicts, both historical and contemporary, by examining their causes, dynamics, and consequences. They learn to identify the underlying factors that contribute to violence and consider alternative approaches to conflict resolution.

2. **Evaluating Sources of Information:** Critical thinking involves the ability to evaluate the credibility and reliability of information sources. Students learn to differentiate between fact and opinion, recognize bias, and assess the validity of arguments. This skill is essential in an era of widespread misinformation and media manipulation.
3. **Questioning Assumptions and Stereotypes:** Peace Pedagogy encourages students to question deeply ingrained assumptions, stereotypes, and prejudices. By challenging these mental models, students can develop a more nuanced understanding of others and reduce the likelihood of conflict arising from misunderstandings or biases.
4. **Considering Multiple Perspectives:** Students are taught to consider multiple perspectives on issues related to peace and conflict. This involves understanding the viewpoints of different stakeholders, including those from diverse cultural, social, and political backgrounds. Considering multiple perspectives helps students develop empathy and fosters a more inclusive approach to problem-solving.
5. **Reflective Thinking:** Reflective thinking is a key aspect of critical thinking in peace pedagogy. Students are encouraged to reflect on their own beliefs, values, and actions in relation to peace and conflict. This self-awareness helps them recognize their role in either perpetuating or resolving conflicts.
6. **Problem-Solving and Decision-Making:** Critical thinking is closely linked to problem-solving and decision-making. Students are taught to approach problems systematically, using logic and reasoning to identify solutions that promote peace and justice.

They learn to weigh the potential consequences of their decisions and consider the broader impact on society.

7. **Ethical Reasoning:** Ethical reasoning is an essential part of critical thinking in Peace Pedagogy. Students are encouraged to consider the ethical implications of their actions and the actions of others, particularly in situations involving conflict or injustice. This helps them develop a strong sense of moral responsibility.
8. **Debate and Dialogue:** Engaging in debates and dialogues on contentious issues is a powerful way to develop critical thinking skills. Students learn to articulate their ideas clearly, listen to opposing views, and engage in constructive discussions that seek common ground. These activities promote respect for differing opinions and the peaceful resolution of disagreements.
9. **Challenging the *Status Quo*:** Critical thinking in Peace Pedagogy often involves challenging the *status quo* and questioning systems of power and privilege. Students are encouraged to think critically about social, economic, and political structures that contribute to conflict and inequality, and to explore ways to create more just and peaceful alternatives.
10. **Creative Thinking:** Alongside analytical thinking, creative thinking is also fostered in Peace Pedagogy. Students are encouraged to think outside the box, generating innovative ideas and solutions for building peace and addressing complex social issues. Creativity is seen as essential for imagining and working towards a better future.

By integrating critical thinking into Peace Pedagogy, educators help students develop the intellectual tools necessary to navigate complex global challenges. This approach not only enhances students' cognitive skills but also prepares them to be thoughtful, informed, and active contributors to a more peaceful and equitable world.

C. Values Education

Values education is a crucial aspect of peace pedagogy, focusing on the development of moral and ethical values that promote peaceful coexistence, respect, and understanding among individuals and communities. By integrating values education into the curriculum, schools can foster a culture of peace that is rooted in the hearts and minds of students.

1. **Promoting Core Values:** Values education emphasizes core values such as empathy, respect, kindness, honesty, tolerance, and compassion. These values are essential for building positive relationships, reducing conflicts, and creating a harmonious society.
2. **Developing Empathy and Compassion:** Students are encouraged to develop empathy and compassion by understanding and sharing the feelings of others. Through activities like storytelling, role-playing, and community service, students learn to see the world from others' perspectives, which helps reduce prejudice and promotes social harmony.
3. **Teaching Respect for Diversity:** Values education teaches students to respect diversity in all its forms, including cultural, religious, ethnic, and social diversity. This respect for diversity is crucial for promoting social cohesion and preventing conflicts that arise from misunderstandings or intolerance.
4. **Fostering Integrity and Honesty:** Integrity and honesty are key components of values education. Students learn the importance of being truthful and acting with integrity in their interactions with others. This helps

build trust and reduces the likelihood of conflicts based on deceit or dishonesty.

5. **Encouraging Responsibility and Accountability:** Values education encourages students to take responsibility for their actions and be accountable for their decisions. This includes understanding the impact of their actions on others and the environment, and taking steps to make positive contributions to their communities.
6. **Instilling a Sense of Justice and Fairness:** A strong emphasis is placed on the values of justice and fairness. Students learn to recognize and challenge injustice, whether it occurs in their immediate surroundings or in the wider world. This understanding of justice helps them advocate for the rights and dignity of others.
7. **Nurturing a Sense of Community:** Values education fosters a sense of belonging and community. Students are encouraged to work together, support one another, and contribute to the well-being of their peers and the broader community. This sense of community is vital for building a peaceful and cooperative society.
8. **Promoting Non-violence:** Non-violence is a fundamental value in Peace Pedagogy. Students learn the importance of resolving conflicts peacefully and are taught to reject all forms of violence, whether physical, verbal, or psychological. This value is reinforced through teachings on conflict resolution, communication skills, and peaceful activism.
9. **Encouraging Environmental Stewardship:** Values education often includes an emphasis on environmental stewardship, teaching students to respect and care for the natural world. This includes understanding the interconnectedness of all life and the importance of sustainable practices to ensure a peaceful and healthy planet for future generations.

10. **Reflective Practice and Moral Reasoning:** Students are encouraged to engage in reflective practice, where they think critically about their values, decisions, and actions. Moral reasoning exercises help students navigate ethical dilemmas and make choices that align with the values of peace, justice, and respect.

By integrating values education into the curriculum, peace pedagogy helps students develop a strong moral foundation that guides their actions and decisions throughout their lives. These values not only contribute to personal growth but also play a critical role in building a more peaceful, just, and compassionate society.

D. Classroom Environment

The classroom environment plays a pivotal role in peace pedagogy, as it directly influences students' ability to learn, interact, and develop values conducive to peace. A peaceful and inclusive classroom environment fosters respect, collaboration, and a sense of community, making it an essential foundation for effective peace education.

1. **Creating a Safe and Inclusive Space:** A key aspect of a peace-oriented classroom is the creation of a safe and inclusive space where all students feel valued, respected, and free to express themselves. This includes ensuring that the classroom is free from bullying, discrimination, and violence, and that every student's voice is heard and appreciated.
2. **Building Positive Relationships:** The classroom environment should prioritize building positive, respectful relationships among students and between students and teachers. Activities that encourage teamwork, mutual support, and trust help create a

strong sense of community and reduce the likelihood of conflicts.

3. **Encouraging Open Dialogue:** An open, communicative environment is essential for peace pedagogy. Teachers should encourage students to share their thoughts, opinions, and feelings openly, and listen to others with empathy and respect. Open dialogue helps students resolve conflicts peacefully and fosters a culture of understanding and cooperation.
4. **Promoting Cooperative Learning:** Cooperative learning strategies, where students work together to achieve common goals, are integral to a peaceful classroom environment. These activities help students develop important social skills, such as collaboration, problem-solving, and mutual respect, while also reducing competition and fostering solidarity.
5. **Implementing Restorative Practices:** Restorative practices, such as restorative circles or peer mediation, can be used to address conflicts and behavioural issues in a way that promotes healing and reconciliation rather than punishment. These practices emphasize accountability, empathy, and the repair of relationships, reinforcing the values of peace and justice.
6. **Celebrating Diversity:** A peace-oriented classroom actively celebrates diversity in all its forms, whether cultural, linguistic, religious, or social. By integrating diverse perspectives and materials into the curriculum, teachers help students appreciate and respect differences, which is crucial for reducing prejudice and promoting inclusion.
7. **Modelling Peaceful Behaviour:** Teachers play a critical role in modelling peaceful behaviour. By demonstrating non-violent communication, fairness, patience, and

respect in their interactions with students, teachers set a powerful example for how to handle conflicts and treat others with dignity.

8. **Creating a Reflective Environment:** A reflective classroom environment encourages students to think critically about their actions, choices, and the impact they have on others. Reflection can be integrated into daily routines through activities such as journaling, group discussions, or mindfulness practices, helping students develop self-awareness and emotional regulation.
9. **Incorporating Peaceful Classroom Management:** Classroom management strategies should align with the principles of peace pedagogy, focusing on positive reinforcement, clear communication, and consistency. Discipline should be approached as a learning opportunity rather than a punitive measure, helping students understand the consequences of their actions and encouraging them to make better choices in the future.
10. **Engaging with the Broader Community:** The classroom environment should extend beyond the four walls, engaging with the broader school community and even local and global communities. This can be done through community service projects, partnerships with local organizations, or global peace initiatives, helping students see the relevance of peace in the wider world.

By cultivating a classroom environment that embodies the principles of peace, teachers create the conditions necessary for students to thrive both academically and socially. This environment not only supports the goals of peace pedagogy but also contributes to the overall well-being and development of each student, preparing them to be active, responsible, and compassionate members of society.

E. Teacher's Role

The role of the teacher is central to the successful implementation of peace pedagogy. Teachers are not just transmitters of knowledge; they are role models, facilitators, and advocates for peace. Their attitudes, behaviours, and teaching methods significantly influence how students understand and practice peace in their lives.

1. **Modelling Peaceful Behaviour:** Teachers serve as role models for their students, demonstrating how to handle conflicts, communicate effectively, and treat others with respect and empathy. By consistently modelling peaceful and non-violent behaviour, teachers provide students with a tangible example of how to live out the principles of peace in everyday interactions.
2. **Facilitating Inclusive and Respectful Dialogue:** Teachers are responsible for creating an environment where open, respectful dialogue can flourish. They encourage students to express their views and listen to others, fostering a classroom culture where differing opinions are valued and considered thoughtfully. This helps students develop the skills needed for peaceful conflict resolution and collaborative problem-solving.
3. **Integrating Peaceful Practices into the Curriculum:** Teachers play a key role in integrating peace education into various subjects across the curriculum. Whether it is through literature, history, social studies, or even science, teachers find ways to incorporate lessons on empathy, justice, and non-violence, helping students connect these values to their broader learning experiences.
4. **Encouraging Critical Thinking and Reflection:** Teachers guide students in developing critical thinking skills by challenging them to question assumptions,

explore multiple perspectives, and reflect on their own beliefs and actions. This reflective practice is essential for helping students internalize the values of peace and apply them in complex, real-world situations.

5. **Supporting Emotional and Social Development:** Teachers support the emotional and social development of students by creating a safe space where they can express their feelings and navigate social relationships. This involves teaching emotional intelligence skills, such as empathy, self-regulation, and effective communication, which are crucial for maintaining peaceful interactions.
6. **Promoting Social Justice and Equity:** Teachers are advocates for social justice within and beyond the classroom. They work to ensure that all students, regardless of their background, have equal opportunities to succeed. This includes addressing any forms of discrimination or bias that may arise and teaching students about the importance of fairness, equity, and inclusion.
7. **Using Restorative Approaches:** When conflicts or disciplinary issues arise, teachers who practice peace pedagogy often use restorative approaches rather than punitive ones. These approaches focus on healing, reconciliation, and restoring relationships, helping students learn from their mistakes and understand the impact of their actions on others.
8. **Fostering a Sense of Global Citizenship:** Teachers help students develop a sense of global citizenship by teaching them about the interconnectedness of people and the planet. This includes raising awareness about global issues such as climate change, poverty, and human rights, and encouraging students to think about their role in creating a more peaceful and sustainable world.

9. **Providing Ongoing Support and Guidance:** Teachers provide ongoing support and guidance to help students navigate their personal and social challenges. They act as mentors, helping students develop the confidence and skills they need to advocate for themselves and others in peaceful ways.
10. **Engaging in Continuous Professional Development:** To effectively teach peace pedagogy, teachers must continually develop their own understanding and skills. This involves participating in professional development opportunities, staying informed about new research and best practices in peace education, and reflecting on their own teaching methods and attitudes.

By fulfilling these roles, teachers become powerful agents of change, helping to cultivate a generation of students who are not only academically proficient but also deeply committed to the principles of peace, justice, and non-violence. Their influence extends beyond the classroom, contributing to the creation of a more peaceful and just society.

F. Community Engagement

Community engagement is a crucial component of peace pedagogy, as it extends the principles of peace beyond the classroom and into the broader society. Engaging with the community helps students connect their learning to real-world contexts, fostering a sense of responsibility and active participation in creating a more peaceful world.

1. **Building Partnerships with Local Organizations:** Schools and teachers collaborate with local organizations, NGOs, and community groups that are dedicated to peacebuilding, social justice, and community service. These partnerships provide students with opportunities

to participate in community-based projects, volunteer work, and advocacy initiatives, deepening their understanding of peace in action.

2. **Encouraging Service Learning:** Service learning integrates community service with academic learning, allowing students to apply their knowledge and skills to address local needs. Through projects that promote social justice, environmental stewardship, or humanitarian aid, students learn the importance of empathy, collaboration, and civic responsibility.
3. **Fostering Cross-Cultural Understanding:** Engaging with diverse community groups helps students appreciate different cultures, perspectives, and experiences. Schools can facilitate cultural exchanges, community dialogues, and collaborative projects that bring together people from various backgrounds, fostering mutual respect and understanding.
4. **Promoting Collaborative Problem-Solving:** Community engagement provides students with opportunities to work alongside others to address shared challenges. Whether through local initiatives or global campaigns, students learn to collaborate, negotiate, and find peaceful solutions to complex problems, developing skills essential for conflict resolution and peacebuilding.
5. **Involving Families in Peace Education:** Schools engage families in Peace Pedagogy by involving them in school activities, workshops, and discussions about peace and social justice. By fostering a strong partnership between the school and the home, students receive consistent messages about the importance of peace, both in their personal lives and within their communities.
6. **Creating Safe Spaces for Dialogue and Action:** Schools can serve as safe spaces where community members can

come together to discuss issues, share experiences, and plan collective actions for peace. These spaces encourage open, respectful dialogue and empower students to take the lead in initiatives that promote social cohesion and conflict resolution.

7. **Empowering Students as Community Leaders:** By engaging with their communities, students develop leadership skills and a sense of agency. Schools can support this by providing opportunities for students to lead community projects, organize events, or participate in local governance. This empowers students to be active contributors to peace in their communities.
8. **Addressing Local and Global Issues:** Peace pedagogy emphasizes the interconnectedness of local and global issues. Community engagement activities help students understand how global challenges, such as poverty, climate change, and human rights, impact their own communities. This awareness motivates students to take action locally while thinking globally.
9. **Celebrating Community Achievements:** Recognizing and celebrating the successes of community-based peace initiatives reinforces the importance of community engagement. Schools can organize events, awards, or exhibitions that showcase student contributions to peace, thereby inspiring others and building a culture of peace within the community.
10. **Sustaining Long-term Engagement:** Effective community engagement in peace pedagogy is not a one-time event but a sustained effort. Schools and teachers work to establish long-term relationships with community partners and continuously involve students in ongoing projects that contribute to lasting peace and social change.

By actively engaging with their communities, students learn to see themselves as part of a larger social fabric, where their actions can make a significant difference. Community engagement in Peace Pedagogy nurtures a sense of interconnectedness, responsibility, and empowerment, helping to create a more peaceful and just society at all levels.

Benefits of Peace Pedagogy

Some key benefits of Peace Pedagogy education are:

1. **Reduced Violence:** Schools that incorporate peace pedagogy often see a reduction in bullying, violence, and other forms of aggression.
2. **Improved Academic Outcomes:** A peaceful, supportive learning environment can lead to better academic performance, as students feel safer and more focused.
3. **Social-emotional Development:** Students develop essential life skills such as empathy, emotional regulation, and effective communication.
4. **Long-term Impact:** By instilling the values of peace and non-violence, Peace Pedagogy contributes to the development of future citizens who are more likely to advocate for peace and justice in society.

Peace Pedagogy in formal education is essential for fostering a generation that values peace, understands the complexities of conflict, and is equipped to contribute positively to a more just and peaceful world.

REFERENCES

Burns, R.J. (2007). *Peace Education: A Review and a Framework.* Routledge, Oxfordshire.

Davis, R.S. & Smith, T.L. (2020). "Restorative Practices in Education: A Review of the Literature". *International Journal of Educational Management, 34*(5): 932-946. https://doi.org/10.1108/IJEM-05-2019-0213

Duffy, A.M. & Wright, P.A. (Eds.). (2004). *Educating for Peace: A Feminist Perspective.* Palgrave Macmillan.

Harris, I.M. & Morrison, M.L. (2013). *Peace education: How we come to love and hatewar.* Teachers College Press, Columbia University.

Johnson, D.M. & Johnson, R.T. (2005). *Peace Education: A Global Approach.* Palgrave Macmillan.

Johnson, E.R. & Clark, M.T. (2017). "Fostering Peace through Education: A Case Study Approach". *Peace Studies Journal, 13*(1): 56-71. https://doi.org/10.1080/15565694.2017.1285711

Lee, S.J. (2018). "Peace Education and Global Citizenship: An Analysis of Curricular Practices". *Educational Review, 70*(4): 462-478. https://doi.org/10.1080/00131911.2018.1472963

McCarthy, J.H. & Williams, J.E. (2021). "The Role of Teachers in Peace Education: A Review of the Literature." *Journal of Peace Research, 58*(3): 334-351. https://doi.org/10.1177/00223433211012857

McEvoy, A.K.C. & McEvoy, P.L. (Eds.). (2008). *Teaching for Peace and Social Justice.* Sage Publications, Los Angeles.

Schaefer, M.A.W. (2019). "Peace Education in Schools: A Review of the Literature". *Journal of Peace Education, 16*(2): 123-145. https://doi.org/10.1080/17400201.2019.1608287

12

Educating for Global Citizenship through Peace Pedagogy

Suman Mazumdar

Introduction

The significance of Peace Pedagogy extends beyond traditional academic subjects to encompass critical thinking, empathy, and global citizenship, in the contemporary interconnected and diverse world. Educators play a pivotal role in fostering a safe and inclusive learning environment where students can explore complex issues related to identity, inequality, and conflict resolution. By incorporating peace education into curriculum frameworks, educators empower students to become active agents of positive change in their communities.

Peace pedagogy in formal education encompasses the deliberate integration of principles, practices, and methodologies that promote peace, social justice, and conflict resolution within educational settings. It represents a proactive approach to cultivating a culture of peace by equipping learners with the necessary knowledge, skills, and attitudes to address societal challenges through peaceful means. Peace pedagogy promotes dialogue, cooperation, and mutual respect for diversity, thereby preparing students to navigate global complexities and contribute constructively to fostering equitable and harmonious societies. This chapter explores how Peace Pedagogy can be integrated into formal education systems, emphasizing its potential to equip students with essential skills for conflict resolution, social justice advocacy, and global citizenship.

Curriculum Development for Peace Education

An effective curriculum design is essential for integrating peace education into formal educational frameworks. Curriculum development for peace education involves intentional design aimed at nurturing attitudes of empathy, conflict resolution skills, and global citizenship among students. It integrates themes of social justice, human rights, and intercultural understanding into various subjects, providing opportunities for critical thinking and dialogue on sensitive issues. A well-structured peace education curriculum emphasizes experiential learning, promoting active participation and collaboration among students. It incorporates diverse perspectives and encourages respectful discourse, fostering a safe and inclusive learning environment. By addressing root causes of conflict and promoting non-violent communication, such curricula empower students to become agents of positive change in their communities. Effective implementation requires continuous teacher training, supportive institutional policies, and collaboration with stakeholders to ensure sustained impact and relevance in addressing contemporary socio-political challenges.

Curriculum Models and Frameworks

Various curriculum models and frameworks prioritize

peacebuilding competencies by integrating critical thinking, empathy, active listening, and conflict resolution skills across educational disciplines. These models are designed to foster a culture of peace, empathy, and social responsibility among students. Here are some notable approaches:

1. **Inquiry-based Learning:** This model encourages students to explore complex issues, including historical conflicts and contemporary social challenges, from multiple perspectives. By engaging in research, discussions, and critical analysis, students develop critical thinking skills and empathy as they examine different viewpoints and understand root causes of conflicts.
2. **Conflict Resolution Education (CRE):** CRE frameworks focus on teaching students the practical skills for managing conflicts constructively. These include active listening, communication strategies, negotiation, mediation, and consensus-building techniques. CRE programmes often incorporate role-playing exercises and simulations to simulate real-life conflict scenarios and practice resolution strategies.
3. **Social-Emotional Learning (SEL) Frameworks:** SEL frameworks emphasize the development of emotional intelligence, empathy, and interpersonal skills as foundational to creating supportive and inclusive learning environments. These frameworks integrate lessons on self-awareness, self-management, social awareness, relationship skills, and responsible decision-making, promoting positive social interactions and conflict resolution abilities.
4. **Human Rights Education:** This framework integrates principles of human rights, justice, and equality into curricula. It emphasizes understanding and respecting the rights and dignity of all individuals, promoting

empathy and social justice advocacy among students. Human rights education often includes discussions on global issues such as discrimination, poverty, and inequality, encouraging students to become agents of positive change in their communities.

5. **Global Citizenship Education (GCE):** GCE frameworks aim to cultivate students' awareness of global interconnectedness and their role as responsible global citizens. This includes understanding diverse cultures, promoting intercultural dialogue, and advocating for social justice and sustainable development. GCE emphasizes critical thinking about global issues and encourages students to take action to address global challenges, fostering empathy and solidarity across borders.
6. **Peace Education Models:** Peace Education models encompass a holistic approach to promoting peacebuilding competencies. They integrate lessons on conflict analysis, non-violent communication, human rights, sustainable development, and intercultural understanding. Peace education emphasizes fostering a culture of peace through cooperative learning, community service projects, and initiatives that promote dialogue, reconciliation, and respect for diversity.
7. **Experiential Learning and Service-Learning:** These models incorporate hands-on experiences and community engagement into the curriculum. Students participate in projects and activities that address local community needs, promoting empathy, active listening, and collaboration while applying critical thinking and problem-solving skills to real-world issues. Service-learning also fosters understanding of social justice and equity, encouraging students to contribute positively to society.

Each of these curriculum models and frameworks prioritizes peacebuilding competencies by providing structured opportunities for students to develop critical thinking, empathy, active listening, and conflict resolution skills. By integrating these competencies into educational settings, educators aim to empower students to become compassionate, engaged, and socially responsible individuals capable of promoting peace and understanding in their communities and beyond.

Teaching Methodologies and Pedagogical Strategies

Effective implementation of peacebuilding competencies in education requires thoughtful teaching methodologies and pedagogical strategies that engage students actively and foster skills such as critical thinking, empathy, active listening, and conflict resolution. Here are several teaching methodologies and pedagogical strategies that can facilitate the integration of peacebuilding competencies:

1. **Experiential Learning:** Experiential learning engages students in hands-on activities, simulations, and real-world experiences that promote understanding of complex issues and practical application of peacebuilding skills. For example, role-playing exercises simulate conflict scenarios where students practice active listening, negotiation, and mediation techniques.
2. **Inquiry-based Learning:** Inquiry-based learning encourages students to investigate questions, issues, or problems through critical thinking and research. Teachers guide students to explore historical and contemporary conflicts from multiple perspectives, encouraging empathy and deeper understanding of underlying causes.

3. **Dialogue and Discussion:** Classroom discussions on peace-related topics create opportunities for students to express diverse viewpoints, listen actively to others, and engage in respectful debate. Facilitators encourage students to analyze different perspectives, challenge assumptions, and seek common ground, promoting empathy and conflict resolution skills.
4. **Collaborative Learning:** Collaborative learning activities, such as group projects and cooperative learning tasks, encourage teamwork and cooperation among students. By working together towards shared goals, students practice communication skills, negotiate differences, and develop empathy for others' perspectives.
5. **Problem-based Learning (PBL):** PBL presents students with authentic, complex problems or challenges that require critical thinking and collaboration to solve. Peacebuilding competencies can be integrated into PBL by framing scenarios that involve conflict resolution, social justice issues, or community-based initiatives where students apply skills such as empathy and negotiation to propose solutions.
6. **Cross-cultural Exchanges:** Virtual or physical exchanges with students from different cultural backgrounds provide opportunities for intercultural dialogue and understanding. Through structured activities and discussions, students learn to appreciate cultural diversity, challenge stereotypes, and develop empathy and respect for others' perspectives.
7. **Reflective Practices:** Reflective exercises, such as journals, essays, or group reflections, encourage students to introspect on their learning experiences, personal biases, and growth in peacebuilding competencies. Reflection promotes self-awareness, empathy development, and continuous improvement in conflict resolution skills.

8. **Service-learning:** Service-learning integrates community service with academic learning objectives. Students engage in meaningful projects that address local community needs, promoting empathy, active listening, and collaborative problem-solving while applying peacebuilding competencies in real-world contexts.
9. **Technology-enhanced Learning:** Digital tools and platforms can support peacebuilding education by facilitating online discussions, virtual simulations, and multimedia resources that promote empathy, critical thinking, and global awareness. Technology can bridge geographical barriers and enable cross-cultural exchanges to broaden students' perspectives.
10. **Teacher Modelling and Role-Modelling:** Teachers play a crucial role in modelling peacebuilding behaviours and values in the classroom. By demonstrating active listening, empathy, respectful communication, and conflict resolution strategies, educators create a positive learning environment where students feel safe to practice and internalize these competencies.

Implementing these teaching methodologies and pedagogical strategies requires ongoing professional development for educators, supportive institutional policies, and collaboration with stakeholders to create inclusive and culturally responsive learning environments. By integrating these approaches, educators can effectively cultivate peacebuilding competencies among students, empowering them to contribute positively to creating a more just, empathetic, and peaceful society.

Role of Educators in Peace Pedagogy

Educators play crucial roles in Peace Pedagogy, which is the practice of teaching and learning focused on fostering peace, empathy, and conflict resolution skills among students. They serve as key facilitators in implementing Peace Pedagogy within classrooms. Their role extends beyond imparting academic knowledge to nurturing students' social and emotional development. Some of the significant roles that educators fulfil in Peace Pedagogy include:

1. **Creating Safe and Inclusive Learning Environments:** Educators establish classroom environments where students feel safe to express diverse viewpoints, discuss sensitive issues, and engage in respectful dialogue. This creates a foundation for empathy and understanding among students.
2. **Modelling Peaceful Behaviour:** Educators serve as role models by demonstrating peaceful behaviour, such as active listening, respectful communication, and conflict resolution strategies. They exemplify the values of tolerance, empathy, and cooperation in their interactions with students and colleagues.
3. **Teaching Peacebuilding Competencies:** Educators integrate peacebuilding competencies, such as critical thinking, empathy, active listening, and non-violent conflict resolution, into their teaching practices across different subjects and grade levels. They design lessons that promote understanding of social justice, human rights, and global citizenship.
4. **Facilitating Dialogue and Critical Reflection:** Educators facilitate structured discussions and activities that encourage students to critically reflect on issues related to peace, justice, and equality. They guide students in analyzing root causes of conflicts, exploring multiple perspectives, and envisioning peaceful solutions.
5. **Promoting Cultural Understanding and Respect:** Educators promote cultural understanding and respect

by incorporating diverse perspectives and experiences into the curriculum. They encourage students to appreciate cultural differences, challenge stereotypes, and celebrate cultural diversity as strengths within the classroom and broader community.

6. **Empowering Student Agency and Advocacy:** Educators empower students to take active roles in promoting peace and social justice through community service projects, advocacy campaigns, and collaborative initiatives. They encourage students to identify local and global issues of concern and take meaningful action towards positive change.
7. **Collaborating with Stakeholders:** Educators collaborate with parents, community members, and organizations to support peace education initiatives both within and outside the classroom. They build partnerships that enhance students' learning experiences and promote a culture of peace within the school and community.
8. **Continuous Professional Development:** Educators engage in ongoing professional development to enhance their knowledge and skills in peace pedagogy. They participate in workshops, conferences, and collaborative learning opportunities to stay informed about best practices and innovative approaches in teaching peace and conflict resolution.
9. **Assessing and Reflecting on Impact:** Educators assess students' progress in developing peacebuilding competencies through various assessment methods, such as portfolios, reflections, and performance-based assessments. They reflect on the impact of their teaching practices and make adjustments to better support students' growth in empathy, critical thinking, and conflict resolution skills.

10. **Advocating for Peace Education Policies:** Educators advocate for policies and initiatives that prioritize peace education in school curricula and educational systems. They participate in advocacy efforts to promote funding, resources, and support for integrating peace pedagogy into national and local education agendas.

Strategies for Training Educators in Peace Education

Training educators in peacebuilding techniques and creating safe spaces for dialogue on sensitive topics related to conflict and identity requires thoughtful strategies that promote empathy, critical reflection, and inclusive teaching practices. Here are several effective strategies for training educators in these areas:

1. **Professional Development Workshops:** Workshops and seminars may be conducted that focuses on peacebuilding techniques, conflict resolution strategies, and fostering empathy among students. These sessions can include experiential learning activities, case studies, and role-playing exercises to help educators understand and practice these skills themselves.
2. **Cultural Competency Training:** Training on cultural competency and diversity awareness may be provided to help educators navigate sensitive topics related to identity and conflict. This training should emphasize understanding different cultural perspectives, challenging biases, and promoting inclusivity in the classroom.
3. **Dialogue Facilitation Skills:** Training sessions on dialogue facilitation techniques that create safe and respectful spaces for discussing sensitive topics may be conducted. Educators can learn how to establish ground rules, manage emotions, and encourage active listening among students to promote constructive dialogue.

4. **Conflict Resolution Workshops:** Workshops on conflict resolution strategies tailored for educators may also be organized. These workshops can cover techniques such as mediation, negotiation, and restorative justice practices that educators can apply in classroom settings to address conflicts peacefully.
5. **Empathy Building Exercises:** Empathy-building exercises should be incorporated into professional development programmes. These exercises may include perspective-taking activities, storytelling, and reflective practices that help educators develop empathy towards students' diverse experiences and backgrounds.
6. **Community Building Activities:** Community building activities during training sessions should be facilitated to create a supportive network among educators. Building strong relationships and trust within the educator community can foster collaboration and shared learning on peacebuilding techniques.
7. **Role-playing and Simulations:** Role-playing and simulations may be used to simulate classroom scenarios involving sensitive topics related to identity and conflict. Educators can practice responding to challenging situations, facilitating discussions, and promoting understanding among students.
8. **Resource Sharing and Case Studies:** Resources, case studies, and best practices should be shared from other educators and experts in peace education. This can include examples of successful initiatives, lesson plans, and curriculum materials that integrate peacebuilding techniques effectively.
9. **Reflective Practice and Feedback:** Reflective practice should be encouraged among educators by providing opportunities for self-assessment and feedback. Reflective

journals, peer observations, and debriefing sessions after classroom activities can help educators refine their approaches and strategies.

10. **Ongoing Support and Mentoring:** Ongoing support and mentoring must be provided for educators implementing peacebuilding techniques in their classrooms. This can include coaching sessions, peer mentoring, and access to expert advice to address challenges and build confidence in applying new skills.

By implementing these strategies, educational institutions can effectively train educators in peacebuilding techniques, foster empathy, and create safe spaces for dialogue on sensitive topics related to conflict and identity. Empowered educators are better equipped to promote inclusivity, respect for diversity, and constructive engagement in addressing social issues within their classrooms and communities.

Impact of Peace Education Programmes

1. **Fostering Empathy and Understanding:** Peace Education Programmes cultivate empathy among participants by encouraging them to see situations from multiple perspectives. Through discussions, role-playing, and experiential learning, individuals develop a deeper understanding of diverse cultures, experiences, and identities. This heightened empathy promotes tolerance and reduces prejudice, fostering inclusive communities where differences are respected.
2. **Developing Conflict Resolution Skills:** Participants acquire practical skills in conflict resolution, negotiation, and mediation. They learn effective communication techniques, active listening, and problem-solving strategies. These skills empower individuals to address

conflicts peacefully, both in personal relationships and community settings, contributing to a culture of dialogue and cooperation.

3. **Promoting Attitudes of Peace and Non-violence:** Peace Education Programmes challenge attitudes that perpetuate violence and discrimination. Participants are encouraged to embrace values of peace, justice, and human rights. They learn to reject stereotypes and biases, fostering attitudes that prioritize reconciliation, mutual respect, and social justice.
4. **Enhancing Social and Emotional Learning (SEL):** These programmes nurture social and emotional competencies such as empathy, self-awareness, and emotional regulation. Participants develop skills that support positive relationships, effective communication, and responsible decision-making. SEL enhances personal well-being and equips individuals to navigate challenges with resilience and empathy.
5. **Empowering Active Citizenship and Civic Engagement:** Participants in Peace Education Programmes become active agents of change in their communities. They engage in civic activities, volunteerism, and advocacy for social justice. These programmes inspire individuals to take leadership roles in promoting peacebuilding initiatives and advocating for equitable and inclusive societies.
6. **Building Knowledge of Peacebuilding Strategies:** Through education on conflict resolution, human rights, and global citizenship, participants gain knowledge of effective peacebuilding strategies. They understand the root causes of conflicts and learn approaches to sustainable peace. This knowledge equips individuals to contribute meaningfully to peace efforts locally and globally.

7. **Strengthening Resilient Communities:** By fostering skills and attitudes conducive to peaceful coexistence, Peace Education Programmes contribute to building resilient communities. Participants contribute to community cohesion, collective problem-solving, and fostering environments where diversity is celebrated and conflicts are managed constructively.
8. **Evaluating Programme Impact and Continuous Improvement:** Effective evaluation mechanisms are employed to assess the impact of Peace Education Programmes. This includes measuring changes in attitudes, behaviours, and knowledge acquisition among participants. Feedback from stakeholders informs programme adjustments and enhancements, ensuring relevance and effectiveness.
9. **Promoting Global Citizenship and Interconnectedness:** Peace Education Programmes promote global citizenship by emphasizing interconnectedness and shared responsibility for global issues. Participants develop a sense of belonging to a larger global community and recognize their role in promoting peace, justice, and sustainability worldwide.
10. **Sustaining Long-term Peacebuilding Efforts:** The long-term impact of Peace Education Programmes is evident in the sustained commitment of participants to peacebuilding efforts. Individuals continue to apply skills learned and advocate for peaceful solutions to conflicts. This sustained effort contributes to creating lasting positive change in communities and societies.

Peace Education Programmes have a transformative impact on individuals and communities by fostering empathy, imparting conflict resolution skills, promoting attitudes of peace, enhancing social-emotional learning, and building knowledge of peacebuilding strategies. These programmes play a vital role in creating a culture of peace where dialogue, cooperation, and respect for human dignity are central to resolving conflicts and building sustainable peace worldwide.

Conclusion

Peace Pedagogy, thus, holds profound significance in formal education as it equips students with essential skills and attitudes crucial for fostering a peaceful and sustainable global society. By embedding principles of peace education into curricula, educational institutions not only empower learners to understand and address conflicts constructively but also promote values of empathy, respect, and cooperation. This pedagogical approach cultivates critical thinking skills that enable students to analyze complex social issues, recognize diverse perspectives, and engage in meaningful dialogue. Moreover, Peace Pedagogy contributes to the development of a civic-minded generation capable of actively participating in democratic processes and advocating for social justice. It emphasizes the importance of human rights, environmental stewardship, and sustainable development, thereby preparing students to address contemporary challenges at local, national, and international levels.

REFERENCES

Bajaj, M. (2011). "Peace Education and the Pedagogy of Non-violence". *Journal of Peace Education, 8*(1): 1-15.

Berking, H. & Van der Zweerde, E. (Eds.). (2006). *Learning to Live Together: Education for Conflict Resolution, Responsible Citizenship, Human Rights and Democracy.* Council of Europe Publishing.

Boulding, E. (2000). *Cultures of Peace: The Hidden Side of History.* Syracuse University Press.

Galtung, J. (1996). "Peace by Peaceful Means: Peace and Conflict, Development and Civilization". *International Peace Research Institute.*

Hicks, D. (2012). *Teaching for Peace: Global Citizenship Education.* Routledge.

International Institute for Educational Planning. (2015). *Education for Peace, Human Rights and Democracy.* IIEP-UNESCO.

Johnson, D.W. & Johnson, R.T. (2013). "Teaching Students to be Peacemakers: A Meta-Analysis". *Peace and Conflict: Journal of Peace Psychology, 19*(4), 417-428.

Noddings, N. (2010). *Peace Education: How We Come to Love and Hate War.* Cambridge University Press.

Peace Education Foundation. (n.d.). *Case Studies in Peace Education.* Retrieved from https://www.peaceeducation.org

Salomon, G. & Cairns, E. (2017). *Handbook of Peace Education.* Routledge.

Smith, A.B. (2007). "Towards a Pedagogy of Peace: Understanding Peace Education as a Pedagogical Process". *Educational Philosophy and Theory, 39*(2): 183-194.

UNESCO. (2019). *Global Citizenship Education: Topics and Learning Objectives.* Paris: UNESCO.

United Nations. (2015). *Transforming Our World: The 2030 Agenda for Sustainable Development.* New York: UN.

13

Critical Analysis of Animated Movie Zootopia within the Purview of Peace and Value Education

Debolina Mukherjee

Introduction

Peace education fosters the understanding, skills, mindsets and values that will allow people to avert conflicts and settle disputes amicably with an eye to establish a peaceful, conducive social environment in which every person will get the opportunity to grow and thrive in life. It is based on the cardinal principles of social justice, equal rights and non-violence. Values like trust, honesty, confidence, autonomy, and respect for humanity—all are examples of non-violence. Justice for all is achieved through the values of solidarity, accountability, love, tolerance and equality (Bhat *et al.*, 2021). Peace and Value education is a must discourse to be integrated in the school curriculum since it assists to teach us about a way of life that is in harmony with oneself, with other individuals and with the natural surroundings (Chaudhry, 2018). Academic institutions have a crucial role in providing youngsters with peace and value education. If we observe the current scenario of Indian education system, unfortunately a decease has been found in the importance of inculcating educational values among the young students. The liability goes to the teachers who, in most of the cases, are overly preoccupied with their respective subject teaching, and thereby, paying little consideration to the students' morality or character-building process (Freakley *et al.*, 2008). It is the educator who has the most important role in helping pupils to develop their educational values. In fact, family and teachers both are equal partners in the endeavour, and they should work together to enhance the values and morals ingrained in children' thoughts and behaviours. Also, the purpose of national education is to develop students' ability, potential, character, and prestigious national culture to educate the nation. This includes developing students' health, erudition, creativity, independence, and sense of faithfulness and their ability to become virtuous, and responsible citizens (Hasanah, 2022).

So, teachers need media which can support them in teaching the subject while simultaneously enriching students with educational value. Additionally, the media ought to be entertaining in order to prevent pupils from becoming disinterested in their studies. Film is one type of that media, the most well-known kind of entertainment in this world. The audio-visual equivalent of storytelling is a movie. In other words, it tells a story with the help of sound-assisted moving images. In addition to being meant to amuse, movies can also serve as educational resources (Walay, 2022). However, films can be utilized to educate viewers about human history, science, art, culture, human behaviour and many other significant issues. Some movies make learning interesting by fusing fun with education. Thereby, selective movies as an engaging learning tool can be introduced to children for instilling educational values in them. Among various types and genres of movies, the most appealing one which tempts all ages, especially children, is animated films. The magic of animated movies with their unique plots, interesting characters and their dialogue delivery, song and music, wonderful visuals, is bound to be felt by every movie lover, particularly young children. Thereby, animated movies can become a great instrument to convey peace and value education. It is the responsibility of teachers as well as parents to appropriately select movies that align with their children's mental development and that serves the role of meaningful learning. Among the most renowned animation enterprises is Walt Disney Animation of every generation. Disney established by Walt Disney in 1921, is among the world's longest-running movie animation businesses (Fanning, 2015). There are numerous massively popular and the most celebrated Disney animated films, including *Toy Story, Up, Zootopia, Frozen, Moana, Up, Aladdin* and so on (Cahya, 2019). The characters of these excellent films impart lessons about purity, never giving up, not being selfish, religious faith loyalty, appreciation, reverence, peace, and persistence etc.

Zootopia, debuted on 4th March, 2016, has become a box office success since its premiere (Pressberg, 2016). The American Film Institute honoured this film as one of the best ten films of 2016 (Hipes, 2016). It has received multiple prestigious awards like Academy Award, a Golden Globe, and Critics' Choice Movie Award. This animated film appears to be aimed towards youngsters. However, at its core, it is intended for everyone. So, apparently, it may seem a light-hearted movie made for children only, but it has many layers to be uncovered to discover that the movie endeavours to make us learn significant lessons of life. This movie is a wonderful instrument for the encouraging value education. Under the mask of entertainment, it also portrays the dark side of reality with the hope for a better future. It pinpoints the negativities or the evil aspects of society like inequality, corruption, discrimination, hatred, jealousy, stereotyping or any form of prejudice that can destroy the humanity, and it tries to uphold moral and social values which can protect humanity from degradation. However, the setting of this film is a metropolitan city named *Zootopia* that is home to anthropomorphic creatures. All the animals in *Zootopia* are somehow able to coexist peacefully side by side, even though some are predators and others are prey. The film is mainly about Judy Hopps, a rabbit who relocates from her small town to the big city of Zootopia in the aspirations of becoming a police officer (Muljadi, 2019).

Objectives of the Study

The following objectives are the focus of this research study:

1. To identify the educational values in *Zootopia* within the context of peace education.
2. To critically explicit or implicit presentation of those values in *Zootopia.*

Research Questions

The research questions, derived from the research objectives are as follows:

1. What are the values identified after the critical analysis of *Zootopia* within the purview of peace education?
2. How have the educational values been presented in *Zootopia* film?

Method

In terms of method this research has adopted qualitative and interpretive approach. After the collection of qualitative data, the researcher has presented them in descriptive way. Noticeably, among various animated movies that could have been examined within the framework of peace education, the researcher purposively selected only one film called *Zootopia* considering it as appropriate text for the desired discourse. To gather meaningful data, she began by watching *Zootopia* and rewatched it for critical analysis, and then conducted this investigation using library studies. The investigation was carried out by going through certain references and searching the internet for more related literature data that had the potential to develop the content analysis. Thus, the movie was examined carefully, and the findings have been descriptively illustrated below.

Discussion & Summarization of the Study Outcomes

Following the critical examination of the narrative, characterization, dialogue, themes, and other facets of the film *Zootopia*, the educational values included in the movie have been highlighted in a descriptive summary.

- *Discarding Inequal Treatment, Stereotypes, Prejudice in Search of Equality:* No individual should be subject to inequal treatment in academic, professional or social life. Equality is fundamental right for everyone. Equalization of opportunity is desirable for all. Discriminatory attitude which makes a clear distinction in favour of or against any individual or thing on account of group, class, race or any other category instead of individual merit, should be abolished. All these get reflected in the popular utterance of Judy, which says "Anyone can be anything". Even though her parents, Stu and Bonnie, discourage her by informing again and again that a rabbit has never worked in the police force since they were never supposed to be law enforcement officers. Judy, on the other hand, sees nothing problematic with her choice to pursue a career as a police officer. She truly believes that everyone has an equal opportunity to achieve their goals and that there are no barriers in the way of success. One further instance of how prejudice and bigotry are accepted as the norm in *Zootopia* can be found in another occurrence. This scene happens at the beginning of the film when Nick, the fox tries to shop at the Jumbeaux Café, which is run by Jerry Jumbeaux, an elephant. But Jerry declines to serve on the grounds that Nick is not an elephant. Additionally, he shows utter shock that how Nick would even consider trying to shop there as an outsider.

A few instances of stereotypes in the film include animals that work as police officers being massive and strong-looking, sloths working as DMV employees, or rabbits working as farmers. Even the Mayor of this city is a lion, who is generally deemed to be the king of beasts. However, Judy's expression "Anyone can be anything" is contradicted by these types of stereotypes, which also bring attention to the true colour of *Zootopia*—people who are trapped in their prejudices (Chinpinyokul, 2021). There should not be any kind stereotypes in assigning roles; people should be judged as per their potential only. Judy was the top student in the police academy, but her captain does not think much of her for the reason that she's the first rabbit who's ever made it to the police force, so she gets placed on mere parking duty. She is treated unfairly due to her diminutive stature. Nevertheless, Judy is intent on proving herself, and she later joins in a case investigation involving 14 missing predatory animals. Judy also gets assistance from a fox, a con artist named Nick Wilde, and they jointly handle the case successfully. Thus, Judy breaks the stereotypes that rabbits cannot play the role of police officer effectively. Nick Wilde experienced a similar situation. Young Nick was being ridiculed and bullied as being a predator he should not dare a scout ranger as the preconceived notion was that scout rangers conduct nice deeds, foxes are generally cunning, thus Nick will not fit in. Due to the bias the other scout rangers mocked at Nick since he does not know where he belongs. Thus, the scenarios shown in *Zootopia* mirror those that occur in our actual world. However, he succeeds in refuting the myth that foxes are inherently shrewd, dishonest and treacherous. At last, he abandons his 'job' as a con artist and chooses to be Judy's partner in the police department.

Biasedness, inequality can lead to nothing but negative forces like hatred, revenge only. In this movie, Bellwether plays a sheep secretary who serves for Mayor Lionheart. Bellwether has a lovely and innocent appearance. Unexpectedly, the suspense is unfolded, it comes out that she is the actual antagonist, transforming predators into ferocious predators. Her animosity towards the predators served as the impetus for her evil scheme. The mayor used to treat her horribly, telling her what to do and referring to her as "Smellwether" or compelling her work in a boiling room instead of an actual office. Bellwether is never respected by Lionheart. She feels as if she is just "a glorified secretary". Bellwether, who has "a grudge against what she saw as an unfair system", is fed up with predators who are always in power undervaluing and underappreciating her. Thereby, she fixed her target to create a world in which prey outnumber predators. Thus, human society in its microcosm may be found across the opulent and successful city of *Zootopia*. This film artistically conveys the message that non-biased attitude, fair treatment, respect are necessary for building of positive attitude towards life and for moral and social development of individuals. Every kind of animal have equal rights just as humans. All must be treated equally and with respect (Zhong, 2016).

- *Advocating the Concept of Equity:* Treating persons justly and equitably according to their respective circumstances is known as equity. It denotes giving individuals the resources which are required for success, even if that necessitates offering varying degrees of assistance (Ainscow, 2016). The film introduces twelve distinct ecosystems in the city to illustrate this idea of equity. The city is seen supplying amenities for various animals as well. A classic example is when Judy lefts for Zootopia bidding her family farewell in the railway station. It is observed that the train doors come in a variety of sizes to accommodate both large and tiny animals. Even the scene with the different-sized garbage can or the scene where Judy pursues the burglar through the tiny city where mice reside depicts the city's egalitarian treatment of all animals. Every animal seems to observe the city to be its ideal setting (Chinpinyokul, 2016).
- *Promoting the Value of Determination:* Never quitting up no matter what, is the sign of determination. When anyone is determined, he/she makes a decision and follow through! The way Judy does not surrender, she does not allow the hindrances to stop from following her dream shows her iron determination. She is never afraid of the obstacles, she is focused, and she solves the case which big animals like rhino, elephant and cheetah could not solve (Shen, 2016). She believes in herself. This is an inspirating tale of perseverance and determination.

The movie can teach students that with the help of right attitude and self-determination one can achieve his/her goal.

- *Principle of Harmony to Encourage Balanced State of Living: Zootopia* depicts a utopian existence in which different types of animals can coexist without bias, prejudice, segregation or stereotyping. In *Zootopia*, all the animals cohabit harmoniously. Predators should not harm or consume prey, and they should not victimize or objectify victims. So, prey and predators can overcome their stereotypes and discover themselves to be different. The two main protagonists in the film, Judy Hoops and Nick Wilde, both express this same viewpoint. Specifically, Judy is found to have a positive and hopeful outlook about the world. She genuinely thinks that each animal of different species can live together peacefully. The film promotes the principle of harmonious living devoid of discrimination, prejudice and stereotyping.
- *Encouraging the Value of Helping Others:* The movie encourages viewers to always be cordial and helpful to others, notably those who are in need. Judy assists in stopping doughnuts in the rodent town, rescues daughter of Mr. Big, and receives "assistance" for herself. Judy meets and assists Nick and his son in purchasing the elephant popsicle. The message of *Zootopia* to is to let benevolence rule the world and always be willing to lend a helping hand to others (Xue, 2016).
- *Championing the Virtue of Love:* In these days of hatred, rage, intolerance and uncertainty, the film offers an uplifting and reassuring celebration of love, friendship, compassion, peace and diversity (Kermode, 2016). One of the main attractions of this movie is Nick Wilde and Judy Hopps' interracial love (Xue, 2016). They get along

well, are amiable, and are funny. Judy is aware that Nick really wished to be a scout ranger and did well, but he is dismayed by the poor treatment he got from everybody around him who thinks a fox will always be devious, discreet and should not be trusted. Back then Nick was bullied by others and lose hope. But Judy therefore gives Nick an opportunity to become her colleague in the police agency. The real strength of their beautiful relation is that they can mend a relationship, take responsibility for their deeds, so they are not easily discouraged. Nick storms out of the press conference, fuming about Judy's remarks on the characteristics of carnivores. Judy acknowledges her error, makes every effort to track down Nick, and offers her sincere apologies to him. Nick accepts with generosity. They have made up and are embracing one another; they are not gloomy or girlie-girly and they are transparent regarding how they feel. Finally, Nick is able to live an honest life and be who he wants to be, all thanks to Judy. Judy and Nick form a partnership at the film's conclusion, and they collaborate as police officers (Muljadi, 2019).

Educational Implication of the Study

Educational implications of any research deals with the ramification of the study, illuminating the significance and effects of the research. The impact of this study can be observed for learners, teachers, parents and researchers. Learners would be capable of gaining a profound understanding of the worth of peace and value education and develop their ability to identify different values in the other films as well. It might be beneficial for teachers as it has the high potential to make the process of teaching learning interesting enough to educate them about educational values. Noticeably, the teachers need to be careful while choosing films considering their suitability. The results of this study may serve as motivation for other researchers who are interested in investigating educational values. Furthermore, this study offers an array of references for any researcher eager to conduct research to explore peace and value education in the domain of animated movies or other mainstream educational movies.

Conclusion

To sum up, there exists a clearly strong connection between education and animated movies. Thereby, both parents and teachers should utilize these movies as an effective vehicle to help their children learn life lessons, develop moral principles (Niemiec & Wedding, 2013). Classroom activities should incorporate educational movies, specially animated ones to provide students learning beyond typical textbook culture. Character building of young learners should be the motto of teachers. And this motto can be easily actualized with the help of peace and value education via engaging educational films (Astuti, *et al.*, 2019). Undoubtedly it helps students undergo positive and transformative learning experiences which they can apply in their everyday lives. Nevertheless, only with strong value system within any individual can prosper in his/her life, be it academic, professional, personal or social one.

REFERENCES

Ainscow, M. (2016). "Collaboration as a Strategy for Promoting Equity in Education: Possibilities and Barriers". *Journal of Professional Capital and Community, 1*(2).

Astuti, R.W., Waluyo, H.J. & Rohmadi, M. (2019). "Character Education Values in Animation Movie of Nussa and Rarra". *Budapest International Research and Critics Institute-Journal* (*BIRCI-Journal*), *2*(4), 215-219.

Bhat, Bilal & Pandey, Dr. (2021). *Peace and Value Education.* Taran Publication ISBN: 978-93-92313-00-4.

Cahya, V.T. (2019). An Analysis of Educational Value in Moana Movie (Doctoral dissertation, UIN Raden Intan Lampung).

Chaudhry, N. (2018). "Peace and Value Education to Foster Inclusion". *International Journal of Latest Trends in Engineering and Technology, 10*(4), pp. 59-62.

Chinpinyokul, P. (2021). "Zootopia (2016)". *The Diversity in Society, Difference, Power, and Discrimination in Film and Media: Student Essays*, Linn-Benton Community College, 978-1-63635-079-0

Fanning, J. (2015). *The Disney Book: A Celebration of the World of Disney.* Dorling Kindersley Ltd.

Freakley, M., Burgh, G., MacSporran, L.T. (2008). *Values Education in Schools: A Resource Book for Student Inquiry.* Aust Council for Ed Research. ISBN, 0864319924.

Hasanah, U. (2022). *An Analysis of Educational Value in Moana Movie Thesis.* State Institute of Islamic Studies Ponorogo.

Hipes, P. (2016). *AFI Awards: Best of 2016 Film List includes 'Silence', 'Hacksaw Ridge' & More.* Retrieved on 9 June, 2024, from https://www.yahoo.com/entertainment/afi-awards-best-film-213416862.html

Kermodode, M. (2016). *Zootropolis Review – Disney's Animated Odd Couple has a Perfect Chemistry.* Retrieved on 3 July, 2024.

Muljadi, H. (2019). "Discrimination in Zootopia: A Critical Reading". *EduLite: Journal of English Education, Literature and Culture.* 4. 236. 10.30659/e.4.2.236-246.

Niemiec, R.M. & Wedding, D. (2013). *Positive Psychology at the Movies: Using Films to Build Character Strengths and Well-being.* Hogrefe Publishing GmbH.

Pressberg, M. (2016). *Anti-Racist 'Zootopia' is Crushing it in Countries where Diversity often Doesn't Play.* Retrieved 9 June, 2024, from https://ibtimes.com/anti-racist-zootopia-crushing-it-countries-where-diversity-often-doesnt-play-2350849.

Shen, C. (2016). "Zootopia: Let the Reality in the Animation". *China Art News.*

Walay, A. (2022). "Use of English Movies as a Pedagogical Tool in Learning English Language". *International Journal of Arts, Sciences and Education, 3*(2), 39-56.

Xue, S. (2016). "Research on the Narrative Art and Social Value of Zootopia in the Film and Television Animation". *Art and Design Review, 4:* 37-40. doi: 10.4236/adr.2016.42006

Zhong, K.L. (2016). "Zootopia: Crazy Animal City in the 'Crazy'". *Real Estate Tribune.*

14

Peace Pedagogy in Formal Education

Girish Chandra Behera and *Pranati Priyadarshini*

Introduction

Peace is the greatest achievement of human life. Education lays a strong foundation for the spread of peace. A life full of wealth and luxuries without mental peace is a life good for nothing. So, education for life must lead to education for peace. Peace is a state of mind which avoids all kinds of internal and external complexes. Peace education has the capacity to sustain peace of mind among the students of all streams, standards, society and states. Peaceful coexistence is the best achievement of the society. So, education in every community should lead to peace education for universal well-being by achieving international peace and world brotherhood. Every religious scripture gives some religious education. The internal tone and tune of every religion sing the songs of peace, pleasure, and prosperity for all the members of the world family. So, every teacher, researcher, academician, policymaker, and social worker should plan, prepare and promote peace education to bring heaven on earth.

Objectives

1. To understand the relevance of peace education.
2. To prepare an innovative curriculum to provide peace education all over the world.
3. To discuss various pedagogical principles of peace education.
4. To study various contents relating to peace education.
5. To focus on curriculum modification for peace education.
6. To understand the role of peace education in resolving disputes.
7. To relate the cultural values with peace education.
8. To maintain peace of mind among the stakeholders of education for social well-being.

Rationale

Education must be ideal reflecting all kinds of humanitarian values to ensure a safe, secure, peaceful social life with a positive mindset. Peace education is the most important trend of education to maintain social discipline amidst the multivarious cultures to celebrate diversity. That's why the saint Swami Vivekananda declared the aim of education is the building of character. This character-building is the base of peace education and an emerging challenge before the educationists of the 21st century. Because the so-called education system becomes career-oriented neglecting the responsibility of character building which generates a self-centric life where interdependence among the individual members is highly neglected and independent life is given high priority but interdependence has been proved to be more ideal in comparison to independent or dependent life which are neither social nor peace promoting in nature. This social quality of interdependence needs to be valued to restore peace in society. So, peace education invites mass cooperation to make people happy for each other. All nations are led by individual statesmen, those statesmen whose minds are shaped in the classroom of that particular nation. So, this article appeals to research scholars, academicians, and policymakers to create a universally accepted culturally sound, and religiously approved curriculum to spread and enrich Peace Education at the world level ensuring a peaceful social atmosphere where there would be no wars, no riots, no disputes, no conflicts, no deprivation, no discrimination, and no destruction of humanity.

Definition of Peace Relating to Peace Education

Different philosophers, educationists, educational theorists, psychologists, and social reformers have defined peace in different ways according to their understanding:

- Mother Teresa speaks, "Peace begins with a smile". Smile is the indication of sound behaviour in education. Peace Education teaches us to smile from the heart.
- Mahatma Gandhi has stated, "There is no 'way to peace', there is only peace." Peace Education tries to explore it.
- Michael Cunningham says, "You cannot find peace by avoiding life." Peace Education systemizes life to earn peace.
- Aristotle states that, "It is not enough to win a war; it is more important to organize the peace." Peace Education prescribes so many activities to create peace in the environment.
- Albert Einstein realises, "Peace cannot be kept by force; it can only be achieved by understanding." Peace Education believes that maintaining peace is a positive attitude.
- Siddharth Goutam defined, "Peace comes from within. Do not seek it without." Peace Education connects peace

with life.

- Dalai Lama XIV interprets, "World peace must develop from inner peace. Peace is not just mere absence of violence. Peace is, I think, the manifestation of human compassion." Peace Education tries to make us compassionate.
- Vincent van Gogh finds that, "There is peace even in the storm." Peace Education develops all the skills and abilities to reach peace of mind.
- Walt Whitman declares that, "Peace is always beautiful." Peace Education beautifies both the internal and external world of life.
- Jimi Hendrix understands that, "When the power of love overcomes the love of power, the world will know peace." Peace is more powerful than any other power or property which makes us materially rich.

Understanding Peace and Peace Education

Peace is a positive state of mind and society as well. Peace is the feeling of highest security in the physical, mental, and social context of well-being. Peace includes both positive peace and negative peace.

Negative peace refers to the absence of direct or physical violence, positive peace refers to the presence of conditions of well-being promoting holistic development of life. The other name of peace is security which includes security of the economy, security of food, personal security, political security, health security, and environmental security. Peace is another form of balancing life and the situation which includes the social, political, economic and ecological, psychological balance of life. Peace is not purchased at the cost of money but rather generated at the cost of Peace Education. Peace Education promotes positive attitudes and managerial skills to build an environment of care and belongingness. It treats the world as a family. It teaches us to feel belongingness and deep attachment with others without having any kind of blood relationship. It teaches us to dedicate ourselves to others' pleasures and give up self-interest for the cause of universal well-being. Peace Education should not be limited to the curriculum of school and college rather it should be part and parcel of our daily life. Peace Education should be a message of transformation shifted from generation to generation with a social commitment to attain international peace and communal harmony to protect and promote peaceful coexistence for all the members of the world family. The smell of peace in the air of love should spread the message of truth or the ultimate reality known as God or the supreme father. All men and women should be taught to love and cooperate as the embodiments of love, in the form of brothers and sisters of one father—the supreme father.

Concept of Pedagogy in Peace Education

The term 'pedagogy' is primarily associated with teacher education. Teacher education consists of ideal teaching and learning practices. In the context of Peace Education, pedagogy refers to all those ways, means and approaches which lead to peace education. Pedagogy is a combination of both theoretical perspectives and practical activities. So, the educationist believes that pedagogy is both the art and science of education. So, it includes the art of living, the art of giving, based on morality, and humanitarian values. The pedagogy of peace education considers the roles and responsibilities of all the stakeholders, i.e. students and teachers, clients and counsellors, *guru* and *shishya*, disciples and prophets, educational policymakers and researchers and so on.

Pedagogical Prospectives in Peace Education

Sl. No.	Peace breaking factor	Standard of education	Strategy of elimination
1	Teasing and irritation, the feeling of absence of the parent, loss of toys, breaking of toys	Pre-primary	Practice of smiling, attitude of thanking, learning to talk sweetly, helping and supporting friends.
2	Defeat in game, failure in exam, quarrel with friends, scolding from parents	Primary	Acquiring the skills of self-management, skills of forgetting sorrows, singing and listening to pain relieving songs, developing attitude of obedience.
3	Confusion in decision making, bad company of friends, immature love attachment, failure in competition, problem in decision making, confusion in career selection, family pressure for marriage upon girls, family pressure for earning upon boys	Upper primary and secondary	Developing sharing habits, reading moral stories, taking the advice of elders, developing the skills of controlling over senses known as *Indriya* sanyam, developing habits of praying and sitting in meditation, taking the support of a suitable counsellor, living under the guidance of parents and teachers, developing the skills of motivation and judgemental capacities, developing various life skills.
4	Facing an accident, delay in the job, failure in the workplace, nega-tive comparison of perfor-mance, failure in love life, work pressure, low income, ideological differences, drug addiction, the victim of mishaps, adjustment problems in the environment	Higher education	Developing spirit of work, enhancing working skills, developing qualities of adjustment, initiatives for self-employment, taking the support of friends and relatives, taking part in spiritual congregation, reading of autobiography of treatment, study of scriptures, avoiding bad company, avoiding drugs and alcohol, avoiding unnecessary experimentation, staying away from ragging in schools and colleges.

Content Development for Peace Education

Peace Education can be incorporated into all the curriculums of arts, science, commerce, and information technology. Content for Peace Education must be age-appropriate, culture-specific, contextual, and content-oriented to suit the needs and demands of people of all categories. The simplicity or complexities of the content of peace education depends upon its characteristics and the beneficiaries or the students. Peace Education is associated with life skill education, spiritual education, cultural education, teacher education and so on. Here is a brief outline of some specific contents which can be included in the Peace Education curriculum:

1. Concept and meaning of peace education.
2. Definition of peace and peace education.
3. Different goals of peace education.
4. Relevance and scope of peace education.
5. Social context of peace and peace education.
6. Strategies and initiatives for global peace prospectives.
7. Difference between positive and negative peace.
8. Importance of peace in institutional management.
9. Connection between leadership and peace management.
10. Factors affecting peace and their elimination.
11. Different practices and approaches for the creation and restoration of peace.
12. Role of great men in the spread of peace in the world.

Components of an Ideal Curriculum for Peace Education

The curriculum of Peace Education must be an integrated curriculum. Though peace is a unique emotional state of mind, Peace Education cannot be treated as a unified curriculum. Because many components are there which creates peace within the individuals and the society. All these components of Peace Education may include religious practice, cultural practice, sustainable practice, individual practice, international practice, spiritual practice, and ethical practice. It means the Peace Education curriculum should focus on religious equity, cultural integration, social cooperation, international cooperation, gender education, life-oriented skills, and all other components that influence peace and peace education in society. It may include the ideal lifestyles of the saints and prophets, and the sacrifice of kings, rulers, and emperors for peace restoration. The divine discourses delivered by eminent sages and great men, ideal mythological stories, religious scriptures and verses from holy books, and all other ways and means of spiritual attainment which leads to peace and peace education.

Global peace is another goal of Peace Education. So, we should imagine a world-class curriculum composed of humanitarian values, religious essence and equity, cultural diversities, divine potentials, peace restoring mechanisms altogether which every university should follow realising the need to protect the world from man-made disasters like terrorist attacks, assassinations, insurgencies, and communal riots. This world-class curriculum should comprise the following valuable components of utmost humanitarian importance:

(a) Need of belongingness for social well-being.
(b) Skills of self-management and life management.
(c) The importance of humanitarian values.
(d) Advantage of spiritual practice.
(e) Different means and ways of spiritual practice.
(f) Place of *yoga* in life.
(g) Similarities in different religions.
(h) The importance of international peace and cultural harmony.

(i) Considering the world as a global village or *Vasudhaiva Kutumbakam*.
(j) The doctrine of divinity and universal brotherhood.
(k) Service as social strength.
(l) Contemplation for inward vision.
(m) Importance of secularism for communal harmony.
(n) Need for sustainability and ecological balance.
(o) Gender equity and respect for women.

Cultural Transformation for Peace Education

Culture transcends boundaries and embraces diversity. Cultural education is associated with peace education because components like culture, cooperation, and community are associated with Peace Education. Cultural harmony is a true aim of cultural education which leads to peace education. It respects individual values and cultural integrity, which inspires peaceful coexistence. Culture should aim at promoting peace and harmony which helps to build up a heavenly atmosphere on earth.

Now-a-days our world is confronting different peace-threatening issues like insurgency, nuclear war, revolution for community identity, communal riots, and so on. These peace-breaking experiences generate instability, restlessness, and loneliness around us. We should extend the value of culture to promote peace and harmony in the whole world. Education should impart values of diverse cultures to constitute a powerful mechanism to regulate and control individual behaviour and drive them towards the building of a peaceful society with deeper attachment and belongingness among different ethnic groups. This Peace Education empowered with cultural values teaches that when we cooperate with others, they become our friend. Peace Education teaches that where there is friendship there is peace. When we create enemies, we lose our peace of mind and the aim of peace education vanishes. So, the quality of peace education depends upon the cultural exchanges being closer to crores of hearts of various cultures. This belongingness helps in promoting and restoring peace everywhere in the society irrespective of geographical and political diversity. So, cultural transmission has its significance to work for Peace Education.

Teaching and Preaching of Secularism for Peace Education

India is the holistic land of secularism. Secularism is another component of Peace Education. Peace Education incorporates all the ethics and values based on secularism to avoid religious disparity which breaks peace in society. If the peace breaks it leads to various kinds of antisocial indiscipline in the form of riots, and communal violence, which sets the base of Peace Education. We are lucky to be Indians. Respect for every religion is the first step in attaining secularism citing an example once Gandhiji preached one's mother gives one's child for breastfeeding but all other mothers are alike holding the same position for their offspring. Every mother is full of love and does not feed me but can bless me like this an individual member may be a follower of a particular religion but every religion has its own importance and particular ways of reaching God. Every religion is against the loss of human life, loss of peace of mind, and loss of cultural harmony in the world. Every religion possesses a sense of the truth of reality, love for all creatures, and a path of light that shows divinity and peace education covers all these facts and principles within its curriculum. So, let us understand the values of secularism associated with Peace Education to establish peace in our hearts and the whole world as well.

Communal Harmony and Peace Education

In the context of music for peace, cultural harmony sings "Ishwar Allah tero naam, sabko sanmati de Bhagwan". Every religion is of the same tune which the evil mind does not realise. Here peace education plays an important role in its realisation. Though there are so many saints in the world who have advocated for a world-class religion, but their teachings and preachings have not been successfully enshrined in the educational curriculum leading to Peace Education. Spiritual education has not been treated as an international compulsion to create peace and harmony for the entire human race. This greater and global thinking is found to be limited within the boundaries of Hindu-temples, Christian-churches, Islamic-masjids, Buddha-viharas, Sikh-gurudwaras, Jain-caves, and other limited spiritual places but Peace Education should not be away of the schools and colleges, from the tolls and tutorials. This is an essentiality on the way of attaining international peace and harmony. So, the Peace Education curriculum may include the *Satsang* movement of Sri Sri Thakur Anukulchandra, the secular principles and social services of Sri Satya Sai, the integral education and yogic atmosphere of Sri Aurobindo, the spiritual sphere of Krishna consciousness, led by Srila Prabhupada. So, political will and educational sanctity should be merged to create a world-class curriculum for Peace Education. It would be dedicated for religious equity and the rapid spread of peace education including all those divine potentials and spiritual essences of every religion in the form of an inevitable subject of Peace Education. If it is true that education is the modification of behaviour and aiming at holistic development of life, peace education must be treated as the most life-scientific instrument to bring positive changes not only in human minds but also in the external world.

Transforming Education for Global Peace

Education is a light that enlightens both the internal world and the external world. When education is in the form of spiritual education it fulfils the needs of life for births. Spiritual education is a crucial part of Peace Education. Because spirituality aims to promote peace both at social and individual levels. It gives many precious gifts of emotional feelings that cannot be stored in the books.

The purpose of spiritual education is to feel the minds and hearts with divine potential which inspires us to won every nation as ours. Spirituality is an essentiality of our life which should be merged with science to improve the quality of life. True spiritual education does not advise searching for places of peace but rather building up peaceful surroundings with a strong commitment and unbeaten determination to achieve international peace and harmony. So, spiritual practice under peace education creates to search for peace within the individuals from the core of their hearts. Now-a-days the world feels to adopt and impose such an ideal system of education which would inspire us to work collectively for peaceful coexistence. Not in our respective locality but rather at the global level. This needs our deep attachment to the world community and valuable attempts at the local level to achieve an endless period of peace for generations to come.

Peace Education and UN Initiatives for Peace Restoration

Peace education is an international concern. So, UN initiatives for ensuring international peace and security should be given an important place in the global peace education curriculum. The following points may be discussed in the context of international peace education:

(a) Use of diplomacy and mediatorship to resolve disputes. Searching for navigating the path from conflict to peace.
(b) Policymaking for multidimensional operations for international peace and harmony.
(c) Encourage leadership to restore peace through political initiatives.
(d) Reintegration of former combatants of different nations.
(e) Mobilization of essential resources for humanitarian assistance to the war victims or common people of war zones.
(f) Creating human rights activists all over the world to ensure social security for the common people.
(g) Formation of international rules and laws and appropriate international authorities to restore peace and resolve conflicts.

Conclusion

ॐ द्यौ शान्तिरन्तरिक्षः शान्तिः पृथ्वी शान्तिरापः शान्तिः रोषधयः शान्तिः। वनस्पतयः शान्तिर्विश्वे देवाःशान्तिब्रह्मा शान्तिः सर्वः शान्तिः शान्तिरेव शान्तिः सा मा शान्तिरेधि ॐ शान्तिः शान्तिः शान्तिः।

Om Dyau Shanti Rantariksha Shanti Prithvi Shanti Rapah
Shanti Roshadhayah Shanti Vanaspatayah Shanti Vishwed Devah Shanti Brahma Shanti
Sarva Shanti Shanti Reva Shanti Sa Ma Shanti Redhi
Om Shanti Shanti Shanti

Which means peace may prevail unto heaven, sky, earth, water, herbs, trees, Gods, and Brahma. May peace own all the people of this war-ful world. May peace stabilise all the stressfull minds busy with their professional career. May peace influence the saints, and prophets of all religions to form a world of peace on earth. Let this be the goal of all lives, all communities, all professions, all institutions and all the countries in the world. Let peace be the base of all forms of education to win overstrain, stress, anxieties, jealousy, intolerance and violence.

REFERENCES

https://www.southernliving.com/peace-quotes-7509990

https://jeasa.jcsaweb.org/peace-education

https://www.unesco.org/en/articles/what-you-need-know-about-unescos-recommendation-education-peace-human-rights-and-sustainable#

15

Ramayana the Epic for Peaceful Existency

Arti Srivastava

Man and Language

According to *Manusmriti*, "Man defines his existence in this world through the process of his thinking capacity and language plays very important role in defining and nurturing this process." ('*manute iti manushyah*').

The essence of a man is defined through his capacity to think and reflect. In fact his capacity of thoughtful expression makes him a special being to contribute and support the harmonious growth of the self and the society. The process of thinking and expression becomes easy and comfortable with the support of language. Man uses different sounds, their combinations and its culture specific manifestations to make himself understood. The beauty of language is such that an idea starts with the language and culminates in a language enabling individual to define himself as a thinking being who evolves through this process as a sensitive being. This sensitive being gets connected to the environment by understanding the expressions and by making himself understood. This process enables him to become a mature being who establishes himself as a sensible and responsible person contributing for the betterment of the society. This is the reason that the language distinguishes human beings from the animal world and characterizes him as a thinking being.

Therefore, knowing a language equips an individual to not only express and communicate but explore his capabilities and therefore, he goes beyond the structural limits of the language and explores the possibilities to enjoy the beauty of language and therefore, lives the language. Living language is a matter of conversation, dialogue and being. This signifies the sensitivities related to that language which can be related to all the spheres of human experiences and which becomes part of human existence. Language has a unique and special way of transcribing thought/perception into language by combining different sounds into meaningful entities of words and sentences and using them for different situation and with different individuals. This beauty and strength of language can be understood only by living the language and experiencing it in natural settings which is enjoyable. The challenge and obstructions emerge when we use predesigned and predetermined methods for understanding it because every language has its own culture and reference, making it different and unique from others. Therefore, if one wants to know a language, it involves individual's continuous interaction with the culture of the language. This understanding of the language facilitates the strength to realise the thought process and manifest the same using appropriate sound. Language, therefore, becomes very important medium to realise and nurture and accelerate the thought process and express the same to facilitate the process of knowing one-self.

Hermeneutics and Language

Hermeneutics refers to the interpretation of given text, speech or symbolic expressions. It involves the understanding of the text and interpretation in terms of understanding and revealing the world. Understanding is achieved through the process of interpretative experience.

> Gadamer states that "understanding is language-bound" (1990: 156). He asserts that "All understanding is interpretation, and all interpretation takes place in the medium of a language that allows the object to come into words and yet is at the same time the interpreter's own language" (Gadamer, 2004: 390) and that "Every interpretation has to adapt itself to the hermeneutical situation to which it belongs" (Gadamer, 2004: 398).
>
> (Main elements of h.-g. Gadamer's communication hermeneutics/pagrindiniai h.-g. Gadamerio komunikacijos hermeneutikos elementa. The free library by farlex)

Therefore, knowing all the aspects and the context of the language is important for the interpretation and understanding of the text for communicating a goodwill is a hermeneutical function.

The process of thinking, its expression, interpretation and understanding are the major concern of philosophy of language. The art of interpretation facilitates the process of understanding the text and explore the possibilities for its contribution for the harmony. The processes involved in it are very natural and require a genuine effort to know the language thoroughly. While speaking, we carry a thought process and the words used to express the same should be able to preserve and express the genuine thought. This involves two aspects:

1. Appropriate sounds/word used to represent the thought; and
2. communication of the word in appropriate manner so that it conveys the intended meaning.

Hermeneutics or art of interpretation is concerned with this aspect of language and helps to understand the language with all its characteristics. In Indian philosophical tradition, the traces of this perspective toward language can be traced from *Vedic* age where each and every sound was uttered with a defined purpose and it was pronounced with appropriate intonations so that it accomplishes the intended purpose.

The *upanishads* and the epics are rich in providing these occasions of language interpretations which have universal values. The framework of epics are rich in providing instances and character descriptions of different roles. They have a scope to be interpreted in present situations for the good of the humans and the society. The hermeneutical analyses of the epic *Ramayana* which is the objective here, has opened many dimensions to understand the humans, their connections and the responsibilities to respond for the harmony of the society.

The way language is expressed in the epic in different contexts and by different characters, it connects to the values and interprets, clarifies and redefines the norms for the betterment of the society. This connection is very natural because the value system of any society seeks dependence and guidance from its literature to continue its existence and recognition in global framework. Therefore, it includes the experiences and the text which has helped man to grow and prove his worth for the well-being of society. The literature provides experiences to live up to our own values and to be of value for the society at large and therefore, it must be included and integrated in our system of education through content and pedagogy. The reasons for this are two:

- One is to understand the values of the classic tradition correctly by connecting it to the contexts of language framework and the context of human connections.
- Another reason for this kind of intervention is because of the value conflicts, the society is facing in the present time.

Technology as Powerful Knowledge

A very important question here can be that why such an important classic reference is not referred so much and is valued only when man requires proof for his religious existence. The answer I understand is the overpowering status of the new knowledge called technology. The technological advancement and the dependence on it has generated many issues in prioritising our life objectives, be it relationships, job, and many more. This has further promoted the value crises among the youth. Modern technologies have started oppressing the society which is labelled as a new progressive value. But this new pattern of values is providing a temporary meaning to their existence and this has invoked the need for our heritage wisdom which is the focus of the NEP2020. The need, therefore, is to create the acceptability and the desire to know the heritage wisdom to develop clarity to discriminate for resolving the conflicts.

Ramayana: A Hermeneutical Analysis

The hermeneutical analyses of the epic *Ramayana* by Valmiki are a great source in this perspective and provides many occasions to understand and reflect for the harmony of the self and society.

For the hermeneutical analyses, the original text was consulted and the understanding and interpretations were based on:

- the letters/symbols used in that language;
- the combination pattern of the letters/sounds in a word;
- the combination pattern of different words in a sentence; and
- the nature and use of sentence and the meanings derived through different combinations of words and other issues related to spoken form of language.

The analyses of the text is done in a manner so that its significance can be realised in the society in a manner so that it can become a guiding force for the generation today.

The Text, Context, Understanding and Interpretations

We all are many times confused and directionless about our choices and it is beautifully mentioned in the epic and it elaborates the importance of following *dharma.* Which means that the choices one makes in his life should be supported by the *dharma*:

यस्मिंस्तु सर्वे स्युरसन्निविष्टाधर्मो यत स्स्यात्तदुपक्रमेत।
द्वेष्यो भवत्यर्थपरो हि लोकेकामात्मता खल्वपि न प्रशस्ता।।2.21.57।।

> [*If actions which combine these three (dharma, artha and kama), cannot be performed, resort to righteousness. One who seeks wealth is abhorred and one who seeks fulfilment of desires does not attract admiration in this world.*]

Dharma, Artha, Kama and Moksha are four *Purusharthas*, the beauty here is that *Dharma* comes in the beginning which signifies that the *Artha* (material wealth) and *Kama* (the desires) should be placed in life according to the *Dharma* (righteousness). If our choices and preferences are in accordance with the righteousness, then it will create harmony inside and in the external world. Therefore, all our economic and earthly desires should follow the *dharma* and that is prescribed in the cultural norms of the society.

Further Valmiki has emphasized the importance of *Patience* for fighting with anger and sorrow which is through the character of *Rama* to *Luxmana* (अवमानं निरस्येमं गृहीत्वा हर्षमुत्तमम्)–

निगृह्य रोषं शोकं च धैर्यमाश्रित्य केवलम्।
अवमानं निरस्येमं गृहीत्वा हर्षमुत्तमम्।।2.22.3।।

(*Control your anger and sorrow. Dismiss this humiliation. Achieve great happiness through courage.*)

If man is overpowered by anger and sorrow, its effects are disastrous which can be a very depressing state for the man and society. The interpretation here can be that the human behaviour is not natural and pure when it is overpowered by anger and therefore, the responsibility is to have patience in those difficult times and not to be swayed away by the temporary emotions. *Rama,* who was to be crowned as the king, even after being sent to the exile did not show anger and disrespect to *Kaikeyee.*

Valmiki has used the word राघवशार्दूल for Rama, meaning, who is the most courageous and brilliant and has the capacity to lead and protect the humanity. This description creates belongingness and assurance for the safety and the security of the people.

यं पालयसि धर्मं त्वं धृत्या च नियमेन च।
स वै राघवशार्दूल धर्मस्त्वामभिरक्षतु।।2.25.3।।

(*The duty which you are carrying out with courage and self-discipline, O tiger among the descendants of Raghu will alone protect you*).

This aspect is further reinforced when *Rama* as the protector of *dharma* tries to guide his brother *Luxmana*. The conversations and dialogues are a very good and effective way to connect and know the people and surroundings but important is to be sensitive about whom to speak, how to speak, what to speak and when to speak because these can strengthen or weaken one's relationships. *Valmiki*, through *Ramayana* has explained life related lessons by *Rama* to *Sita* and patient hearing by her, especially in the situation of crises to protect his wife and to protect the relationships for a secure living. (*The context is when Rama was planning to go for exile all alone and wanted Sita to live in the palace*) *Rama* tells *Sita*—

बुद्धियुक्ता हि पुरुषा न सहन्ते परस्तवम्।
तस्मान्नते गुणाः कथ्या भरतस्याग्रतो मम।।2.26.25।।

(*You should never praise me in the presence of Bharata because intellectuals cannot tolerate others being praised before them. You should never extol my virtues before him.*)

When one is dependent on others, they have to be careful while praising their close ones and loved ones because that can become a reason for their insecurity. This is a social skill one should learn to be able to get accepted in the environment. Further *Rama* clarifies one more point that in order to stay in the palace where *Bharata* will be the king, *Sita* should not expect special treatment, (नापि त्वं तेन भर्तव्या विशेषेण कदाचन) rather her conduct should be such that her acceptability is created.

नापि त्वं तेन भर्तव्या विशेषेण कदाचन।
अनुकूलतया शक्यं समीपे त्वस्य वर्तितुम्।।2.26.26।।

(Never expect special treatment from Bharata. You can stay with him by conducting yourself in a favourable manner.)

Our culture defines and sustains our existence. The place of father in our system is like God, (पिता ही देवतं) therefore, he should get the divine place in the life of children, *Valmiki* has beautifully mentioned this in his epic through *Rama* and he says that Place of father is higher than Gods, therefore, he should be respected. *Rama* says:

पिता हि दैवतं तात देवतानामपि स्मृतम्।
तस्माद्दैवतमित्येव करिष्यामि पितुर्वचः।।2.34.52।।

(Father is divine even for the gods as cited in scriptures, therefore, looking upon father as my god, I will carry out his words, O father.)

The purpose of equating the father to God seems to be the assurances related to the belongingness and the security of both father and son. Father is full of experiences and the son is immature and new to the world, the purpose is to create a relation of faith between father and son. The interpretation is very much required for the society today because the new knowledge power in the name of technology has introduced many logical parameters for understanding and defining the relationships which are temporary and does not satisfy the humanistic parameters.

Another relationship example can be traced in the form of husband and wife in *Valmiki's Ramayana* when *Valmiki* through the sage *Vashishtha* clarifies the status of wife by taking the threads from the divine concept of *ardhnareeshwar.* Wife, according to *shastras* is the soul of their husband (आत्मा ही दारास्सर्वेषां) and therefore, can take up the responsibilities and enjoy the privileges as her husband enjoys. Sri *Vasishtha* says:

आत्मा हि दारास्सर्वेषां दारसङ्ग्रहवर्तिनाम् ।
आत्मेयमिति रामस्य पालयिष्यति मेदिनीम् । ।2.37.24 । ।

(*For every householder, his wife is the soul. Since Sita is the soul of Rama, she can rule this earth.*)

Therefore, the authority of *shastras* is used as a righteous way to acknowledge the individuals, their rights and their duties for a conflict free harmonious society. This is further enriched by *Valmiki* through *Kaushalya* when she tries to sensitise *Sita* for her relationship with her husband *Rama*. She clarifies the basic fundamentals for a happy relationship and uses the metaphor of *Veena* and Strings, and chariot and wheels for the purpose (नातन्त्री वाद्यते वीणा नाचक्रो वर्तते रथः). Through *Kaushalya Valmiki* has suggested a healthy and beautiful dialogical relationship pattern between a mother-in-law and a daughter-in-law where *Sita* is receptive and respectful for the advices of *Kaushalya*:

नातन्त्री वाद्यते वीणा नाचक्रो वर्तते रथः ।
नापतिस्सुखमेधेत या स्यादपि शतात्मजा । ।2.39.29 । ।

(*A veena (lute) sans strings cannot be played. A chariot without wheels cannot move. Similarly, a woman without her husband finds no happiness even though she has one hundred sons.*)

मितं ददाति हि पिता मितं माता मितं सुतः ।
अमितस्य हि दातारं भर्तारं का न पूजयेत् । ।2.39.30 । ।

(*While the happiness that the father, mother and son give is limited, a husband gives unlimited happiness. Which wife will not worship such a husband?*)

अमितस्य हि दातारं भर्तारं, literally means that the husband give unlimited happiness, therefore, he is respect worthy. The interpretation of this is very valuable for the sustenance of natural relationship pattern of the society. Husband and wife together create the basic structure of the society with love, dependence, sacrifice and belongingness. The new choices of the youth today (example—gay marriage, live-in relationship) for this togetherness are very dangerous for the future society because they obstruct the natural process of development of human society. The changes and the modifications are necessary for the healthy growth of any society but the basic and fundamental parameters cannot be compromised.

The essential character of human being is portrayed by *Valmiki* through *Rama's* behaviour which is observable in him through his patience (न क्रुध्यत्यभिशप्तोऽपि), tolerance (क्रोधनीयानि वर्जयन्) and his equal treatment to all mothers (न्सर्वान् सम) can be interpreted well for the clarification and understanding of the situation and responsibility.

न क्रुध्यत्यभिशप्तोऽपि क्रोधनीयानि वर्जयन्।
क्रुद्धान्प्रसादयन्सर्वान् समदुःखः क्व गच्छति।।2.41.3।।

(*Where is he who, even if reviled, never gets angry, never does acts that provoke anger, pacifies those who are enraged and shares the sorrows of others going now?*)

These traits of a personality as projected by *Valmiki* through *Rama* may appear difficult to follow but if this is practiced in the family, it becomes naturally the character of the family. Many a times we have heard the observations of the people when they guess the family through the behaviour of its members. ***Values are Caught and not Taught.***

The basic element of society is to nurture acceptability for each other for the sustenance and growth. How do we create this in the present context is mechanically defined and accepted, therefore, does not last for long. The need is to understand the universal parameters to create a harmonious society. *Valmiki* has projected this aspect through the character of *Rama*. He has portrayed him as one who is well-versed with the righteous behaviour and practiced the same in his life and that's why people accepted him and became more and more convinced by observing him. Therefore, the acceptability of a leader is more when he is able to follow *dharma* (दाशरथिर्धर्मएवास्थितो) and become inspirable:

यथा यथा दाशरथिर्धर्म एवास्थितोऽभवत् ।
तथा तथा प्रकृतयो रामं पतिमकामयन् । ।2.45.11 । ।

[*The more the son of Dasaratha* (*Rama*) *committed to righteousness, the more the subjects desired that he should be their king.*]

The responsibility lies with all of us to develop the capacity to differentiate between happiness and pleasure, *Shreyas* and *Preyas* (*Kathopnishad*) and accordingly consult the directives as mentioned in our classical text. This will further generate the wisdom to integrate it in the present context. The efforts should be to be more sensitive towards our commitments so that we become inspiration for each other.

Valmiki has touched a very sensitive and important aspect which connects to the generation today. King *Dashratha* learnt the skill of hunting through sounds. He used it and unfortunately *Shravana Kumar* was killed and he was cursed for this by his parents. King also realised that learning the skill of killing animals by listening to the sound was not a right choice because he killed someone without intending to kill him.

The choice of course/skill has to be examined closely and its impact on the environment and society need to be assessed properly. *Valmiki,* through *Dashratha* is also clarifying this the skill he chose to learn was not appropriate. He realised that it was just an attraction to learn the skill (कश्चित्पलाशैर्मोहितो).

यथान्यः पुरुषः कश्चित्पलाशैर्मोहितो भवेत्।
एवं ममाऽप्यविज्ञातं शब्दवेध्यमयं फलम्।।2.63.13।।

(*Like someone who is deluded by palasa trees I too did not realise the consequences of shooting the target following the direction of the sound.*)

The interpretation is very important for the generation today. While selecting the course or knowledge to be gained, one should not go by popular choices but by the utility and relevance of the same.

Addressing the sensitivities of humans is highlighted very beautifully in *Ramayana* in the context of relationships and in the context of nature also. Man as a part of nature owes responsibility to understand its expressions and nurture by not disturbing its natural process. *Valmiki* through the different expression of his characters glorifies the beauty of the nature and man's capacity to understand and sensitize himself towards its expressions. At one place while going for exile *Rama* after listening to the sound of nature identifies the place through the sound (श्रूयते शब्दो वारिणो वारिघट्टितः) and says that two rivers are meeting nearby which is *Ganga* and *Yamuna*:

नूनं प्राप्ताः स्मसम्भेदं गङ्गायमुनयोर्वयम्।
तथा हि श्रूयते शब्दो वारिणो वारिघट्टितः।।2.54.6।।

(*We have surely reached the confluence of Ganga and Yamuna which can be ascertained from the sounds of clashing water.*)

The interpretation suggests that nature has its own way of expression. Different weathers, different creatures express through the sounds and visuals which carry significant meaning for our physical, mental and emotional existence. As a part of nature we have the responsibility to understand this without trying to have control over it. The sound of the instrument *sitar* can be created through synthesizer but creating it through the real instrument in the lap of nature can create magic.

Further, the message for protecting our trees and understanding their coexistence with humans, specially banyan tree is very beautifully explained by *Valmiki* to the extent that he made *Sita* to worship the tree (तस्मै सीताञ्जलिं कृत्वा प्रयुञ्जीताशिषश्शिवाः).

ततो न्यग्रोधमासाद्य महान्तं हरितच्छदम् । ।2.55.6 । ।
विवृद्धं बहुभिर्वृक्षै श्श्यामं सिद्धोपसेवितम् ।
तस्मै सीताञ्जलिं कृत्वा प्रयुञ्जीताशिषश्शिवाः । ।2.55.7 । ।

(*There you will find a large banyan tree with its lush green leaves, looking dark with its densely grown trees. It is inhabited by siddhas. Sita should offer with folded palms invocations for her well-being.*)

Many a times worshipping the nature is considered as a ceremonial practice of a religion and that's why their true meaning is misinterpreted. All the natural resources are part of our existence, be it physical, mental or emotional, therefore, it is our responsibility to ensure their sustenance for the protection of humans. This is done in the religion through different ways, by dictating guidelines, logical reasoning or attaching a faith to it. As per faith, if we worship something, we will not destroy that and banyan tree has all those qualities which are good for the sustenance.

Ramayana has beautiful occasions where one can celebrate humanity. An example of this is when someone leaves, he leaves with a *swastivachan* (words of welfare) (स्वस्त्ययनं) by the sender for his well-being and safe journey, a reason to meet again and continue the relationship.

तेषां चैव स्वस्त्ययनं महर्षिस्सचकार ह।
प्रस्थितांश्चैव तान्प्रेक्ष्य पिता पुत्रानिवान्वगात्।।2.55.2।।

(*Seeing them setting forth, the great sage blessed them for a safe journey and followed them like a father following his children.*)

These *swastivachan* may still be part of many households but the meanings are lost, and therefore, the intentions are always doubted or misinterpreted. As a result human relationships are getting weak day by day.

Happiness and grief constitute the web of life and its human to be sad and happy. *Valmiki's* intention of creating a happy society and moving further without getting depressed is the message for the youth today who get easily swayed away by a small failure. Falling into a grief state is natural but prolonged lamenting weakens a person, (शोको नाशयते सर्वं), therefore, it is considered as being enemy to oneself which results in destroying the qualities of the affected person:

शोको नाशयते धैर्यं शोको नाशयते श्रुतम्।
शोको नाशयते सर्वं नास्ति शोकसमो रिपुः।।2.62.15।।

(*Grief destroys fortitude. Grief destroys knowledge of the scriptures, grief destroys everything. There is no enemy equal to grief.*)

There are many more occasions in the epic which can be interpreted hermeneutically for creating and clarifying the value choices for the society today. By analysing through this qualitative approach, it is apparent that the values of the epic are relevant for:

(a) clarity of objectives towards achieving life goals and the attached responsibility,
(b) about righteous attitude and behaviour,
(c) human values and their need,
(d) value of compassionate behaviour,
(e) value of tolerance,
(f) selfishness and selflessness,
(g) society and our responsibilities, and so many other interpretations are possible in different contexts. They can be a reference for sensitising the youth today through the processes of education to create a culture of harmony in their environment.

The hermeneutical analysis opens many dimensions for the interpretation of the text. The use of different words and sentences and their combinations in different contexts clarifies and glorifies the virtues which can provide a basis for understanding the righteous way of living in the present context. The acceptability of the same is possible if it can be integrated with the requirement of the present society. The necessary condition for this is to create occasions for dialogue and discussions on the classical wisdom through the process of education. The schools and colleges can create a platform with this objective and provide opportunity for academic discussions. This will promote a healthy approach of understanding our heritage wisdom and associate it with our existence.

REFERENCES

Alston, William P. (1964). *Philosophy of Language*, Prentice Hall, Foundation of Philosophy Series.

Arapura (1986). *Hermeneutical Essays on Vedantic Topics*, Motilal Banarsidass.

Blackwell (2002). *Companion to Philosophy*, Edition II. Nicholas Bunnin, Eric Tsui-James (Eds.).

Buber, M. (1970). *I and Thou*. New York: Charles Scribner's Sons.

Cenkner, William (1976). *The Hindu Personality in Education*, Manohar.

Gadamer, H.-G. (2008). *Philosophical Hermeneutics*. Berkeley, Los Angeles, London: University of California Press.

Gerald, L. Gutek (2009). *New Perspectives on Philosophy and Education*, Pearson.

Joshi Kireet (1988). "A Philosophy of Education for Contemporary Youth". Indian Council of Philosophical Research.

Main Elements of H.-G. Gadamer's Communication Hermeneutics/ Pagrindiniai H.-G. Gadamerio Komunikacijos Hermeneutikos Elementai. (The free library by Farlex, Humanities > Philosophy and religion > COACTIVITY: Philosophy, Communication > March1, 2017 The Free Library > Date > 2017 > March > 1 > COACTIVITY: Philosophy, Communication)

Othmar Gachter (1983). *Hermeneutics and Language in Purvamimansa: A Study in Sabar Bhasya*, Motilal Banarsidass.

Ricoeur, P. (2004). *The Conflict of Interpretations: Essays in Hermeneutics*. Ihde, D. (Ed.). London, New York: Continuum.

Sri Aurobindo and the Mother (2014). *A New Education for a New Consciousness*, Sri Aurobindo Ashram, Delhi Branch.

Valmiki Ramayana, Part-1, Geeta Press, Gorakhpur.

16

Integrating Gandhian Educational Philosophy into Contemporary Indian Education

Pradip Das

Introduction

> "An eye for an eye will only make the whole world blind...Be the change that you wish to see the world". – M.K. Gandhi.

Gandhian Philosophy and thought on education had brought a new dimension and fundamental changes for building up of a new social order based on mutual cooperation, tolerance, truth and non-violence. But a dismal picture in the sphere of education is seen today as we have been failed to follow his glorious thought in the field of education. Educational Institutions have been the breeding ground of violence, communal conflicts, racial discrimination and social disintegration. Moreover, education of today has become completely out of touch both with the realities of national life and the upsurge of national aspirations. It has failed to cope up with the socio-economic problem stirring up in our country. The morality and human values of the youth of our country have been decreasing day by day as the system of education gives the youth a little insight in their national heritage, culture and values. But, if we go through the Gandhian thought, we will find that he categorically emphasized on the development of social, cultural, economic, environmental and aesthetic values through the adoption of 'Learning by doing' which will cause 'all round drawing out of the best in child and man—body, mind and spirit.' Gandhi wanted to make the child to be more practical rather than depending upon the accumulation of bookish knowledge. Gandhiji's purpose of education as to raise man to a higher order through full development of the individual and the evolution of a new man. The Indian Education System, with its diverse and dynamic landscape, faces numerous challenges, including rote learning, lack of practical skills, and insufficient emphasis on moral and ethical development. Mahatma Gandhi's educational philosophy, often encapsulated in his concept of "Nai Talim" or Basic Education, emphasizes learning by doing, self-sufficiency, and the development of body, mind, and spirit. This chapter seeks to bridge the gap between Gandhian educational ideals and modern educational practices, proposing ways to harmonize the two for the benefit of contemporary learners.

Statement of the Research Problem

In almost 66 years of our Independence, education in India still continues with some such blemishes that have hindered not only individual progress but also national development. Some of such weaknesses are being discussed below: Human civilization is on the brink of several crises and progress. This is due to lack of efficient Human Resources. Tremendous progress has been made in the field of Science and Technology. The work of social and economic reconstruction has reached to a zenith of considerable pitch. But all social, political and economic reconstruction involves many complicated problems of high intense due to lack of humanistic approach to education. The development of Science and Technology and rapid growth of populations have given a new dimension of problems in the 21st century and we are not preparing human resources with the help of qualitative education to tackle the new problems. The task of education is not merely turning out first-rate scientists, engineers, technicians and doctors but making a good human being with the help of planning to impart proper education that creates both technical efficiency and human efficiency. Roborts can never take the place of human beings having the quality of truth, beauty and goodness. A scientist or engineer or doctor who can manipulate his machines or apparatus and conduct his experiments successfully but becomes an unsuccessful poor human being if he fails to understand and empathize his fellow workers and fellow men associated with him. It is true education which makes a man responsive to decent emotion and structure of character and personality. Neglecting the value based education we are simply trying to make the wall of civilization on the base of sands. Human civilization will fall like a house of cards if our education fails to advocate and cherish practical efficiency and high technical skill, appreciation to dignity of labour, clarity of mind, community interests, and loyalties to fellow citizen, compassion and tolerance.

Objectives of the Study

The objectives of the study are as follows:

1. To find out the impact of Gandhian educational thought on all aspects of life.
2. To search out the trends of Indian Education System in

pre- and post-Independence period and the influence of Gandhian views for the reconstruction of education and generation of human resource.

3. To assess the influence of Gandhian thought in the process of all round development particularly in Life Skills of the learners.
4. To search out the relevance of Gandhian educational thought in the present Indian socio-economic and educational scenario for the progress of our nation.
5. To find out the impact of Gandhian values and ideologies for the development of Human Resource and for solving the educational crises arising in educational institutions in the 21st century.
6. To find out the process of development of education of women and untouchables leading to the national progress by following Gandhian line.
7. To search out the impact of educational thought of Mahatma Gandhi in developing environmental consciousness for sustainable development.
8. To help the future researchers by showing the new areas of research to reconstruct the Secondary Education on Gandhian line.

Needs and Scope of the Study

Students, of all stages whether it may be primary, secondary or higher education, are engaged themselves in accumulating bookish knowledge. Learning to them becomes a burden and monotonous. Intrinsic motivation in them is rare for achieving true knowledge or empirical knowledge. Education today does not help them to become self-sufficient and self-dependent in future. Even education of today is not so related to the new changes in the global perspectives and growing socio-economic problems stirring up in our country in the present century. In educational scenario what we notice today is indiscipline, impatience, violence, lawlessness, hatred, decrease of human values, lack of self-confidence, self-sufficiency and self-reliance, mental insecurity, stress, depression, anxiety, consumerisation of foreign culture etc. The skills of problem solving attitude, decision making capacity, communication, interpersonal relation, empathy, social awareness, self-awareness, coping up with emotion and stress are not inculcated due to lack of active involvement of the learners in the teaching-learning process. So 'all round drawing out of the best'—the goal of education is not fulfilled. As a result, unemployment, student's unrest, violation of human rights, violation of rules and regulations, religious fanaticism, inhuman treatment to women, caste conflicts prevailed to greater extent in the present century. Mahatma Gandhi was a philosopher in one hand and a 'Karmayogi' on the other. The researcher tries to find out the truth as to how and whether the Gandhian theories and principles of education are the solution of all these crises prevailed in the field of education. How his thought on education could guide us to make the secondary education more purposive and more objective based is the main object of the research problem. This is an attempt to prove if his principles and practices of education show a new dimension to reach the goal of secondary education and prevent the value erosion in the sphere of education and in all aspects of life.

Research Problem

Education is a powerful tool to develop individual a complete human being. Secondary education, as it lies in the middle of the primary and higher education, is a very important stage of education. Teachers of primary section are selected from this stage and at the same time it is the gate way to higher education. Education of today has become completely out of touch with the realities of life and the upsurge of national aspiration.

The researcher has tried to find out the truth as to how and whether the Gandhian theories and principles of education are the solution of the problem for development human resource. Moreover, his political, socio-economic, cultural views and educational thought could guide us as to how human beings are developed as resources which is treated as the main object of the research problem. This is an attempt to prove if his principles and practices of education show a new dimension to the ways to develop human resource and to prevent the value erosion in all aspects of life for an ideal human civilization.

Data Collection or Literature Review

This step involves identifying, locating, and collecting information pertaining to the research topic. The information sources are often contained in documents such as diaries or newspapers, records, photographs, relics, and interviews with individuals who have had the experience with or have knowledge of the research topic. Interviews with individuals who have knowledge of the research topic are called oral histories. The documents, records, oral histories and other information sources can be primary or secondary sources. A primary source is a source that has a direct involvement with the event being investigated like a diary, an original map, or an interview with a person that experienced the event. Whereas, a secondary source is a source that was created from a primary source such as books written about the vent. Secondary sources are considered less useful than primary sources.

Methodology of the Study

There is no one approach that is used in conducting historical research although there is a general set of steps that are typically followed. These include the following steps although there is some overlap and movement back and forth between the steps:

(i) Identification of the research topic and formulation of the research problem or question.
(ii) Data collection or literature review.
(iii) Evaluation of materials.
(iv) Data synthesis.
(v) Report preparation or preparation of the narrative exposition.

Each of these steps is discussed briefly below:

- Identification of the research topic and formulation of the research problem or question.
- This is the first step in any type of educational research including historical research. Ideas for historical research topics can come from many different sources such as current issues in education, the accomplishments of an individual, a government policy, or the relationship between events.

Sustainable Development and Gandhi's Framework through Education

Gandhian views on education harmonises the economic, political, social, moral-religious aspects of life in the context of man's rising aspirations to sustain life in harmony with men and nature. 'Naitalim Education' is the process of a new type of education to keep balance between ecology and technology to ensure labour intensive production for proper use of resources. So it is assumed that if the curriculum of secondary education is designed on Gandhian line as the essence of sustainable development lies in his philosophy, the students of this stage will learn the main objectives of sustainable development and will come forward to save the nature and natural resources. The environment education introduced in secondary level may be designed on Gandhian line to sustain life in harmony with men and nature. The examination of the statement shown in the graphical figure corroborates the views.

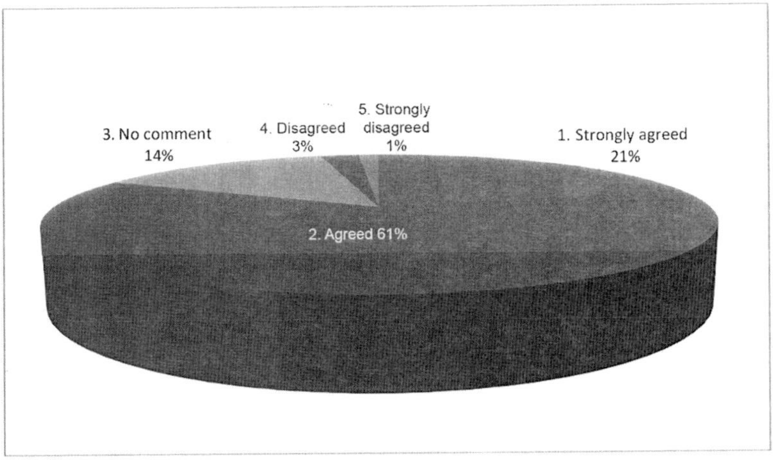

Fig. 16.1

The New Area of Research in Secondary Education on Gandhian Thought

In India, quantitative output has affected the quality of research in education with the growth of educational technology, modes of preparing research tools, advances in data collection, use of electronic devices. It is hoped that quality of research will be improved in the educational perspective. The development of educational research is based on priority of fields. In India, contemporary issues are given more emphasis. The priority is decided according to the national needs. Different commissions have suggested and recommended for appropriate and better system of education in the country. But various educational problems are not solved till the date. The researcher has suggested to follow the educational philosophy of Mahatma Gandhi and to make attempt for further research on the following topics related to education.

(a) The research work may be undertaken to study on the aims and values of secondary education.
(b) The research work may be taken into consideration to initiate further research on the study of changing values in the 21st century.
(c) The projects may be considered for the research on educational and social mobility, secularization and modernization.
(d) There are further scope of research on education for environmental consciousness and sustainable development.
(e) The project may be undertaken on the role of teachers for character building education.
(f) Research work may be undertaken on education of women sect for the equalization of educational opportunity.
(g) The project may be undertaken on problems posed by multilingualism at secondary level.
(h) Research work may be undertaken on the curriculum design in the changing circumstances of education.
(i) The project may be undertaken on the development of human resource and the progress of education.

(j) Research work may be undertaken on the development of life skills and education for future living.
(k) The project may be undertaken on the development of norms of adolescent behaviour in Indian culture.
(l) There is scope for further research on the educational development of the village and the change in village politics.

Key Aspects of Gandhian Educational Philosophy

1. **Holistic Development: Learning by Doing:** A cornerstone of Gandhian education is the integration of productive work with learning. This approach not only imparts practical skills but also reinforces the dignity of labour.
2. **Self-reliance and Sustainability:** Gandhi advocated for education that promotes self-sufficiency, encouraging students to learn skills that make them independent and capable of contributing to their communities.
3. **Value-based Education**: Gandhi's vision stressed the inculcation of values such as truth, non-violence, and social responsibility, aiming to create conscientious and responsible citizens.
4. **Community-centric Learning:** Gandhi's model of education was deeply connected with the local community, promoting local culture, traditions, and languages, and addressing the community's needs.

Implications for Contemporary Indian Education

1. **Curriculum Reforms:** Integrating Gandhian principles necessitates a shift from rote learning to experiential learning. Curricula should include practical activities, community projects, and value education.

2. **Skill Development:** Emphasizing vocational training and skill development can prepare students for real-world challenges, reducing the mismatch between education and employment.
3. **Character Education:** Introducing programmes that focus on moral and ethical education can help in nurturing responsible and socially aware citizens.
4. **Teacher Training:** Educators need to be trained in Gandhian principles to effectively impart these values. This includes fostering an environment of respect, empathy, and cooperation in classrooms.
5. **Community Engagement:** Schools should strengthen their ties with local communities, involving them in educational processes and making learning more relevant and contextual.

Strategies for Integration

1. **Project-based Learning:** Encourage projects that involve community service, environmental conservation, and local crafts, promoting hands-on learning and social responsibility.
2. **Ethics and Value Education:** Incorporate ethics and value education into the curriculum, with regular classes and activities focused on Gandhian values like non-violence, honesty, and simplicity.
3. **Vocational Training:** Establish vocational training centres within schools to teach skills such as agriculture, weaving, carpentry, and other local trades, ensuring students gain practical knowledge and self-reliance.
4. **Teacher Empowerment:** Conduct workshops and training sessions for teachers on Gandhian Educational philosophy, equipping them to create a more engaging and value-driven learning environment.

5. **Community-based Initiatives:** Develop community-based initiatives where students participate in local development projects, fostering a sense of responsibility and connection with their surroundings.

Challenges and Solutions

Challenges

- *Resistance to Change:* Traditional mindsets and existing educational structures may resist the adoption of new methodologies.
- *Resource Constraints:* Implementing practical and community-based learning can require additional resources and infrastructure.
- *Teacher Preparedness:* Educators may lack the training or motivation to adopt Gandhian principles effectively.

Solutions

- *Gradual Implementation:* Start with pilot programmes and gradually scale up successful initiatives, demonstrating their effectiveness to stakeholders.
- *Government and NGO Support:* Seek support from government bodies and NGOs to provide resources, training, and infrastructure.
- *Continuous Professional Development:* Invest in ongoing professional development for teachers to keep them motivated and equipped to implement new teaching methods.

Conclusion

In the 21st century, a number of progressive methods of

teaching and a variety of audio-visual aids are implemented to make the teaching-learning process in classroom more effective and attractive. But proper man making and character building education is not being imparted. Theory has been given more importance rather than practice. In the present system of education students are being failed to achieve self-reliance and self-confidence. Total development of personality of the student at secondary level is not occurred. Students have been losing their faith towards the glorious tradition and culture of India. Social, political, economic and moral values have been eroded. Self-learning or auto-learning is not gained. The relation between students and teachers has been decreased. Teachers are losing their respect and dignity in society. Dependence on private tuition is tremendously grown. Students at secondary stage have lost their interest to go to schools. It is a great concern of poor attendance of students in classes X and XII when the terminal external examinations are held. Students do not feel necessary to make contact with the teachers. Only achieving the degree or diploma has become the target of the students. Behavioural changes are not truly taken place. Education of today is not related to the new changes in the global perspectives and growing socio-economic problems stirring up in our country in the present century. What is a great concern in the perspective of education today is indiscipline, impatience, violence, lawlessness, hatred, decrease of human values and lack of self-confidence, self-sufficiency and self-reliance, mental insecurity, stress, depression, and anxiety. Integrating Gandhian educational philosophy into the contemporary Indian education system holds the potential to address current challenges and foster a more holistic, value-based, and practical approach to learning. By embracing these timeless principles, India can develop an education system that not only imparts knowledge but also builds character, self-reliance, and a deep sense of social responsibility among students.

REFERENCES

Dehury, D. (2008). "Mahatma Gandhi's Contribution to Education". *Orissa Review*, Orissa, LXV (5).

Gandhi, M.K. (1951). *Basic Education.* Navajivan Publishing House.

Gangrade, K.D. (2003, October-December.). "Gandhian Approach to Empowerment of Women". *IASSI Quarterly. 22*(2), pp. 5-33.

Gangrade, K.D. (2004). *Gandhi's Autobiography and Moral Lessons.* Rajghat, New Deihi: Gandhi Smiriti, and Darshan Smriti, Retrieved from www.mkgandhi.org

Gangrade, K.D. (2004, January-June). *Gandhian Approach to Empowerment of Women*, Roshni, pp. 19-24.

Gudavarthy, A. (2008, 31 May-6 June). "Gandhi, dalits and feminists: recovering the convergence". *Economic and Political Weekly. 43*(22); pp. 83-99.

Jha, S. (2004, 10-16 July.). "Charkha, 'Dear forgotten Friend' of Widows: Reading the Erasures of a Symbol". *Economic and Political Weekly. 39*(28), pp. 3113-3120.

Kumar, K. (1999). *Political Agenda of Education: A Study of Colonialist and Nationalist Ideas.* Sage Publications.

Ministry of Education, Government of India (2020). *National Education Policy 2020.*

Parekh, B. (1997). *Gandhi: A Very Short Introduction.* Oxford University Press.

Prabhu, R.K. & Rao, U.R. (1967). *The Mind of Mahatma Gandhi.* Navajivan Publishing House.

Tendulkar, D.G. (1953). *Mahatma.* Publications Division, Ministry of Information and Broadcasting, Government of India, Vol. 111.

Tennyson, O. (1999). *Mahatma Gandhi, the Missing Laureate,* Nobel e-museum Peace Editor.

Varkey, C.J. (1940).*The Wardha Scheme of Education: An Exposition and Examination.* London, Oxford University Press.

Veeraiah, B. (2003). *Education in Emerging India.* New Delhi: Himalay Publishing House.

17

Role of Sports Entertainment in Peace

Bimal Soreng, Soumya Ranjan Panigrahi, Anupam Kumar Patel, Sonalita Nayak and *Jubraj Khamari*

Introduction

Sport and entertainment play crucial roles in promoting peace by bridging divides, fostering understanding, and conveying messages of unity. These platforms transcend cultural, ethnic, and national boundaries, offering common ground for diverse groups to connect. Global sporting events like the Olympics and the FIFA World Cup serve as powerful symbols of international cooperation, uniting participants and spectators from around the world. On a local level, community sports can break down barriers, bringing together people from different backgrounds in a spirit of teamwork and respect.

Entertainment, particularly music, film, and television, also has a profound impact on peacebuilding. Music, with its universal appeal, can unite people across cultures, while concerts for peace, such as "Live Aid", bring global attention to important causes. Films and documentaries that depict the human cost of conflict, like "Hotel Rwanda" or "Schindler's List", foster empathy and understanding, challenging viewers to consider perspectives beyond their own.

Moreover, athletes and entertainers often use their platforms to advocate for peace and social justice, becoming ambassadors of change. Examples include Muhammad Ali's stance against war and Didier Drogba's role in ending civil conflict in Côte d'Ivoire. These figures show how sport and entertainment can be more than just leisure—they can be powerful forces for positive social change.

In an increasingly connected world, sport and entertainment provide shared experiences that can promote a culture of peace. By celebrating diversity, encouraging dialogue, and highlighting the importance of unity, these arenas contribute significantly to global peacebuilding efforts.

Sport as a Catalyst for Peace

1. Fostering Social Cohesion

Sport plays a crucial role in fostering social cohesion and building a sense of community, as it brings people from diverse backgrounds together around a shared passion. Whether through local football matches or international sporting events, sport serves as a unifying platform that helps break down social and cultural barriers. By creating spaces where individuals can connect over common interests, sport promotes a collective identity that transcends differences. Additionally, sport is particularly effective in engaging young people, offering them positive outlets for their energy and diverting them from potentially harmful activities. Programmes that emphasize teamwork, discipline, and fair play not only develop essential life skills but also contribute to peaceful coexistence within communities. Through these means, sport becomes a powerful tool for social cohesion and community building.

2. Platforms for Dialogue

Sport serves as a powerful platform for diplomacy, providing neutral grounds where conflicting parties can engage in dialogue. A notable example is "ping-pong diplomacy", where table tennis matches between the United States and China in the 1970s played a significant role in easing tensions and improving relations between the two nations. Such events illustrate how sport can transcend political boundaries and foster communication in situations where traditional diplomacy might struggle. Additionally, sport is a key avenue for promoting human rights. Organizations and athletes frequently use their visibility to advocate for peace and social justice, leading campaigns against racism, gender inequality, and violence on global stages. By highlighting these issues during major sporting events, they bring widespread attention to critical causes, using the universal language of sport to unite people around the values of equality and respect.

3. Healing and Reconciliation

In conflict societies, sport plays a crucial role in healing divisions and fostering reconciliation. By engaging former adversaries in cooperative sports activities, these programmes help rebuild trust and create opportunities for positive interactions. Sport serves as a common ground where individuals can come together, setting aside past grievances and working towards shared goals. Beyond its impact on social relationships, sport also significantly contributes to mental health and well-being, particularly in communities recovering from conflict. The routine and structure provided by regular sports participation offer a sense of normalcy, helping individuals cope with trauma and stress. By promoting both physical and emotional recovery, sport becomes a vital tool in the broader process of post-conflict rehabilitation and peacebuilding.

Entertainment's Role in Peacebuilding

1. Promoting Cultural Understanding

Film and music have a profound ability to act as bridges between cultures, telling stories that foster empathy and understanding. By showcasing diverse perspectives, these forms of entertainment challenge stereotypes and promote a more nuanced understanding of global issues. Movies and music can transcend language barriers and cultural differences, allowing audiences to connect with experiences and emotions that might otherwise seem distant or unfamiliar. This connection helps to break down prejudices and build a sense of shared humanity. Furthermore, celebrities and entertainers often use their platforms to advocate for peace and social justice. Through concerts, films, and social media, they can reach millions of people, raising awareness and mobilizing support for peace initiatives. Their influence is powerful, as they can inspire action and drive change by leveraging their global reach to highlight important causes. In this way, entertainment not only entertains but also educates and unites people in the pursuit of a more just and peaceful world.

2. Creating Safe Spaces for Expression

In conflict-affected areas, theater and drama serve as crucial therapeutic tools, providing individuals with safe spaces to express their experiences and emotions. These artistic forms facilitate healing by allowing participants to explore and articulate their trauma in a controlled environment. Through role-playing and storytelling, people can confront their experiences, gain insights into their feelings, and process the psychological impacts of conflict. This not only aids in personal recovery but also fosters communal understanding and empathy, contributing to broader reconciliation efforts.

Additionally, art becomes a form of peaceful resistance in regions facing oppression. Creative expression through visual art, music, and performance critiques and challenges unjust systems, offering a voice to marginalized communities. Artists use their work to highlight social injustices and inspire movements for change, mobilizing communities to advocate for justice and equality. By addressing societal issues through art, these creators drive social change and promote a culture of resistance against oppression. Together, theatre, drama, and other artistic expressions play a vital role in healing individuals and communities while challenging and transforming oppressive systems.

Synergies Between Sport and Entertainment

The intersection of sport and entertainment enhances their impact on peacebuilding, as collaborative efforts often amplify their effectiveness. Charity events that combine sports and entertainment, such as benefit concerts featuring sports stars or sports-themed film festivals, leverage the strengths of both domains to promote social change. These events not only raise awareness and funds for important causes but also demonstrate the combined power of sport and entertainment in addressing global issues. The synergy between these fields enhances their ability to foster unity and drive positive change, showcasing how creative and collaborative approaches can lead to significant social impact.

In summary, sport and entertainment are more than sources of enjoyment—they are vital tools in the pursuit of global peace. By promoting social cohesion, facilitating dialogue, and providing means for healing and education, both domains contribute significantly to building a more understanding and united world. As the challenges of our time continue to evolve, the roles of sport and entertainment in peacebuilding will remain crucial, offering innovative and impactful ways to address pressing global issues and foster a culture of peace.

Conclusion

Sport and entertainment transcend mere enjoyment, emerging as vital instruments in the pursuit of global peace. Both fields foster social cohesion by bringing together individuals from diverse backgrounds and creating a shared sense of community. Sport unites people through teamwork and competition, while entertainment—through film, music, and theater—promotes empathy and understanding by showcasing diverse perspectives and experiences. These domains also facilitate dialogue and healing, with sport serving as a neutral platform for diplomatic engagement and entertainment offering therapeutic spaces for emotional expression and resistance against oppression.

Moreover, sport and entertainment play crucial roles in raising awareness about social issues. Athletes and entertainers use their platforms to advocate for human rights, challenge injustices, and mobilize support for peace initiatives. Their influence helps highlight critical issues and inspire action. As global challenges evolve, the roles of sport and entertainment in peacebuilding are likely to become even more integral. By leveraging their unique capacities to connect people, promote dialogue, and drive social change, these fields offer innovative and impactful ways to address pressing global issues and build a more understanding and united world.

REFERENCES

Abdul-Jabbar, K. (2022). *Entertainment Nation: How Music, Television, Film, Sports, and Theater Shaped the United States*. Smithsonian Institution.

Bosshart, L. & Hellmuller, L. (2009). "Pervasive Entertainment, Ubiquitous Entertainment". *Communication Research Trends, 28*(2), 3-26.

Gesser Edelsburg, A. (2011). "Entertainment-Education: Dilemmas of Israeli Creators of Theatre About the Israeli-Palestinian Conflict in Promoting Peace". *Journal of Peace Education, 8*(1): 55-76.

Leonard, D. (2004). "Unsettling the Military Entertainment Complex: Video Games and a Pedagogy of Peace". *Studies in Media & Information Literacy Education, 4*(4): 1-8.

Macaulay, S. (1987). "Images of Law in Everyday Life: The Lessons of School, Entertainment, and Spectator Sports". *Law & Soc'y Rev., 21*: 185.

McGoldrick, A. (2017). *News as Entertainment. Preventing War and Promoting Peace: A Guide for Health Professionals*, 129.

McLaughlin, G. & Baker, S. (2010). *The Propaganda of Peace: The Role of Media and Culture in the Northern Ireland Peace Process*. Intellect.

Quessard, M. (2020). "Entertainment Diplomacy". *Global Diplomacy: An Introduction to Theory and Practice*, 279-295.

Reid, H.L. (2006). "Olympic Sport and its Lessons for Peace". *Journal of the Philosophy of Sport, 33*(2): 205-214.

Schulenkorf, N. (2010). "The Roles and Responsibilities of a Change Agent in Sport Event Development Projects". *Sport Management Review, 13*(2): 118-128.

18

Forgoing a Future of Peace through Education in India

Bhawani Shankar Gadatia

Introduction

Education is the foundation for building more peaceful, just, and sustainable societies, as it shapes every aspect of our daily lives and our future opportunities. However, it is deeply influenced by our health and environment, especially in a global context marked by worsening climate change, democratic backsliding, persistent inequalities, and the rise of discrimination, hate speech, violence, and conflict (UNESCO, 2023). As a tool to address and prevent these problems, education can be a long-term benefit with increasing returns if shaped and implemented effectively. Universally recognized as a cornerstone for fostering peace, promoting understanding, and nurturing tolerance among diverse groups, education is critical in a culturally and socially complex nation like India. With over 1.4 billion people belonging to various ethnicities, religions, and languages, India's educational system holds the potential to bridge divides, build common ground, and create a peaceful society. However, recent trends in India's educational policies and practices indicate a deviation from these ideals. Issues such as curricular biases, rote learning, educational inequality, and political interference raise concerns about the country's ability to nurture a peaceful future through its education system. Addressing these challenges and leveraging the transformative potential of education through comprehensive reforms is essential to ensure India does not forgo a future of peace.

Concept of Peace Education

Peace education is a vital component in the broader mission of fostering a harmonious global society. It goes beyond merely avoiding conflict and war; it involves cultivating a culture where justice, equality, and human dignity are upheld. This holistic approach to education aims to provide individuals with the essential tools, insights, and competencies needed to actively contribute to creating a more sustainable, just, and peaceful world. Peace education encompasses a range of definitions and perspectives, with no single, universally accepted understanding. According to UNESCO (2005), peace education involves exploring ways to create more just and sustainable futures. It is education for life, not merely training for a vocation. The goal of peace education is to equip individuals with the values, skills, and attitudes needed to lead fulfilling lives, foster harmonious relationships, and actively contribute as responsible and engaged citizens (NCERT, 2006). This form of education is not just about imparting knowledge but also about shaping the character and conscience of learners to empower them to contribute to peaceful coexistence and sustainable development (Bajaj & Hantzopoulos, 2016).

Peace education strives to cultivate the knowledge, skills, attitudes, and values essential for fostering a culture of peace. It is a proactive, long-term strategy aimed at developing peaceful individuals who manage conflicts using non-violent approaches (UNESCO, 2023). This approach encompasses the physical, emotional, intellectual, and social development of children within a framework grounded in human values (Schmidt & Friedman, 1988). By embedding peace education in the curriculum, educators can create learning environments that encourage empathy, critical thinking, and a commitment to justice, which are essential for the prevention of violence and the promotion of a culture of peace (Reardon, 1988). "Peace Education cultivates the knowledge base, skills, attitudes, and values that seek to transform people's mindsets, attitudes, and behaviours that, in the first place, have either created or exacerbated violent conflicts. It seeks this transformation by building awareness and understanding, developing concern, and challenging personal and social action that will enable people to live, relate, and create conditions and systems that actualize non-violence, justice, environmental care, and other peace values" (Navarro-Castro & Nario-Galace, 2019). This transformation is crucial in a world where violent conflicts often arise from misunderstandings, intolerance, and injustice. Peacebuilding is the responsibility of every individual and a challenge for the entire human family (UNESCO, 2005). It requires collective action and a shared commitment to fostering environments where peace can flourish. Peace Education is, therefore, not just an educational goal but a societal necessity, integral to achieving long-lasting peace and sustainable development worldwide.

Historical Context

Pre-Independence Educational System

The educational landscape in India has undergone significant transformations over the centuries. During the pre-Independence era, education in India was a blend of traditional systems, such as the *Gurukul* system, and colonial influences introduced by the British. The *Gurukul* system focused on holistic education, including moral and spiritual teachings, while the British introduced a more formal, structured education system aimed at creating a class of educated individuals to serve the colonial administration.

The British colonial education system, however, was not designed to promote critical thinking or inclusivity. It primarily served to reinforce colonial dominance and propagate a limited perspective of history and knowledge. This system created a divide between the educated elite and the masses, contributing to social stratification.

Post-Independence Reforms and Visionaries

After gaining Independence in 1947, India embarked on a journey to reform its education system, aiming to build an inclusive, equitable, and progressive nation. Visionaries like Mahatma Gandhi and Jawaharlal Nehru envisioned an education system that would promote scientific temper, critical thinking, and social harmony.

Mahatma Gandhi emphasized "Nai Talim" or basic education, which integrated practical skills with academic learning and moral development. Nehru, on the other hand, advocated for a secular and modern education system that would foster unity in diversity. The establishment of institutions, like the Indian Institutes of Technology (IITs) and the Indian

Institutes of Management (IIMs), was part of this vision to create centres of excellence in education.

Despite these efforts, the legacy of colonial education persisted, and various challenges continued to impede the realization of a truly inclusive and peaceful educational system.

Current Challenges in the Indian Education System

Curricular Bias and Historical Revisionism

One of the pressing issues in the current Indian education system is the presence of curricular biases and historical revisionism. Recent years have seen a trend of modifying school textbooks to reflect certain ideological perspectives, often at the expense of a balanced and comprehensive portrayal of history.

These changes can lead to the marginalization of certain communities and the propagation of a singular narrative that does not reflect the pluralistic nature of Indian society. Such biased education can sow seeds of discord and resentment among different groups, undermining social harmony and peace.

Emphasis on Rote Learning Over Critical Thinking

The Indian Education System has long been criticized for its emphasis on rote learning. Students are often encouraged to memorize facts and figures rather than engage in critical thinking and problem-solving. This approach stifles creativity, hinders intellectual growth, and limits the ability of students to understand and address complex social issues.

A lack of critical thinking skills can lead to a populace that is easily swayed by misinformation and extremist ideologies, posing a significant threat to social peace and stability.

Inequitable Access to Quality Education

Educational inequality remains a major challenge in India. There is a stark disparity in the quality of education received by students from different socio-economic backgrounds. While urban areas often have access to well-resourced schools and qualified teachers, rural and marginalized communities face significant barriers to quality education.

This inequality perpetuates cycles of poverty and social exclusion, leading to discontent and potential conflict. Ensuring equitable access to quality education is essential for building a cohesive and peaceful society.

Political Influence and Academic Freedom

Increasing political interference in educational institutions poses a threat to academic freedom and the integrity of education. When political agendas drive educational content and policies, it can lead to the propagation of biased ideologies and the suppression of diverse perspectives.

Academic freedom is essential for creating an environment where critical inquiry and diverse viewpoints can flourish. Without it, the education system risks becoming a tool for ideological indoctrination rather than fulfilling its role in promoting critical thinking and social harmony.

Role of Education in Promoting Peace: A Strategic Recommendation

Comprehensive reforms are needed in the Indian Education System to realize the transformative potential of education in promoting peace. These reforms should focus on creating an inclusive, critical, and equitable education framework.

Inclusive and Balanced Curriculum

Developing an inclusive and balanced curriculum is essential for fostering social harmony. The curriculum should reflect the diverse cultural, religious, and historical narratives of India. It should promote respect and appreciation for different communities, helping students understand and value the richness of India's pluralistic heritage.

- ***Diverse Representation*:** Include content from various cultures, religions, and communities in textbooks and learning materials. Ensure that the contributions of marginalized groups, such as *Dalits, Adivasis*, and women, are highlighted.
- ***Local Histories and Cultures*:** Integrate regional histories, languages, and traditions into the national curriculum. This approach helps students connect with their local heritage while appreciating the broader national context.
- ***Regular Curriculum Reviews*:** Establish an independent body to review and update the curriculum regularly. This body should include educators, historians, sociologists, and community representatives to ensure a balanced and inclusive perspective.
- ***Interdisciplinary Approach*:** Promote interdisciplinary learning that connects history, literature, geography, and social studies to provide students with a comprehensive understanding of social dynamics.
- ***Cultural Exchange Programmes*:** Encourage schools to organize cultural exchange programmes and activities that expose students to different traditions and practices, fostering mutual respect and understanding.

Promotion of Critical Thinking and Problem-Solving Skills

Educational strategies should prioritize the development of critical thinking and problem-solving skills. Encouraging students to question, analyze, and engage in debates can cultivate a more thoughtful and tolerant citizenry. This approach helps counteract extremist ideologies and promotes rational discourse.

- ***Pedagogical Training for Teachers*:** Provide ongoing professional development for teachers on pedagogical methods that promote critical thinking and problem-solving. Workshops, seminars, and certification programmes can be part of this initiative.
- ***Active Learning Techniques*:** Encourage the use of active learning techniques, such as group discussions, debates, project-based learning, and case studies, in the classroom.
- ***Assessment Reform*:** Shift from traditional rote-based examinations to assessments that evaluate critical thinking, creativity, and problem-solving abilities. Introduce project work, open-book examinations, and continuous assessment methods.
- ***Integration of Technology*:** Utilize digital tools and platforms to create interactive and engaging learning experiences that foster critical thinking. Online forums, virtual labs, and educational apps can support this goal.

Civic and Moral Education

Integrating civic education that emphasizes democratic values, human rights, and responsibilities can empower students to become active, informed citizens committed to peace and justice. Moral education should also be a key component, teaching students' empathy, ethical reasoning, and respect for others.

- ***Civic Education Curriculum***: Introduce a comprehensive civic education curriculum that covers topics such as democracy, human rights, the Constitution of India, environmental sustainability, intercultural education and global citizenship.
- ***Moral and Ethical Education***: Integrate moral and ethical education into the curriculum, focusing on empathy, respect for diversity, and ethical decision-making.
- ***Experiential Learning***: Encourage experiential learning opportunities, such as community service, internships, and civic engagement projects, to help students apply their civic and moral knowledge in real-world contexts.
- ***Debates and Model Parliaments***: Organize debates, model parliaments, and mock elections to provide students with practical experiences in democratic processes and governance.

Equitable Education Opportunities

Ensuring equitable access to quality education for all, regardless of socio-economic background, is crucial. Policies aimed at reducing educational disparities can help bridge social divides and foster a more inclusive society. This includes investing in schools in rural and marginalized communities, providing scholarships and financial aid, and ensuring that all students have access to qualified teachers and educational resources.

- ***Resource Allocation***: Ensure equitable allocation of resources to schools in rural and marginalized communities. This includes infrastructure development, provision of learning materials, and access to technology.
- ***Scholarships and Financial Aid***: Expand scholarship programmes and financial aid schemes to support students from low-income families. This can include

need-based scholarships, fee waivers, and stipends for school supplies.

- ***Inclusive School Policies***: Develop school policies that promote inclusivity and accommodate the needs of diverse learners, including those with disabilities. Implement measures such as accessible infrastructure, special education programmes, and inclusive classroom practices.
- ***Community Involvement***: Engage local communities in the educational process by forming school management committees, involving parents in decision-making, and promoting community-based education initiatives.

Teacher Training and Support

Investing in comprehensive teacher training programmes is essential for equipping educators with the skills needed to handle diverse classrooms and promote inclusive education. Teachers play a critical role in shaping students' attitudes and values. Providing ongoing professional development and support can help teachers create a positive and inclusive learning environment.

- ***Comprehensive Training Programmes***: Develop teacher training programmes focusing on inclusive education practices, culturally responsive teaching, and strategies for promoting critical thinking. Include modules on new pedagogical methods and the use of technology in education.
- ***Continuous Professional Development***: Establish mechanisms for continuous professional development, such as regular workshops, online courses, and peer learning networks. Provide teachers with opportunities to update their skills and knowledge.

- ***Mentorship Programmes***: Create mentorship programmes where experienced teachers can guide and support novice teachers. This can help new teachers navigate challenges and improve their teaching practices.
- ***Support Systems***: Provide access to counselling and support services for teachers to address professional and personal challenges. This includes mental health support, career counselling, and professional guidance.
- ***Incentives and Recognition***: Recognize and reward teachers who demonstrate excellence in promoting inclusive and critical education. Implement awards, public recognition, and career advancement opportunities as incentives.
- ***Collaborative Platforms***: Encourage collaboration among teachers through professional learning communities, forums, and conferences. These platforms can facilitate the sharing of best practices and innovative teaching strategies.

Protecting Academic Freedom and Institutional Autonomy

Protecting academic freedom and institutional autonomy is vital for fostering an environment where diverse ideas can flourish. Minimizing political interference in educational institutions can help maintain objectivity and balance in educational content. Institutions should be free to pursue academic excellence and critical inquiry without fear of political repercussions.

- ***Legislation for Academic Freedom***: Enact legislation that explicitly protects academic freedom and institutional autonomy. This legislation should safeguard against undue political influence in curriculum development, faculty appointments, and administrative decisions.

- ***Independent Oversight Bodies*:** Establish independent bodies to oversee the functioning of educational institutions and ensure adherence to principles of academic freedom. These bodies should include representatives from academia, civil society, and the legal profession.
- ***Transparent Governance*:** Promote transparent and accountable governance structures within educational institutions. Ensure that decision-making processes are inclusive and representative of various stakeholders.
- ***Support for Research and Innovation*:** Provide funding and support for research and innovation in education. Encourage institutions to pursue independent research agendas that address social issues and contribute to knowledge creation.

Encouraging Community and Stakeholder Engagement

By fostering collaboration between schools, families, local organizations, and businesses, educational institutions can create inclusive and supportive learning environments. This partnership enriches educational experiences, addresses community needs, and promotes shared responsibility for nurturing well-rounded, socially responsible, and globally aware citizens.

- ***Public Awareness Campaigns*:** Launch campaigns to raise awareness about the importance of inclusive and equitable education. Use media, social platforms, and community events to disseminate information and engage the public.
- ***Collaborative Platforms*:** Create platforms for collaboration among government agencies, educational institutions, NGOs, and the private sector. These platforms can facilitate sharing of best practices, resources, and expertise.

- ***Parental Involvement*:** Encourage parental involvement in the educational process through regular parent-teacher meetings, workshops, and participation in school governance.
- ***Community-based Initiatives*:** Support community-based education initiatives that address local needs and promote social cohesion. Examples include after-school programmes, literacy campaigns, and cultural exchange activities.

Monitoring and Evaluation

Monitoring and Evaluation in Peace Education are vital for assessing programme effectiveness, guiding improvements, and ensuring accountability. They provide data to refine educational strategies, track progress, and adapt to changing needs. M&E also support the replication and scaling of successful programmes, contributing to policy development and enhancing the broader field of Peace Education.

- ***Establish Monitoring Frameworks*:** Develop comprehensive monitoring frameworks to track the implementation and impact of educational policies. These frameworks should include clear indicators, data collection methods, and evaluation tools.
- ***Regular Assessments*:** Conduct regular assessments of educational programmes and policies to identify strengths, weaknesses, and areas for improvement. Use findings to inform policy adjustments and resource allocation.
- ***Stakeholder Feedback*:** Gather feedback from students, teachers, parents, and communities to evaluate the effectiveness of reforms. Use participatory approaches, such as surveys, focus groups, and town hall meetings, to ensure diverse perspectives are considered.

- ***Transparency and Accountability***: Ensure transparency and accountability in the monitoring and evaluation process. Publish evaluation reports and make them accessible to the public. Hold policymakers and educational institutions accountable for their performance.

Future Prospects

As India navigates the challenges and opportunities within its educational landscape, the future prospects for leveraging education as a tool for peace are both promising and complex. Implementing the recommended policies can set the stage for transformative changes that foster social harmony and prepare the nation for a peaceful and prosperous future.

Enhanced Social Cohesion and National Unity

Students will gain a comprehensive understanding of India's pluralistic society by incorporating diverse cultural and historical narratives. This approach will foster mutual respect and reduce social tensions.

Promoting critical thinking and problem-solving skills will create a more informed and tolerant populace. Students will be better equipped to analyze and address social issues, contributing to a more cohesive society.

Reduction in Educational Inequality

Ensuring equitable access to quality education for all students, particularly those from marginalized communities, will help bridge social and economic divides. This can lead to increased social mobility and reduced poverty.

Implementing inclusive school policies will ensure that all students, regardless of their background or abilities, have equal opportunities to succeed. This will create a more level playing field and promote social justice.

Strengthened Civic Engagement and Democratic Values

Integrating civic education into the curriculum will empower students to become active, informed citizens. Understanding democratic processes, human rights, and responsibilities will enhance their participation in civic life and strengthen democratic institutions.

Providing experiential learning opportunities will enable students to apply their knowledge in real-world contexts, fostering a sense of responsibility and commitment to societal well-being.

Improved Quality of Education

Investing in teacher training and professional development will enhance the quality of education. Well-trained teachers will be better equipped to handle diverse classrooms, promote critical thinking, and support inclusive education.

Shifting from rote-based examinations to assessments that evaluate critical thinking and problem-solving will improve learning outcomes and prepare students for the challenges of the 21st century.

Protection of Academic Freedom

Enacting legislation to protect academic freedom and institutional autonomy will create an environment conducive to independent inquiry and intellectual growth. This will ensure that educational institutions can function without undue political influence, promoting a balanced and objective education.

Long-term Vision for Education and Peace in India

Education as a Pillar of Sustainable Development

Education will be recognized as a fundamental pillar of sustainable development, contributing to economic growth, social equity, and environmental sustainability. By fostering a well-educated and socially conscious populace, India can achieve its development goals while maintaining social harmony.

A Knowledge-based Society

With a focus on critical thinking, innovation, and research, India can transition to a knowledge-based society. This will not only enhance the country's global competitiveness but also promote a culture of continuous learning and intellectual curiosity.

Inclusive and Just Society

An education system that promotes inclusivity and social justice will lead to a more equitable society. By addressing educational disparities and ensuring that all individuals have access to quality education, India can reduce social inequalities and promote a sense of belongingness and cohesion among its citizens.

Global Leadership in Education

India can emerge as a global leader in education by implementing progressive educational policies and practices. Sharing best practices and collaborating with other countries can enhance India's influence on the global stage and contribute to international efforts to promote education for peace.

Conclusion

The journey toward forging a peaceful future through education in India is both an ambitious and essential endeavour. The proposed reforms and policy recommendations aim to transform the Indian education system into a cornerstone for peace and development. By prioritizing inclusivity, critical thinking, equitable access, and academic freedom, India can harness the transformative power of education. This approach will not only enhance social cohesion and national unity but also prepare the country for a sustainable and prosperous future. With the collective efforts of all stakeholders, India can create an education system that serves as the foundation for lasting peace, ensuring that the nation does not forgo its future of peace.

REFERENCES

Bajaj, M. & Hantzopoulos, M. (Eds.). (2016). *Peace Education: International Perspectives*. Bloomsbury Publishing.

National Council of Educational Research and Training (NCERT). (2006). *Education for Peace: A framework*.

Navarro-Castro, L. & Nario-Galace, J. (2019). *Peace Education: A Pathway to a Culture of Peace* (3rd edn.). Center for Peace Education, Miriam College.

Reardon, B.A. (1988). *Comprehensive Peace Education: Educating for Global Responsibility*. Teachers College Press.

Schmidt, F. & Friedman, A. (1988). *Peace Making Skills for Little Kids: A Guide for Teachers, Counsellors, and Parents*. Miami, FL: Peace Education Foundation.

UNESCO (2005). *Peace Education Framework for Teacher Education.*

UNESCO (2023). *Recommendation on Education for Peace and Human Rights, International Understanding, Cooperation, Fundamental Freedoms, Global Citizenship and Sustainable Development* (42 C/40).

19

Students' Conflict Resolution through *Ananda* Parisar in the Schools

Arnab Kumar Dutta

Introduction

Conflict resolution is the skill of resolving a problem cordially. In the inclusive environment, there is a high need for this skill within the country's contemporary education process. Conflict is a natural process in every part of the world that involves human relationships. But, the point is that having good handling of resolution skills brings a healthy, happy, and peaceful relationship with other stakeholders. Conflict resolution is a collaborative process to find out the probable solution rather than pulling them apart. The conflict-free environment in the field of education is not possible as learners come from different parts of society and they have different queries and outlooks. To handle these conflicts professionally, it is necessary to bring innovative ways to figure out the problem and draw out maximum output and an effective engagement of the learners. If the learners of our education system have many conflicts and confusion in their minds, it is not possible to confirm their all-round development and bring out all their possibilities. Conflict resolution creates a respectful environment for the students to clarify their doubts, solve their problems, and engage in the work of learning assuring their full potential, and strong collaborative relationships of trust.

Now-a-days classroom interaction is confined by a specific boundary of knowledge and is limited within the assigned syllabus. Hence, there is no chance of solving the queries of the students' minds other than the prescribed knowledge. The timetables or routines of the schools are constructed only for classroom interaction for specific subjects. Practically, there is no chance of clarifying the conflicts within the minds of students other than subject-specific content that constructs obstacles in front of the all-round development of the students. In most cases, students clarify their queries from their friends of the same age who also have limited knowledge. They play with their friends in the time of recess or tiffin without the guidance of any teacher or expert. As they have no practical knowledge of teamwork, the team making by themselves provoke exclusion practices as they make their team according to their own choice without considering the diversification. Actually, they have very little knowledge about the governmental system and structure in our state and country. So, to overcome these problems, it is necessary to bring resolution for solving the problem in a peaceful manner.

Background of the Study

In 2018, the Delhi Government introduced happiness classes in schools for the mental and emotional well-being of the students up to class eight. In the handbook for happiness, which was introduced by the government for classes 6 to 8, four divisions are there. These are mindfulness, storytelling, activities, and expression. The view of the Education Minister of Delhi was that happy learners have more orientation towards fast learning, creative thinking, acceptance of failures, and making strong relationships and friendships. It is introduced as a process of keeping the students stress-free and joyful engagement despite the monotony of studies.

NEP 2020 found alarming data that though the enrolment in school education has increased due to the SSA and RTE Act even the dropout rate also increased according to the grade. The dropout rate from 6-8 to 9-10 is 11.6 per cent. This policy document noted that a high amount of dropouts occurs after grade five and especially after grade eight. The policy recommended that, by 2030, from preschool to secondary school, the dropout rate should be zero through holistic educational opportunities from the beginning of the preschool.

NEP 2020 advised two overall initiatives to overcome the above-mentioned problems. One is effective and sufficient infrastructures in the schools and another is universal participation for quality and equitable education.

The experts of this policy found that only quality may retain the students in the field of education by their interest. There should be the chance to learn formal as well as non-formal modes.

The document pointed out that the main motto of the curriculum and pedagogical changes should be focused on real understanding and the proper learning of the students through cognitive development as well as character building, holistic and well-rounded development of contemporary skills. Proper engaging processes of teaching-learning interaction should be the only way to reach the goal of the aforesaid developments.

One of the most significant observations of the document is that more fun, collaborative, creative, and exploratory works for learners in the classroom sessions will be the way to reduce curriculum content and increase essential deeper learning and critical thinking.

Art integration and sports integration in classroom transactions are mostly helpful for the students for a joyful classroom and fit India movement through the integration of Indian art and culture and the development of social skills. These integrations are the part of the holistic development of the students through physical and psychological well-being and cognitive abilities.

NEP 2020 also recommended bag less days throughout the year to confirm the participation of the learners in various activities like quizzes, arts, sports, and vocational crafts rather than only cognitive engagement in the classroom.

These observations and recommendations of NEP 2020 have a common belief that students are the centre of the education system and their queries, curiosity, and conflict of thoughts should be addressed as they find the joy of peace through education.

Objectives of the Study

Objectives of the study are to:

1. Understand the policy documents of *Ananda Parisar.*
2. Clarify the recent scenario of the *Anada Parisar* in the schools.

Methodology

In this study, researcher applied the qualitative technique of research. To understand the policy documents, researcher took help of the secondary sources of data and for the clarification of recent scenario, he scheduled a focus group discussion of six teachers from primary and secondary schools of Hooghly district, West Bengal.

Discussion

In 2022, West Bengal Board of Secondary Education implemented various activities for the overall development of the school students. One of these most important activities is *Anada Parisar*. The department constructed policy guideline regarding the formation of each activity. *Anada Parisar* is a bundle of activities that target to develop soft skills of the students and develop communication between teachers and students. *Ananda* means Happy and *Parisar* means space. Through this effort, the School Education Department of West Bengal tries to build up a space where the students can share happily their feelings, queries, opinions and conflict of thoughts that they face in family, school and society. This space should be free from fear and judgements and is a consequence of socio-emotional development of the students. In this space, as students have the scope to play and fun with their friends, also teachers have an advantage to understand the abilities, needs and psychology of their students in a better way. This understanding of the teachers will help them to motivate and engage the students effectively.

Salient features

The salient features of the *Ananda Parisar* are:

- It will be carried out for the learners from class 1 to class 10.
- The activities will take place at last period of every week for every class.
- It will be a fear free discussion between teachers and students regarding confusion, queries, conflicts and opinions of the different issues faced by the students.

Activities of Anada Parisar

Anada Parisar is constituted with some activities. These activities are mainly related to the promotion of students all and well-rounded development. As the students think that the school is their second home, so, it is necessary to make a fear-free environment where they can exchange their thoughts, feelings, queries, and confusion. In this space, they will produce their opinion freely whatever it is right or wrong. Through these activities, they can find out the source of happiness. These activities are:

- Informal interaction between teachers and students.
- Improve communication skill.
- Development of morality.
- Improve soft skills.
- Classroom decoration with the students' photographs.
- Display board of teachers' bio-data and photograph.

Through a focus group discussion researcher found that these activities are helpful for the retention of the students in the school. Teachers have the chance to understand the students more deeply and students have the chance to clarify their queries. They pointed out that when some students are involved in any activity, other students get inspiration from them and in this time, teachers motivate them to join those activities. As there is no boundary of specific work, the students engage in the works without any fear and their smiles on face promote that they get joy and happiness from these activities. They agreed with each other that it is a training of good human being and citizenship.

Teachers informed that, at the last period of the end of a week, students build-up their self-satisfactions that boost them to come in school for the next week. They added, when the students find their photos hanging on the wall, makes them happy. This period is actually a preparation, organisation and participation in a cultural programme to them. Then they remain free from pressure, stress and fear and join in the activities through a collaborative way. They feel from the bondage of curriculum content even they are in their school. They told that teachers also participate in different activities with them as a result, students easily communicate with them freely without any hesitation.

Though there are some extremely positive feedbacks, even the group members pointed out some problems related to execution of the *Anada Parisar*. They argued that in some cases, the higher authority send some questions for quizzes are not age specific. Another problem is that the selected period is the last period of Saturday, in this day; as it is a half day of the school hour, the number of the students comparatively less in number so, not all students have the chance to join the activities in every week. The financial problem is one of the most significant problems in this regard. They gave emphasis that there is no specific fund for continuing of these activities. There are much expenditure for essential equipments for games and decorations.

Conclusion

Anada Parisar is a great planning in the field of education for the students of classes 1 to 10. It significantly increases the number of participants in activities that enhance their skills. Students, especially from government schools are from underprivileged sections of society will not be able to clarify their queries, curiosity, and conflict of thought scientifically. The *Anada Parisar* gives the chance to those students to clarify their thoughts as well as effectively engage in different activities that bring happiness and peace to their minds.

Now-a-days it is a complex situation in the field of education to retain students in the school, especially in government schools. There are many conflicts in this field but the conflict of thought of the students can be addressed through the planning conflict resolution. Conflict resolution is a process of solving problems professionally. *Ananda Parisar* is a process of conflict resolution of the students by the teachers through the proper planning of the School Education Department of the Government of West Bengal.

REFERENCES

Ay, Ş. Ç., Keskin, H. K. & Akilli, M. (2019). "Examining the Effects of Negotiation and Peer Mediation on Students' Conflict Resolution and Problem-Solving Skills". *International Journal of Instruction, 12*(3), 717-730. https://doi.org/10.29333/iji.2019.12343a

Boroş, S., Meslec, N., Curşeu, P. L. & Emons, W. (2010). "Struggles for Cooperation: Conflict Resolution Strategies in Multicultural Groups". *Journal of Managerial Psychology, 25*(5): 539-554.

Chowdhury, A. & Mete, J. (2018). "A Study on Peace Education in Purulia District in West Bengal". *J. Emerg. Technol. Innov. Res, 5*.

Cohen, T.R. (2010). "Conflict Resolution", in I.B. Weiner & W.E. Craighead (Eds.), *The Corsini Encyclopedia of Psychology*, 4th edn, Volume 1 (pp. 390-391). Hoboken, NJ: John Wiley & Sons, Inc. Available at: http://dx.doi.org/10.1002/9780470479216.corpsy0219

Deutsch, M. & Coleman, P.T. (Eds.). (2000). *The Handbook of Conflict Resolution: Theory and Practice*. San Francisco: Jossey-Bass.

https://www.hindustantimes.com/delhi-news/in-a-class-for-happiness/story O7D3oLdBAPlhT67rL8sL5L.html

https://meruinternationalschool.com/tellapur/happy-hour-where-education-is-joy/

https://www.ritzmagazine.in/happy-hours-to-be-introduced-in-schools/

https://wbbse.wb.gov.in/ReadWriteData/Notification/133147040609378515.pdf

Iqbal, K., Khalil, U. & Khan, A. (2017). "Perceptions of Secondary School Teachers Regarding the Role of Education in Social Conflict Resolution". *Bulletin of Education and Research, 39*(3), 157-170. https://doi.org/eric.ed.gov/fulltext/EJ1210308 Management

National Education Policy 2020. https://www.mhrd.gov.in/sites/upload_files/mhrd/files/nep/ NEP_Final_English.pdf referred on 10/08/2020.

Sarkar, S.R. (2016). "Peace Situation among the Students of Secondary Level in West Bengal". *Arts and Social Sciences Journal, 7*(6), 1-4.

Valente, S. & Lourenço, A.A. (2020, February). "Conflict in the Classroom: How Teachers' Emotional Intelligence Influences Conflict Management", in *Frontiers in Education* (Vol. 5, p. 5). Frontiers Media, SA.

20

Promoting Peace Education in Schools

Suhana Begum

Introduction

Peace education in the UNICEF conception as quoted by Fountain (1999) refers to advancing the knowledge, skills, attitudes, and values required to produce behavioural changes that will enable children, adolescents, and adults to prevent conflicts and violence. These changes are real and designed to solve disputes peacefully and to establish intrapersonal, interpersonal, intergroup, national, and worldwide peace-promoting environments.

Peace will be attained when all people on the planet are aware of and capable of resolving conflicts on a global scale, work toward maintaining justice without resorting to violence, live by upholding equality and human rights norms, value cultural variety, and show respect for one another. All of these can be accomplished through methodical peace education (Solomon and De Rivera, 2009).

Peace education is a multifaceted and comprehensive approach to both content and process. A tree with numerous branches that have different topics and forms might be compared to Peace Education. Castro and Galace (2008) proposed that Peace Education is an umbrella with a diverse context, namely disarmament education, human rights education, global education, conflict resolution education, education for international understanding, interfaith education, development education, gender-fair/non-sexist education, and environmental education. Peace Education has a distinct focus, encompassing a range of normative skill sets and orientations.

Objectives of the Study

1. To understand the concepts of Peace Education.
2. To know the different strategies for creating a Peaceful Classroom.
3. To examine the different teaching-learning approaches in Peace Education.

Creating a Peaceful Classroom

Creating a peaceful classroom environment can assist students in appreciating and respecting one another regardless of differences. The following are some strategies to support the development of an accepting and loving atmosphere in our classrooms:

1. **Declare your Classroom a Peaceful Area and Provide Guidelines for Achieving it:** Introduce the idea of a quiet classroom to your pupils throughout the first few days of instruction. Find out from them what they believe is required to foster a peaceful environment in the classroom. Request that they make a poster explaining

that their classroom is a Zone of Peace and outlining the rules that must be followed to make that happen.

2. **Reinforce Your Students:** When the chance arises, say something kind or constructive to someone. Acknowledge the contribution of their concept. Express interest in the opinions of the students. Give them an eye contact or a nod.
3. **Encourage Students to Express their Emotions Constructively:** Avoid responding aggressively to situations that irritate you. When our patience is tested, our thermometers rise, and we tend to respond angrily. It is common knowledge that teachers will occasionally yell at their students, kick or shove furniture, or toss objects out of frustration. Anger management is a skill that educators should acquire.

   Students who experience a sense of welcome and belonging are in a peaceful classroom. Therefore, people should not be made fun of or excluded, especially because of traits that are out of their control.
4. **Create more Cooperative than Competitive Practices:** Cooperative practices allow the class to collaborate to achieve a common goal. On the other hand, cooperative learning activities foster positive interdependence by teaching students how to work together and communicate to accomplish a common goal. With cooperative learning, students discover how to use one another's unique abilities, skills, and strengths to solve problems together.
5. **Encourage the Students on Peaceful and Constructive Dispute Resolution Techniques:** Encourage them to take proactive measures to avoid harmful situations. In instances where there is a dispute, mediate. Use a strategy for problem-solving. Show students how to apply this

strategy and engage in productive discussion. Remind them that courteous language is necessary for productive dialoguing amongst disputants. Establish a quiet space for kids to discuss their worries, such as a peaceful corner in the classroom or a quiet place on the school's property.

6. **Encourage Students to Practice their Communication Skills:** Miscommunication, misinterpretation, and misunderstanding are the main causes of many problems in the classroom. Sometimes, others misinterpret what we say or perceive what we do. Teaching pupils how to clarify and paraphrase is one technique to help prevent conflicts that result from misunderstandings.

When students feel comfortable and safe, the classroom is peaceful. It is a place where they can be themselves without feeling bound by obligations. They may develop as people there without worrying about being made fun of, left out, or injured. Teachers can assist in the construction of these classrooms. Learners will find it simpler to transfer these beliefs and skills to different contexts of interaction if the principles of peace are taught and practised in the classroom. Furthermore, Peace Educators ought to feel content that they have contributed to creating a culture in which peaceful norms have taken hold.

Teaching-Learning Approaches and Strategies in Peace Education

Many Teaching-Learning strategies are compatible with the approaches to Peace Education described above. They are as follows:

1. **Discussion:** One method for ensuring that each participant's voice is heard is the small group discussion. A well-considered and well-researched foundation is necessary for a discussion to be most productive.

2. **Pair Share:** Partnership groups are formed throughout the discussion process. A discussion starter is posed by the facilitator. Person A listens while B answers the question without interruption. Roles are switched after a predetermined amount of time. Subsequently, A links the ideas B made to the class, and the other way around. Enhancing listening abilities is a beneficial practice.
3. **Exercise of Visualization and Imagination:** The practice of visualization increases the participants' use of imagination. It enables individuals to envision alternatives to, say, contentious circumstances. Students are challenged to "propose" remedies rather than merely "expose" and "oppose" bad situations.
4. **Perspective-taking:** By using this strategy, students are expected to comprehend and value the perspectives of others. It is a technique for solving problems. "Stepping in the other person's shoes and walking in them for a while" is what this means (Lee, 1960). It is common practice to use this tool to foster tolerance and empathy.
5. **Role-playing:** With the usage of this technique, participants are given the chance to "feel" the circumstance instead of just thinking about it. It also fosters empathy and a deeper comprehension of different points of view through role-playing. Cognitive and emotive learning can both be fostered by it.
6. **Simulation Games:** By creating violent scenarios, for example, students can better understand the state of unrest and be more imaginative when coming up with solutions to unfair circumstances. One such instance is the "Sharing the Earth's Resources" simulation of wealth distribution.
7. **Problem-solving:** Among the best learning strategies is the ability to solve problems. Utilizing other important

cognitive abilities like analysis, generation, and evaluation of possibilities is made possible by it.

8. **Taking Stances and Conducting Issue Polls:** This activity aims to highlight participants' contrasting opinions on a contentious claim, such as the one that "Wars will happen in the future, whether we like it or not." Regarding contentious assertions, there can be at least three possible responses: agree, disagree, and not sure/neutral.
9. **Encouraging Action:** As a way of putting what they have learned into practice, participants are asked, when appropriate, to declare their resolve or commitment to taking specific actions.
10. **Citing or Writing a Reference:** When a lesson begins or ends with the reading of a peace-related quotation, it inspires students to reflect on or gain a deeper understanding of the material covered.
11. **Web Charting:** At the start of a lesson, writing a word like "peace" or "war" on the board and asking students to write or draw what they associate with it will engage their minds. It is also a useful starting point for a conversation about a specific idea connected to peace.
12. **Using Film and Photographs:** The students' brains are helped to form vivid images through the use of video and/or photos. A discussion of the messages delivered and the students' responses can come next.
13. **Telling Stories Including Personal Stories:** Sometimes, the anecdotes and stories we tell help learners retain the information we aim to impart. It would be easier to understand the arguments you wish to convey if you share any personal experiences you have with the matter. Using this tactic also fosters a more intimate relationship between you and your students.

14. **Song/Poem Analysis:** Peace is a theme found in many songs and writings. Your students will learn the principles you wish to still in them in a more imaginative way if you give them the freedom to read or listen to them, choose their favourite lines, and analyze messages.
15. **Completion of Sentences:** Teachers can discover more about the ideas and opinions that students may have about a given issue by encouraging them to finish sentences that are not quite full. They can also use this method to ask participants for ideas for actions.
16. **Reciprocal Teaching:** As facilitators, students take turns with one another. "We usually forget what we see, but we remember what we hear. But when we do something, we better understand it." When allowed to instruct, students are more likely to comprehend the concepts, values, and skills we hope to preserve.
17. **Using a Brainstorm:** It is an approach that fosters creativity by allowing pupils to freely express their thoughts without fear of criticism from their peers. As this is for highly contentious subjects, the use of a third person is very beneficial.

Conclusion

Education is the best choice for creating a culture of peace. Peace Education has the power to change because it emphasizes creating mental, ethical, and behavioural frameworks for coexistence. In the framework of education, maintaining peace is not only necessary as a goal, but also as a climate that covers teaching-learning interactions. The teacher has a crucial role in creating a peaceful classroom atmosphere, which starts with intrapersonal harmony. To create a comprehensive and long-term system of peace, a peaceful school classroom must be built using a variety of methods and techniques. Thus, holistic and comprehensive efforts in the constellation of interpersonal connections are necessary for the establishment of peaceful schools. At the level of the image, the school's vision and mission reflect a spirit of peace, fostering a collective awareness of all aspects of the school that are framed by moral, ethical, and spiritual norms and in line with good values around the world. A variety of extracurricular activities can also be linked to the establishment of peaceful schools. With these many approaches, the establishment of a school peace culture is accomplished both simultaneously with individual intervention and structurally through organizational intervention.

REFERENCES

Fountain, S. (1999). *Peace Education in UNICEF.* Unicef, Programme Division.

Johnson, D.W. & Johnson, R.T. (2011). "Peace Education in the Classroom: Creating Effective Peace Education Programmes", in *Handbook on Peace Education* (pp. 223-240). Psychology Press.

Johnson, D.W. & Johnson, R.T. (2013). "Essential Components of Peace Education", in *Peace Education Tip V44# 4* (pp. 280-292). Routledge.

Salomon, G. & Nevo, B. (2005). *Peace Education: The Concept, Principles, and Practices around the World.* Psychology Press.

Setiadi, R. (February 2020). "Peace Education Pedagogy: A Strategy to Build Peaceful Schooling", in *International Conference on Educational Psychology and Pedagogy "Diversity in Education" (ICEPP 2019)* (pp.161-166). Atlantis Press.

21

Peace Pedagogy for *Viksit Bharat* in 2024

Mou Banerjee and *Lokanath Mishra*

Introduction

The current era is exhausting, fraught with chaos, technological advancement, political tension and various adversities. All the so-called exciting things in life always make one feel helpless, then the key to getting out of that emptiness lies within oneself. It is well-known that peace is not defined by the omission of conflict—it is actually a changing state of mutual respect, justice and harmony. The pursuit of peace and upholding fundamental human ideals is crucial. Due to the increasing noise around and the confusion arising from it, most people today abandon the journey towards self-identification and personal development at the very beginning. To remain in harmony with the environment, peace education is needed, which includes principles and standards of values, motivates to distinguish between right and wrong, and act according to principles. In the face of growing international conflict, social divisions, and multiple crises across societies, peace education is particularly essential because it provides people with the knowledge, skills, and attitudes necessary to avoid conflict, resolve disagreements peacefully, and build a culture of tolerance. Peace Education can help reduce violence at the personal, political, and societal levels by teaching empathy, non-violent communication, and conflict resolution techniques. Peace Education develops an understanding of human rights and social injustice, which also encourages civic engagement to combat injustice and prejudice. As the world grows more interconnected, Peace Education becomes more and more important in tackling complicated global challenges like migration and climate change, where understanding and collaboration are essential.

Concept of Peace

> "Peace is not merely the absence of war but the presence of justice, of law, of order—in short, of government." **—Albert Einstein**

The concept of peace is dynamic and complex, involving a wide range of elements, types, and characteristics. Peace is the inner satisfaction of a person. There are various sources of peace, the most notable of which are pleasant feelings and knowledge of values that help a person reach a higher level. Peace is a feeling of well-being and a sense of positivity in the surroundings of life. The reverse of mental unrest, peace encourages people to think in a healthy way. We can endeavour to create a more harmonious and peaceful world by understanding the complexity of peace.

Concept of Peace Education

Establishing an atmosphere of peace in society is one of the most important goals of education. The family is the starting point for Peace Education, which continues at school. Peace

Education aims to provide students with the knowledge, values, and attitudes necessary for peaceful living in a diverse context. Peace Education desires to identify and address root issues including poverty, inequality, and the lack of basic necessities of people, going beyond merely managing conflict. Peace Education encourages people to become change agents in their communities by fostering critical thinking abilities and the capacity for productive discourse. Peace Education has discussed two types of peace: Negative Peace and Positive Peace.

Negative Peace refers to the absence of conflict or direct violence.

Positive Peace is defined as the presence of social and economic justice (Reardon, B.A., 2012).

According to UNICEF, Peace Education is the action of developing the knowledge, attitudes, skills and values necessary for behaviour change, so as to enable children, youth and adults to avoid overt and structural forms of conflict and violence, to resolve challenges peacefully and to establish the necessary conditions for promoting peace at the national, international, interpersonal or intergroup levels.

Peace Education in Educational Context

Peace Education is essential for mutual coexistence and living together in an inclusive manner. Peace Education aims to discover new ways of learning based on individual differences. It is important to identify the inequalities that exist in the current situation. Peace Education can be practiced in both regulated and non-regulated educational settings. Some important purposes are as follows:

(a) To take necessary steps to make the world a better and more humane place to live in.

(b) To develop values and skills for students to strive for contentment in life.
(c) To help students develop a better perspective on building a functioning world society.
(d) To develop constructive behaviour to deal with problems, so that mutual conflicts can be reduced and eliminated.
(e) To build an active state to promote positive human relations for the purpose of peace building.

Peace Education in Cultural Context

Peace Education always tries to organize a special kind of cultural environment with the aim of providing consistency between the objectives and the results of any work process. There is no specific path or table for achieving peace in the world because peace itself is a path or means. It is possible to analyze the nature of peace education properly only based on a suitable curriculum objective. Characteristic peace education is the process of acquiring knowledge, attitudes, skills, character building and basic understanding through which everyone can live in unity and harmony with each other. Peace Education refers to the creative and constructive thinking process of the person. Individuals always try to achieve peace in the physical and spiritual state through experience. Teaching non-violence, love, compassion, trust, honesty, cooperation etc. and respecting human society and all living beings on earth is the main vision of Peace Education.

Peace Education in Social Context

Peace Education provides the knowledge necessary to understand the dynamics of any group. Humanity has lived in different groups since ancient times. These are—family, hunting party, nation, tribe, village, city, army, political party, state, country, international organization etc.

Gandhian Approach to Peace Building

Gandhiji's vision of peace, or positive notion of peace, emphasizes the power of non-violence, the pursuit of truth, compassion, forgiveness, and active peacemaking. In Gandhiji's philosophy, the core idea is "*Ahimsa*" or non-violence, which is the accepted standard of love, life, and creation as opposed to violence, which begets jealousy, death, and destruction. To avoid conflict, he believes that the universal human ideal of non-violence should be promoted not just at the personal level, but also at the societal, national, and international levels. Gandhiji's method is based on moral principles since he thinks that conflict and all forms of violence originate from moral degradation. Mahatma Gandhi dedicated his life to promoting peace, equality, and respect for all people, as well as tolerance, respect for all ethnic groups and religious views, and the resolving of conflicts. Gandhiji's non-violence is not just a weapon for the weak; it is also a weapon for the courageous and powerful. The fundamental framework of many educational programmes in India and many other nations includes the promotion of peace education through Gandhian studies and ideas. Gandhi intended for non-violent action to refer to non-violent, constructive mass action. Although Gandhi did not specifically write about Peace Education, his life and ideology definitely had a significant impact on the subject of peace studies and Peace Education, not only for India but also for other countries throughout the world (Prasad, 1998). Gandhi's worldview is integrated from his ideas of non-violence and peace. The idea of "self" and human nature served as the foundation for Gandhiji's worldview. Gandhi highlighted the ability of all people to reach their full potential with non-violence, acknowledging the inherent goodness of man. He believed that all people are part of the divine and are interdependent, interrelated or connected each other. Gandhi's idea of peace is likewise based on principles. For him, peace emerged from the way of life. Consequently, justice, development, and the environment are all intimately related to peace.

Establishing Peace Education for Promoting Development of India

Peace Education programmes are becoming increasingly popular around the world, as states, international organisations, and civil society organisations recognise their relevance. However, as this acknowledgement grows, coincides with discussion regarding the broader aim and nature of peace education initiatives (S.P. Udayakumar, 2009). The *Vedas*, *Puranas*, and *Upanishads* demonstrate India's ancient tradition of encouraging peace, international understanding, tolerance, and self-control. The ancient Indian sages regarded the world as a global community. They imagined it as "*Vasudhaiva Kutumbakam*"—which means the entire universe is a family.

Implementation of Peace Education in Indian Education System

1. Determining the fundamentals of peace studies.
2. Develop a curriculum structure.
3. Give teachers the appropriate training.
4. Reviewing and adopting the programme.
5. Inclusion of experiential and student-centred learning.
6. Spreading knowledge through initiatives involving social action.
7. Encouraging volunteers in order to offer learning opportunities.
8. Keeping up a steady level of enthusiasm for establishing peace.

9. Promoting peace and collaboration in education.
10. Selection and assessment of information.
11. Removing bias from information about conflicts.
12. Holding presentations, seminars, and campaigns for peace.
13. Supplying every aspect of society with peace educator training.
14. The focus should be on independent and active learning.

Strategies for Integrating Peace Education into Teacher Education Curriculum

The integration of peace as a perspective in the school curriculum is an idea whose time has come. Education for peace aims to cultivate a culture of peace, making learning both meaningful and joyful. While Peace Education focuses on specific topics, education for peace seeks to shape the overall educational enterprise Clarke-Habibi, S. (2018).

For effective implementation, the curriculum should reduce its load to incorporate peace concepts contextually and pedagogically. The connection between peace and justice must be highlighted, ensuring justice takes precedence in cases of conflicting interests, as this promotes long-term peace. Addressing the needs of teachers through mechanisms like Teachers' Tribunals is also essential to achieving educational goals. Inner peace is recognized as the foundation of broader peace, though caution must be exercised to avoid misinterpreting it as escapism or selfishness.

The NCERT (2005) developed a new Teacher Education curriculum for junior secondary schools to improve its relevance. However, Wisdom and Imo (2010) critiqued it for inadequately addressing peace education, advocating for the inclusion of co-curricular activities. Similarly, earlier studies by Amucheazi (1980) and Enu (2005) highlighted gaps in the curriculum and called for further integration of Peace Education concepts (Mishra, L., 2011, 2013). Deutsch (1993) emphasized that families and schools are the two key institutions shaping children's understanding of love and hate. He proposed that fostering a cooperative learning environment, initiating conflict management programmes, utilizing constructive controversy, and establishing school-based dispute resolution centres can cultivate positive relationships and prepare children to live peacefully. Similarly, Salomon (2002) highlighted the importance of creating opportunities for children to express their opinions freely, which could strengthen their moral courage and contribute to their character development. Weigert (1999) advocated for experiential learning as an effective pedagogy to enhance understanding of peace and violence while nurturing the skills, motivations, and ideas necessary for creating a better world. Building on this, Hettler, Linda, and Johnston (2009) demonstrated a clear connection between peace education and experiential learning, suggesting that such approaches could shift school culture toward peace, offer youth opportunities to influence society positively, and equip them to practice conflict resolution and violence prevention. Participants in experiential programmes also gained insights into their role in fostering environmental stewardship, developing peaceful relationships, and taking responsibility for community well-being (Hartmut, B., Nick, M., & Jane, C. 2018; Joseph, P.B., & Duss, L.S. 2009).

Peace Education in the Context of 21st Century

Most educators and practitioners in the 21st century acknowledge that the social and political goals of Peace Education are focused on eradicating violence in all of its forms (negative peace) and creating the conditions required for the growth of peace on a national, international, intergroup, and interpersonal level (positive peace). With many different educational purposes and objectives, peace education is conducted in numerous settings worldwide. The majority of initiatives concentrate on peace education. This education fosters critical thinking, a critical understanding of violence, and relevant knowledge about how to bring about peace. Peace Education aims to improve attitudes and abilities to attain peace on an individual, interpersonal, social, and political level. It is transformative and forward-looking.

Dimension	Learning Goals	Transformative Learning Approaches
Personal	Developing inner strength and confidence. Managing life's schedule. Nurturing positivity with a positive mindset. Becoming physically and mentally strong through physical training.	• Self-efficacy • Self-realization • Sense of ethics • Independence lifestyle
Political	To develop a political perspective based on acceptance. To develop a sense of democracy. To understand constitutional values. To fulfil civic duties. To respect the opinions of others.	• Learning human rights • Dialectic thinking • Leadership skills • Social justice • Non-violent attitude • Sense of equality
Cultural	Understanding the roots of culture. Maintaining cultural heritage. Developing aesthetic thinking. Being aware of morality; what is right and what is wrong and why.	• Adapt own culture • Respect other culture • Moral values • Aesthetical knowledge
Social	To be responsible towards society. To respect social norms and values. To strive to build a society free from prejudice. To develop oneself as a member of society through the process of socialization.	• Socialization • Social adjustment • Communication skills • Helping attitude • Peer adjustment • Belongingness

(*Contd.*)

Dimension	Learning Goals	Transformative Learning Approaches
Rational	Developing a rational perspective. Moving forward in solving problems. Striving to increase emotional intelligence. Developing a thoughtful attitude. Searching for innovation in a systematic way. Developing a scientific attitude regarding social awareness.	• Critical thinking skills • Decision making skills • Systematic approaches • Creative thinking skills • Sense of novelty • Problem solving skills
Physical	Understanding the ontological perspective. Protecting the ecosystem. Taking care of all elements of the environment. Adapting to one's own environment.	• Environmental knowledge • Sustainable development • Acclimatization

Conclusion

Peace Education honour humane principles for dealing with conflict at both the individual and societal levels. It has its origins in societies with a strong tradition of peace. Religious sources have played an important role in changing people's mindsets towards constructive peace, thereby contributing to world peace. Many peace educators and educators have made important contributions to this issue. Gandhi was a key figure in developing educational strategies that promote peace. With the advancement of expertise and modern methods, peace education is gradually being implemented in various educational programmes around the world, with significant support from state and national governments as well as international organizations such as UNESCO.

REFERENCES

Bajaj, M. (2016). "In the Gaze of Gandhi: Peace Education in Contemporary India". *Peace Education: International Perspectives*, 107-122.

Fountain, S., 1998. "Peace Education/Conflict Resolution Evaluation Methods". New York, UNICEF (unpublished paper, available from the author).

Hicks, D., 1985. "Education for Peace: Issues, Dilemmas and Alternatives". Lancaster: St. Martin's College.

Okamoto, M. (March 1982). "Peace Education Around the World", *Treatises*, 51.

Prasad, S.N. (1998). "Development of Peace Education in India (Since Independence)". Peace Education Miniprints No. 95.

Reardon, B.A. (2012). "Education for Sustainable Peace: Practices, Problems and Possibilities, in Psychological Components of Sustainable Peace" (pp. 325-352). New York: Springer.

Salomon (2004). "Does Peace Education Make a Difference in the Context of an Intractable Conflict?" *Peace and Conflict: Journal of Peace Psychology*, *10*(3): 257-274

Tint, B.S. & Prasad, G.K. (2007). "Peace Education in India: Academics, Politics, and Peace". *Peace Research*, 23-37.

Udayakumar, S.P. (2009). "Peace Education in India: A Proposal". *Peace Prints: South Asian Journal of Peace Building*, *2*(1): 1-6.

22

Cultivating Peace in the Classroom Environment

Ankur Nandi, Tapash Das and *Tarini Halder*

Introduction

Over the past decades, global events and human experiences have heightened the urgency for the pursuit of peace. Violence has emerged in human society in ways never seen before. Observing the world today, any thoughtful individual may feel discouraged and even horrified by the violent actions being carried out by humans against each other and nature. It is distressing to acknowledge that we are living in an era characterized by unprecedented violence in the forms of terrorism, war, crime, injustice, oppression, and exploitation, which exist alongside superficial development enjoyed by a select few. Most of the humanity remains in severe poverty, struggling for mere survival. Society, as constructed by humans, is plagued by disorder and confusion, with the most unfortunate aspect being the impact of this chaos on the innocent minds of children. Children naturally absorb the violence in their environment, and will eventually grow into the next generation of those who perpetuate violence. In a world fragmented by competing nuclear-armed forces, peace education may be the only hope for the survival of life on Earth (UN, 2020; Brander *et al.*, 2023; Chandra & Halder, 2013). Dr. S. Radhakrishnan, the first President of independent India, aptly noted, "It is essential for us not to live apart but to live together, understanding one another, knowing one another's fears and anxieties, aspirations, and thoughts." The concept of a "Culture of Peace" began to take shape in the late 1980s. Indeed, two of the four pillars of education proposed by the Delors Report (1996), namely "learning to live together" and "learning to be", are linked to peaceful living. Peace gained significant focus as the UN declared 2001-2010 as the International Decade for a Culture of Peace. Consequently, cultivating peace in the hearts of children has become a critical issue that demands immediate attention.

Objectives

1. To understand the role of major disciplines in promoting peace in the classroom environment.
2. To study the role of different pedagogical mechanisms to promote peace in the classroom.
3. To discuss Social and Emotional Learning (SEL) programmes for the improvement of peace in the classroom environment.
4. To analyze the attributes and role of the teacher as a peace builder in the classroom environment.

Methodology

For this chapter, research on scholarly databases such as Google Scholar, JSTOR, ScienceDirect, and many more websites was searched using the keywords "peace education", "cultivation of peace", "role of teacher", "teacher as a peace builder", "disciplines in promoting peace", "major disciplines in promoting peace" and "Social and Emotional Learning (SEL) programmes". The search, limited to English-language articles from 2001 to 2024, yielded 364 relevant sources. After screening for relevance, credibility, and recency, 64 peer-reviewed articles from reputable journals were selected. Emphasis was laid on the emerging themes and trends on the subject under study regarding creating peace in the classroom environment. The method used was a qualitative synthesis done by organizing data into categories and themes.

Discussion

Role of major disciplines in promoting peace in the classroom environment.

Language

Through language, educators can impart essential skills and values, such as conflict resolution and the understanding of diversity. This can be achieved through various classroom activities that focus on language skills, social interaction skills, critical thinking skills, and understanding diversity (Ghosh & Mete, 2014; Tatsumi, 2018). To facilitate this learning, teachers can arrange a variety of programmes that encompass reading and writing, speaking, and listening exercises (D'Argenio, 2022). Implementing weekly spelling programmes alongside communication skills practice enhances students' ability to articulate their thoughts and engage in meaningful discussions. Additionally, activities such as writing scripts for plays, organizing debates, and conducting discussions on pressing social issues can foster critical thinking and negotiation skills among students, empowering them to confront complex topics in a supportive setting (Lanier, 2024). These experiences empower students to confront complex topics in a supportive setting, promoting both personal and academic growth (D'Argenio, 2022).

Social Science

Social science subjects like History, Geography, Economics, Political Science, and Sociology provide scope to know their surroundings and the world and help to explore world peace (Agnihotri, 2017; Folorunso & Adegboye, 2024). In social science with the help of multisensory teaching approaches students will be able to know about their identity depth of universal value and love for others, tolerance, peace, justice, equality, human rights, honesty, cultural contexts, social systems, and lifestyle of different regions (Ghosh & Mete, 2014). Historical knowledge is fundamental in learning from past experiences of war and peacebuilding, which can inform contemporary perspectives on conflict and resolution (Folorunso & Adegboye, 2024; Chakraborty, 2014). Historical knowledge provides important lessons on the dynamics of social relationships, governance, and community resilience necessary for fostering peace. Additionally, understanding the geographic distribution of various cultures helps students comprehend how environmental and socio-economic factors uniquely influence social welfare in different regions, aiding in the analysis of local, national, and international conflicts (Agnihotri, 2017).

Science

Students have learned the role of science in everyday life and science is treated with living things and environment with care and sensitivity. Such a lesson improves the awareness of the ethics of science, social responsibility, the role of science in sustainable global development, and skills for peace among the students (Gulhan, 2023; Chakraborty, 2014). With the help of science, we can create a sense of how they can achieve environmental sustainability (UNESCO, 2024) by caring about nature, the effect of nuclear war on the environment, nuclear waste and its management, deforestation, biodiversity, land mine, dams, and their ecological impact, sharing resources, power of the nuclear weapon, understanding its uses, form of energy production etc. (Ghosh & Mete, 2014). These experiences empower students to confront complex topics in a supportive setting, promoting both personal and academic growth (D'Argenio, 2022) which contributes to peaceful relationships between different groups of pupils (Syafril *et al.*, 2020; Harrison, 2023; Chakraborty, 2014).

Mathematics

With the help of mathematics, we can develop problem-solving skills, creative and critical thinking skills, the relation between mathematics and culture, and awareness of the environment (Ghosh & Mete, 2014; Harrison, 2023; Tatsumi, 2018). Processes of collecting, presenting, interpreting data, and calculating probabilities can develop skills in communicating meaning with integrity which contributes to peaceful relationships between different groups of pupils (Syafril *et al.*, 2020; Harrison, 2023; Chakraborty, 2014).

Role of Different Pedagogical Mechanisms to Promote Peace in the Classroom

Project Work

Project work serves as an effective pedagogical strategy for promoting peace by fostering collaboration and teamwork among students. This collaborative learning approach encourages students to engage in problem-solving activities that address real-world issues related to peace and conflict resolution, helping them to develop essential social skills such as empathy, communication, and mutual respect (Setiadi, Kartadinata, Ilfiandra, & Nakaya, 2017; Chakraborty, 2014). Through project work, educators can create a conducive environment that promotes dialogue and collaboration, essential components for cultivating a culture of peace. By focusing on themes such as social justice, environmental sustainability, and human rights, students can identify and address local and global issues in ways that foster understanding and cooperation among diverse groups (Dutta, Andzenge & Walkling, 2016; Brooks & Hajir, 2020).

Problem-solving

Problem-solving strategies within educational settings promote active participation and collaboration among students. This collaborative approach not only enhances critical thinking but also builds a sense of community and respect among peers, crucial elements for fostering a peaceful classroom environment (UNESCO, 2017; Setiadi & Ilfiandra, 2019). Engaging in problem-solving activities encourages students to analyze conflicts from multiple perspectives, which fosters empathy and understanding essential for peaceful coexistence (Setiadi *et al.*, 2017; Chakraborty, 2014). Problem-solving encourages students to consider the feelings and perspectives of others, thereby promoting empathy and respect. Developing these qualities is vital for peaceful interactions and understanding in diverse environments, making it an essential component of peace education (Setiadi *et al.*, 2017; UNICEF, 2005).

Cooperative Learning

Cooperative learning is a vehicle for fostering peace (Jenkins & Jenkins, 2010). Cooperative learning is an effective pedagogical strategy that substantially contributes to peace education by promoting collaborative skills among students. It fosters an environment where students learn to work together towards common goals, which is essential for building mutual respect and understanding necessary for peaceful interactions (Zezima, 2017; Chakraborty, 2014). Cooperative learning in promoting peace is its emphasis on developing essential social skills such as communication, negotiation, and conflict resolution. These skills are vital in managing interpersonal relationships and addressing conflicts effectively, thereby creating a non-violent classroom environment (Martinez Lirola, 2016; Jenkins & Jenkins, 2010; Chadar & Chadar, 2018).

Team Learning

Through team learning, students develop a sense of belonging and support within their learning environment. This supportive atmosphere encourages open dialogue and collaboration, which are necessary for constructive discussions related to peace and conflict (Kollies & Zapri, 2024). This exposure fosters empathy and understanding, fundamental qualities for peacebuilding and reducing prejudices among peers (Chakraborty, 2014; Kollies & Zapri, 2024). So, this approach enhances pupils' understanding and ability to advocate for peace.

Simulated Learning

Simulated learning is a powerful pedagogical strategy that deepens students' understanding of conflict and peacebuilding by immersing them in practical scenarios (Gelot, 2019). Through simulations, students can engage in complex social interactions and practice resolving conflicts in a controlled, reflective environment (Rudy, 2017; Gelot, 2019; Chakraborty, 2014). Students learn not only the mechanics of conflict resolution but also the values of empathy, respect, and cooperation, which are foundational to peaceful communities (Park, 2024; Rosen, 2022; Rudy, 2017).

Case Studies

Case studies are effective pedagogical strategies that facilitate a deep understanding of complex social issues, including peace and conflict. They allow students to explore real-world scenarios and learn from historical and contemporary examples of conflict resolution and peacebuilding efforts. This method enhances critical analysis and reflection, which are essential for understanding the nuances of peacebuilding processes (Wallach, 2020; Setiadi *et al.*, 2017). Through case studies, students engage actively with social issues, fostering a sense of responsibility and agency in their learning (Chakraborty, 2014). This engagement helps them to empathize with different perspectives and understand the historical context of conflicts, which is crucial for promoting peace and non-violence (Setiadi *et al.*, 2017).

Social and Emotional Learning (SEL) Programmes for the Improvement of Peace in the Classroom Environment

Second Step Programme

The Second Step programme is a universal, school-based social-emotional learning initiative aimed at reducing violence and enhancing academic success among middle school students. It focuses on teaching social and emotional skills such as empathy, emotion management, and conflict resolution. Research has demonstrated that these skills contribute to a reduction in physical aggression among students within one year (Espelage, Low, Polanin, & Brown, 2015; Low, Cook, Smolkowski, & Buntain-Ricklefs, 2015). Additionally, studies have shown that the programme increases students' feelings of school belonging, which correlates with lower rates of bullying and aggression, thus fostering a more peaceful classroom environment (Espelage, Low, Van Ryzin, & Polanin, 2015; Grossman *et al.*, 1997; Neace & Munoz, 2012; Sullivan, Sutherland, Farrell, & Taylor, 2015).

Promoting Alternative Thinking Strategies (PATHS)

The PATHS programme demonstrates significant effectiveness in fostering a peaceful classroom environment through measurable outcomes. Research indicates that it reduces reported aggressive behaviours by 32 per cent, increases self-control by 36 per cent, and enhances students' emotional vocabulary by 68 per cent (Collaborative for Academic, Social, and Emotional Learning CASEL, Programme Guide, 2024). The programme is recognized as a promising practice for improving children's social and emotional competence, with significant effects on peer ratings of aggression and hyperactive-disruptive behaviour, as well as observer ratings of classroom atmosphere (Domitrovich, Cortes, & Greenberg, 2007; Conduct Problems Prevention Research Group, 1999). Moreover, social-emotional learning programmes like PATHS can have meaningful preventive effects on population-level rates of aggression, social competence, and academic engagement during the elementary school years (Conduct Problems Prevention Research Group, 2010). These improvements in emotional and social competencies lead to a more harmonious classroom atmosphere.

Mind UP Programme

The Mind UP programme is designed to cultivate mindfulness among students, facilitating better emotional regulation and positive social interactions in the classroom focused on enhancing social-emotional skills, which in turn improve classroom dynamics and overall behaviour (Schonert-Reichl *et al.*, 2015; Mind UP, The Goldie Hawn Foundation, 2024). Evidence suggests that participation in Mind UP positively influences classroom environments, leading to decreased disruptive behaviours and increased student engagement.

RULER Programme

Marc Brackett is the lead developer of RULER, an evidence-based approach to Social and Emotional Learning (SEL) developed at the Yale Centre for Emotional Intelligence. RULER, an acronym for the five skills of emotional intelligence (Recognizing, Understanding, Labelling, Expressing, and Regulating), supports entire school communities in understanding the value of emotions, building the skills of emotional intelligence, and creating and maintaining a positive school climate. RULER aims to infuse the principles of emotional intelligence into the immune system of schools, enhancing how students learn, teachers teach, family's parents, and leaders lead. It has been proven to boost academic performance, decrease school problems like bullying, enrich classroom climates, reduce teacher stress and burnout, and enhance teacher instructional practices. This evidence-based approach has substantially improved classroom climates and dynamics, leading to better teacher-student relationships and a reduction in bullying behaviour. Schools that have implemented RULER have reported significant benefits related to student behaviour and overall school climate (Yale Centre for Emotional Intelligence, 2024).

CASEL Framework Programmes

The Collaborative for Academic, Social, and Emotional Learning (CASEL) framework incorporates various evidence-based SEL programmes that emphasize the integration of social and emotional learning across different settings. Programmes under this framework have shown measurable improvements in student behaviour, emotional regulation, and interpersonal relationships, contributing significantly to peaceful and supportive classroom environments. Schools utilizing CASEL-endorsed programmes report enhanced classroom interactions and reduced conflict.

Attributes and Role of the Teacher as a Peace Builder in the Classroom Environment

The role of teachers as peacebuilders in the classroom is multifaceted, where they act as both agents of change promoting harmony and as influencers on social behaviour among students. Their impact is highlighted in how they can foster respect, justice, and inclusiveness in diverse classroom settings (Horner *et al.*, 2015; Sayed & Novelli, 2015).

Attributes of the Teacher as Peace Builder

The following attributes are highlighted in the work of a globally renowned, expert, and experienced peace educator Betty Reardon (2001):

1. Teachers should embody the qualities of responsible global citizens and active proponents of a culture of peace. They need to be visionaries who inspire hope and drive positive change, understanding that education is a tool for constructive transformation.
2. Teachers should be motivated and engaged in their communities, viewing themselves as accountable and responsible members of society.
3. They should commit to lifelong learning, continually enhancing their skills and expanding their knowledge base.
4. Teachers should act as both preservers and transmitters of culture, serving as effective agents of social and cultural change.
5. They should seek to build and maintain relationships that foster peace and a sense of community.
6. Teachers need to be sensitive to gender issues, staying vigilant to avoid and address any gender biases in themselves or their students.

7. They should be critical in a constructive manner, aiming to eliminate harmful behaviours rather than causing harm to others.
8. Teachers should respect individual differences, which will help them address varying learning styles and abilities among students.
9. They should demonstrate a caring and supportive attitude, ensuring that students feel valued and supported.
10. Effective communication and conflict resolution skills are essential for teachers to foster a peace-building environment. In a teacher training workshop by the Centre for Peace Education in the Philippines, participants identified these attributes as vital for educators dedicated to peace.

During a teacher training workshop organized by the Centre for Peace Education in the Philippines, participating teachers identified key characteristics essential for a teacher dedicated to peace.

> "Passionate for peace, Compassionate, concerned and kind, Caring encouraging, understanding, Respect other people, Gentle and non-threatening, Fair and impartial, Having faith in god, inspired by spirituality, Facilitator of learning, rather than sources of authority, Tolerant, open, respectful of ideas of others, Sensitive to diversity of classroom, Ability to accept learner as they are, Open to sharing relevant personal stories, Skilled in eliciting thoughts and posing reflective questions, Motivated, enthusiastic, inspiring, Joyful and filled with vibrant energy, Bearer of hope rather than despair, Model of behaviour and attitude what they teach."

Based on the discussion of the qualities of a peace teacher, we can observe similarities between the views of Betty Rearber and those of educators in the Philippines. This suggests that despite different cultural contexts, peace teachers must embody common principles, values, and characteristics. A peace teacher should be approachable and foster positive relationships with students, colleagues, parents, and the broader community. They should also be firm, fair, and consistent in matters of discipline. As role models for the learning community, teachers should create a supportive and harmonious environment through their attitudes, behaviour, democratic practices, and interactions, promoting the goal of learning to live together.

Role of a Teacher as a Peacebuilder

- Incorporating Peace Education into the curriculum allows teachers to explicitly address themes of conflict resolution, social justice, and respect for diversity (Parmar, 2014; Chandra & Halder, 2014). Teacher-centred and subject-centred approaches are ineffective in peace education, as these methods often limit student engagement and ownership of learning (Chandra & Halder, 2014). Instead, the most effective approach is child-centred education, which serves as a natural extension of the notion of child rights within the classroom and school environment. In the child-centred method, the teacher adopts multiple roles, including that of a facilitator and a planner, enabling them to set goals and select the most suitable learning activities for students. Peace-oriented pedagogy emphasizes that education should not solely focus on the retention of concepts, memorization of texts, or achieving individual goals, but rather on fostering reflection, sharing, care, and collaboration among students (UNESCO, 2001).

- As a catalyst for learning, the teacher sparks interest among students by implementing engaging activities and strategies tailored to their needs. Effective teaching methods include asking questions, telling stories, sharing anecdotes, playing games, conducting experiments, leading discussions, and using techniques like value clarification, examples, analogies, metaphors, role-play, and simulations (James, 2024; Chandra & Halder, 2014). These methods are particularly effective in promoting peace by fostering collaborative learning and critical thinking, which are crucial for conflict resolution (James, 2024). By employing diverse teaching techniques, teachers create a classroom environment that supports peace and mutual respect (James, 2024). Consequently, the teacher's role as a facilitator is crucial in developing a peaceful learning atmosphere where students can address complex issues related to peace and conflict resolution (James, 2024).
- In their role as climate builders, teachers foster a supportive, caring, safe, and inclusive classroom environment. The quality of the learning environment is as important as the content taught, and teachers play a vital role in creating a positive classroom climate (Kennedy, 2023; Chandra & Halder, 2014). The teacher's attitudes, patience, empathy, democratic values, and humanistic approaches significantly influence the classroom climate (Qiu, 2022; Kennedy, 2023). Teachers must maintain impartiality towards all students, regardless of their social backgrounds (Kennedy, 2023). A warm and engaging approach is essential for establishing a positive climate that supports Peace Education, enabling students to interact respectfully and understand each other better (Hawthorne, 2022; Kennedy, 2023).

- As guides and prompters, teachers direct the learning process towards specific goals by supporting students, addressing gaps in their understanding, and offering personalized assistance. The methods used should be creative, child-centred, experiential, and participatory. This includes designing customized learning experiences and using discussions, debates, presentations, and collaborative projects suited to students' maturity levels and subject content. This approach highlights the importance of active learning, where the teacher encourages student participation and collaboration, thereby enriching their educational experience (Brame & Biel, 2015).
- In their role as mediators, teachers help resolve conflicts between groups or individuals by fostering positive interactions and experiences. Mediators assist students in gaining a deeper understanding of themselves, encouraging inquiry through relevant questions, and exploring new ideas. Teachers also guide students in discovering and applying essential values, which enhances the overall learning experience and creates a supportive educational environment (Gross, 2016).
- As an organizer of knowledge, the teacher consolidates the learners' understanding by facilitating discussions after activities. This presents a significant opportunity for the peace teacher to instill the importance of employing peaceful methods to resolve disagreements and conflicts (Chandra & Halder, 2014). Through these discussions, the teacher can highlight the benefits of conflict resolution techniques rooted in peace education, emphasizing mutual respect and understanding. By guiding students in reflective dialogue, they can explore various perspectives and approaches to resolving conflicts

constructively (Sindhi, 2016, Chandra & Halder, 2014). This process not only enhances students' comprehension of the subject matter but also reinforces the values of peace and collaboration, ultimately fostering a more harmonious classroom atmosphere (Sindhi, 2016).

- Finally, as an evaluator, the teacher assesses the extent to which educational goals have been accomplished. A teacher who can critically analyze their attitudes, habitual modes of thinking, and teaching approaches from a peace-oriented perspective proves to be invaluable to education for peace (Harris, 2003; Del Felice, Karako, & Wisler, 2015). This reflective evaluation includes considering what is taught, the underlying values of the content, and the pedagogical methods employed (Harris, 2003). Such evaluative practices enable the teacher to identify areas for improvement and reinforce peace principles within the educational framework (Gross, 2016). By doing so, educators not only support student learning but also contribute to the formation of a more peaceful society (Harris, 2003; Chandra & Halder, 2014).

So, the teacher plays a dynamic role in the classroom in promoting peace through education.

Conclusion

In conclusion, major academic disciplines, and pedagogical mechanisms, along with Social and Emotional Learning (SEL) programmes and teachers play an important role in cultivating and promoting peace within the classroom climate. Language education, social sciences, science, and mathematics together to the development of critical thinking, cultural awareness, ethical behaviour, and problem-solving skills among the learner population towards the establishment of a peaceful society. Pedagogical approaches, of which some are cooperative learning and case studies, offer the means for collaboration, empathy, and conflict resolution. These SEL programmes help in controlling the emotional regulation of students and hence decrease aggression. These elements make the teacher a peace-builder when using them to bring out the components of understanding in a curriculum that leads the student towards peace, justice, and respect for each other and finally, towards peace in society.

REFERENCES

Agnihotri, S. (2017). "Social Science as a Panacea for Creating a Peaceful World: Myth or Reality", in *Proceedings of the 4th International Conference on Social Sciences* (Vol. 4, pp. 90-97). TIIKM. https://doi.org/10.17501/icoss.2017.41094

Brander, P., De Witte, L., Ghanea, N., Gomes, R., Keen, E., Nikitina, A. & Pinkeviciute, J. (2023). "COMPASS: Manual for Human Rights Education with Young People" (2nd edn.). *Council of Europe*. https://rm.coe.int/compass-2023-eng-final-web/1680af992c

Brooks, C. & Hajir, B. (2020). "Peace Education in Formal Schools: Why is it Important and How can it be Done?" *International Alert*. https://www.international-alert.org/app/uploads/2021/07/Peace-Education-Schools-formal-EN-2020.pdf

Chadar, K. & Chadar, S.N. (2018). "Inculcating Best Practices in Education for Peace and Values". *International Journal for Innovative Research in Multidisciplinary Field*, *5*(5): 146-148.

Chakraborty, A. (2014). "Peace Education: The New Pedagogical Approaches to Conventional Teaching Learning Process", in B.C. Mondal, S.K. Biswas & B. Saha (Eds.), *Peace Education: Present and Future* (pp. 201-220). Sponsored Teachers Training College.

Chandra, B. & Halder, T. (2014). "Teacher's Role is to Promote the Value and Culture of Peace", in B.C. Mondal, S.K. Biswas & B. Saha (Eds.), *Peace Education: Present and Future* (pp. 221-235). Sponsored Teachers Training College.

Collaborative for Academic, Social, and Emotional Learning (CASEL). (2024). "Promoting Alternative Thinking Strategies (PATHS)". *CASEL Programme Guide.* https://pg.casel.org/promoting-alternative-thinking-strategies-

Conduct Problems Prevention Research Group (1999). "Initial impact of the Fast Track prevention trial for conduct problems: II. Classroom effects". *Journal of Consulting and Clinical Psychology, 67*(5), 648-657. https://doi.org/10.1037/0022-006X.67.5.648

Conduct Problems Prevention Research Group (2010). "The Effects of a Multiyear Universal Social-Emotional Learning Program: The Role of Student and School Characteristics". *Journal of Consulting and Clinical Psychology, 78*(2), 156-168. https://doi.org/10.1037/a0018607

D'Argenio, L. (2022). *Teaching Critical Thinking Skills in the ESL Classroom.* Bridge. https://bridge.edu/tefl/blog/teaching-critical-thinking-skills-esl-classroom/

Domitrovich, C.E., Cortes, R.C. & Greenberg, M.T. (2007). "Improving Young Children's Social and Emotional Competence: A Randomized Trial of the Preschool 'PATHS' Curriculum". *Journal of Primary Prevention, 28*(2), 67-91. https://doi.org/10.1007/s10935-007-0081-0

Dutta, U., Andzenge, A.K. & Walkling, K. (2016). "The Everyday Peace Project: An Innovative Approach to Peace Pedagogy". *Journal of Peace Education, 13*(1): 1-26. https://doi.org/10.1080/17400201.2016.1151773

Espelage, D.L., Low, S., Polanin, J.R. & Brown, E.C. (2015). "Clinical Trial of Second Step Middle-School Programme: Impact on Aggression & Victimization". *Journal of Applied Developmental Psychology, 27*: 52-63.

Espelage, D.L., Low, S., Van Ryzin, M.J. & Polanin, J.R. (2015). "Clinical Trial of the Second Step Middle School Program: Impact on Bullying, Cyberbullying, Homophobic Teasing, and Sexual Harassment Perpetration". *School Psychology Review, 44*(4): 464-479.

Folorunso, C.O. & Adegboye, A.A. (2024). "The Role of Social Studies Education in Achieving a Global Peace". *International Journal of Research in Social Sciences and Information Technology, 11*(7): 1-12. https://doi.org/10.51244/IJRSI.2024.1107045

Gelot, L. (2019). "Training for Peace, Conscientization through University Simulation". *Journal of Peace Education, 16*(2): 195-214. https://doi.org/10.1080/17400201.2019.1576514

Ghosh, B. & Mete, J. (2014). "Integrating Peace Education in Our School Curriculum in the Light of NCF with Reference to Practical Steps", in B.C. Mondal, S.K. Biswas & B. Saha (Eds.), *Peace Education: Present and Future* (pp. 174-183). Sponsored Teachers Training College.

Gross, O. (2016). *Restore The Respect: How to Mediate School Conflicts and Keep Students Learning.* Paul H. Brookes Publishing.

Grossman, D.C., Neckerman, H.J., Koepsell, T.D., Liu, P.Y., Asher, K.N., Beland, K., ... & Rivara, F.P. (1997). "Effectiveness of a Violence Prevention Curriculum among Children in Elementary School: A Randomized Controlled Trial". *Journal of the American Medical Association, 277*(20): 1605-1611.

Gulhan, F. (2023). "Environmental Sustainability in Science Education in the Anthropocene: A View from STEAM Education". *Science Insights Education Frontiers, 14*(2): 2129-2143. https://doi.org/10.15354/sief.23.re088

Harris, I.M. (2003). *Peace Education Evaluation.* https://files.eric.ed.gov/fulltext/ED480127.pdf

Harrison, K. (2023). *Editors' Notes: Critical Mathematical Thinking Skills Create More Engaged Citizens, Says Expert.* Phys.org. University of New South Wales. https://phys.org/news/2023-11-critical-mathematical-skills-engaged-citizens.

Hawthorne, H. (2022). *How to Create a Positive Learning Environment. High Speed Training.* https://www.highspeedtraining.co.uk/hub/how-to-create-a-positive-learning-environment/

Horner, L., Kadiwal, L., Sayed, Y., Barrett, A., Durrani, N. & Novelli, M. (2015). "Literature review: The role of teachers in peacebuilding". *Sussex Centre for Migration Research.* https://educationanddevelopment.wordpress.com/wp-content/uploads/2014/11/the-role-of-teachers-in-peacebuilding-literature-review.pdf

James, H. (2024). "Strategies for Integrating Peace Education into the Curriculum". *Medium.* https://medium.com/@hj819734/strategies-for-integrating-peace-education-into-the-curriculum-04344542a274

Jenkins, K. & Jenkins, B. (2010). "Cooperative Learning: A Dialogic Approach to Constructing a Locally Relevant Peace Education Programme for Bougainville". *Journal of Peace Education, 7*(2): 185-203. https://doi.org/10.1080/17400201.2010.502371

Kennedy, J.J. (2023). "How to create peaceable classrooms". *Deccan Herald.* https://www.deccanherald.com/education/how-to-create-peaceable-classrooms-2700465

Kollies, U. & Zapri, D. (2024). "Teaching Peace: in an era marred by Escalating Conflicts and Diminishing Peacefulness, the Question of Education's Role in Peacebuilding has Never Been More Urgent". *United Nations Today.* https://untoday.org/teaching-peace/#:~:text

Lanier, A. (2024). "World Readiness for a World in Conflict", *Language Magazine.* https://www.languagemagazine.com/2024/02/12/world-readiness-for-a-world-in-conflict/

Low, S., Cook, C.R., Smolkowski, K. & Buntain-Ricklefs, J. (2015). "Promoting Social-emotional Competence: An Evaluation of the Elementary Version of Second Step". *Journal of School Psychology, 53*(6): 463-477.

Martinez Lirola, M. (2016). "A Proposal to Combine Cooperative Learning and Peace Education in a Foreign Language Subject". *Journal of Global Research in Education and Social Science, 5*(2): 101-111. https://ikprress.org/index.php/JOGRESS/article/view/1821/1725

Mind Up, The Goldie Hawn Foundation (2024). *Building Stronger, Healthier Brains for a Better Future.* https://mindup.org

National Institute of Justice (2019). *Effects of the Second Step Programme in Middle School on Violence, Victimization, and Substance Use in High School.* https://nij.ojp.gov/topics/articles/effects-second-step-program-middle-school-violence-victimization-and-substance-use

Neace, W.P. & Munoz, M.A. (2012). "Pushing the Boundaries of Education: Evaluating the Impact of Second Step: A Violence Prevention Curriculum with Psychosocial and Non-Cognitive Measures". *Child & Youth Services, 33*(1): 46-69.

Park, J. (2024). "Conflict Resolution Pedagogical Effects of Applying Simulation Games: An Exploration Through Case Studies". *Jung, Suk-in; Park, Jin-woo, 2*(3): 33-45. https://doi.org/10.59227/ch.2023.2.3.33

Parmar, R.M. (2014). "Role of Teacher for Peace Education". *The International Journal of Indian Psychology, 2*(2): 1-8. https://ijip.in/wp-content/uploads/2019/01/18.01.004.20140102.pdf

Qiu, F. (2022). "Reviewing the Role of Positive Classroom Climate in Improving English as a Foreign Language Students' Social Interactions in the Online Classroom". *Frontiers in Psychology, 13*: 1012524. https://doi.org/10.3389/fpsyg.2022.1012524

Reardon, B. (2001). *The Role of Teachers in Peace Education.* Center for Peace Education, Philippines.

Rosen, A.M. (2022). "Simulations and Games to Teach Conflict and Political Violence", in *Oxford Research Encyclopedia of International Studies.* International Studies Association and Oxford University Press. https://doi.org/10.1093/acrefore/9780190846626.013.709

Rudy, J. (2017). *Using simulations and scenarios to teach peace. Elizabethtown College Centre for Global Understanding and Peacemaking.* https://www.globalpartnership.org/blog/using-simulations-and-scenarios-teach-peace

Sayed, Y. & Novelli, M. (2015). *The Crucial Role of Teachers in Peacebuilding: Education and Teachers Hold One of the Keys to Building Successful and Sustainable Peace in Post-Conflict Situations around the World.* Centre for International Education, University of Sussex. https://www.globalpartnership.org/blog/crucial-role-teachers-peacebuilding

Schonert-Reichl, K.A., Oberle, E., Lawlor, M.S., Abbott, D., Thomson, K., Oberlander, T.F. & Diamond, A. (2015). "Enhancing cognitive and social-emotional development through a simple-to-administer mindfulness-based school programme for elementary school children: A randomized controlled trial". *Developmental Psychology, 51*(1): 52-66. https://doi.org/10.1037/a0038454

Setiadi, R. & Ilfiandra (2019). "Peace education pedagogy: A strategy to build peaceful schooling". In *Advances in Social Science, Education, and Humanities Research: Proceedings of the International Conference on Educational Psychology and Pedagogy* (ICEPP 2019) 399, 161-166. https://www.atlantis-press.com/proceedings/icepp-19/125933647

Setiadi, R., Kartadinata, S., Ilfiandra & Nakaya, A. (2017). "A Peace Pedagogy Model for the Development of Peace Culture in an Education Setting". *The Open Psychology Journal, 10*(1): 182-191. https://doi.org/10.2174/1874350101710010182

Sindhi, S. (2016). "Teachers: Agents of Peace Building in the Conflict Zones". *Greater Kashmir*. https://www.peace-ed-campaign.org/teachers-agents-peace-building-conflict-zones/

Social and Character Development Research Consortium (2010). *Efficacy of Schoolwide Programmes to Promote Social and Character Development and Reduce Problem Behaviour in Elementary School Children* (NCER 2011-2012). Washington, DC: National Centre for Education Research, Institute of Education Sciences, U.S. Department of Education.

Sullivan, T.N., Sutherland, K.S., Farrell, A.D. & Taylor, K.A. (2015). "An Evaluation of Second Step: What are the Benefits for Youth with and without Disabilities?" *Remedial and Special Education, 36*(5): 286-298.

Syafril, S., Aini, N.R., Netriwati, Pahrudin, A., Yaumas, N.E. & Engkizar. (2020). "Spirit of Mathematics Critical Thinking Skills (CTS)". *Journal of Physics: Conference Series, 1467*(1): 1-8. https://doi.org/10.1088/1742-6596/1467/1/012069

Tatsumi, A. (2018). *Teaching Critical Thinking in the Language Classroom*. Cambridge University Press. https://www.cambridge.org/elt/blog/2018/04/04/teaching-critical-thinking/

UNESCO (2001). *Learning the Way of Peace: A Teachers' Guide to Peace Education United Nations*. https://unesdoc.unesco.org/ark:/48223/pf0000125228

UNESCO (2017). *Transformative Pedagogy for Peace-Building: A Guide for Teachers*. https://unesdoc.unesco.org/ark:/48223/pf0000261349

UNESCO (2024). *Climate Change and Sustainability in Science and Social Science Secondary School Curricula*. https://www.unesco.org/en/articles/climate-change-and-sustainability-science-and-social-science-secondary-school-curricula

UNICEF (2005). *Come Together, Talk Together, Work Together: Practicing Peace: A Peace Education Module for Youth and Young Adults in Solomon Islands* (4th draft). https://www.creducation.net/resources/Practicing_Peace_Youth-Young_Adult_Curriculum_Solomon_Islands.pdf

United Nation (2020). *Shaping Our Future Together*. https://www.un.org/en/un75/new-era-conflict-and-violence#:~:text

Using cooperative learning groups effectively. Vanderbilt University Centre for Teaching. http://cft.vanderbilt.edu/guides-sub-pages/setting-up-and-facilitating-group-work-using-cooperative-learning-groups-effectively/

Wallach, D. (2020). *Ways to Peace: Case Studies in Peace and Diplomacy. A Reader for High School & College Students* [Master's thesis, University of Maine]. https://digitalcommons.library.umaine.edu/cgi/viewcontent.cgi?article=4395&context=etd

Yale Centre for Emotional Intelligence. (2024). *RULER Program Positively Impacts Student Behaviour and Achievement.* Yale University. https://www.ycei.org/ruler-program

Zezima, A. (2017). "Best Practice Classroom Activities for Improving Students' Cooperative Skills". *SCSD Behaviour Matters.* https://scsdbehaviourmatters.weebly.com/blog/best-practice-classroom-activities-for-improving-students-cooperative-

Index

S.B.D